# BRITAIN

## FROM CALLAGHAN
## TO THATCHER

### About the series

(Ramline Political ...) ... between conventional textbooks ... reporting. Each title examines the key polit... economic and social changes of the country providing a ... brief contextual background to each development ...

## About the series

Chambers Political Spotlights aim to provide a bridge between
conventional textbooks and contemporary reporting. Each title
examines the key political, economic and social changes of the
country, providing, in addition, a brief contextual background to
each development discussed.

# POLITICS IN BRITAIN

# FROM CALLAGHAN TO THATCHER

J Denis Derbyshire, Ph.D. Lond
and
Ian Derbyshire, Ph.D. Cantab

# Chambers

© J Denis Derbyshire and Ian Derbyshire 1988

First published by Sandpiper Publishing as a Sandpiper Compact, 1986
This edition published by W & R Chambers Ltd, 1988
Reprinted 1988

**British Library Cataloguing in Publication Data**

Derbyshire, J Denis
    Politics in Britain: From Callaghan to
    Thatcher.—(Chambers political spotlights).
    1. Great Britain—Politics and
    government—1979-
    I. Title II. Derbyshire, Ian
    941.088'8    DA589.7

ISBN 0-550-20742-2


Typeset by Blackwood Pillans & Wilson, Edinburgh
Printed in Great Britain at the University Press, Cambridge

**Acknowledgements**

This book is based on a wide range of contemporary sources including *The
Times, The Guardian, The Independent, The Observer, The Sunday Times,
The Economist, Newsweek, Time, Keesing's Contemporary Archives, The
Annual Register* and *Europa: A World Survey.*

Every effort has been made to trace copyright holders, but if any have
inadvertently been overlooked the publishers will be pleased to make the
necessary arrangements at the first opportunity.

# Contents

# Preface

This book, as one of the Chambers Political Spotlights, was conceived as a bridge between the conventional textbook and contemporary events, with the aim of providing the student, teacher and general reader with a guide through political developments during recent years.

We have looked, as objectively as possible, at key political, economic and social changes during the past decade, providing, in addition, a brief contextual background to each development. Wherever possible, the narrative and analysis have been supported by relevant statistical material.

It has been said that a week in politics is a long time. On that basis, we have attempted to cover, in these brief pages, a millennium. We have looked at a rapidly-changing scene, whose record will never be completely up to date. Nevertheless, we felt it a task worth tackling and hope that we have achieved some measure of success.

# Part One

# THE BRITISH POLITICAL SYSTEM

## The Politics of Tradition

Britain is unique in Western Europe in being free from invasion for more than nine hundred years and having escaped violent revolution during the last three centuries. Its social and economic development since the 1640–60 'Great Revolution' has, instead, been continuous and uninterrupted, involving the gradual growth in the power of the House of Commons and the extension of the franchise through the Reform Acts of 1832, 1867, 1884, 1918, 1928, 1948 and 1970. It lacks a written constitution or external 'supreme court' watchdog and has evolved instead an unwritten constitution composed of Acts, the common law and 'conventions'. This unwritten constitution has the virtues of flexibility and ease of adaptation, but has the weakness of ambiguity and runs the risk of misapplication.

A key feature of the British political system is the unfettered sovereignty of Parliament and the imperfect separation of the executive from the legislative branch of government. This contrasts with many political models overseas, in particular with the separation of powers enshrined in the American constitution. The British political executive is, in theory, accountable to the legislature: the Houses of Commons and Lords. However, its members sit in the legislature and command a parliamentary majority exercised through disciplined party machines. Its majority in the elected House of Commons is, in a non-coalition situation, firm and dependable. Support from the unelected House of Lords is more uncertain, but its powers of obstruction have been progressively reduced during the present century by the Parliament Acts of 1911 and 1949. These factors, combined with the unusual centralisation of political authority, have made the British executive potentially the most powerful in the western world.

At the heart of the executive is the Prime Minister and the cabinet of twenty or so ministers who work in conjunction with the professional civil service. During the mid and later 19th century the Prime Minister was seen by contemporary observers as merely the 'first among equals'. However, with the growth in the departmental responsibilities of ministers and the increased personalisation of electoral campaigns, so the role of the Prime Minister, as the broad co-ordinating and policy making figure, has extended. Much still depends upon personality, and the input of ministers in their own spheres remains significant. Nevertheless, there has been a clear movement towards prime ministerial government during the last two decades, with policy being framed by small and select cabinet committees and sub-committees and the input of the Number 10 private office and policy units has become considerable. The election of the Prime Minister by the broad ranks of parliamentary colleagues, and in the case of the Labour, Liberal and Social Democratic parties by the membership at large, has furthered this authority. The cabinet nevertheless continues to function as a disciplined body with its members adhering to collective responsibility once a decision has been made. This solid support extends to the eighty or more junior ministers and parliamentary private secretaries, the so-called 'payroll voters'. Lord Hailsham once described this powerful executive machine as an 'elective dictatorship'. However, considerable initiative and authority is also wielded by the non-elected bureaucracy who provide expertise and continuity.

With the steady shift of political power towards the apex of the political system there have been signs of growing backbench rebellion. This became particularly evident during the 1970s when the proportion of divisions ending in cross-voting tripled and when first the Heath and then the Wilson-Callaghan governments were defeated 6 and 23 times respectively by backbenchers on controversial issues (see Table 1). Such rebellions and defeats were unprecedented in the postwar era. By comparative standards, for example those of the US Congress, members of Parliament remain unusually disciplined. Loyalty to, and dependence upon, the party for nomination and electoral support and the desire for political advancement and patronage remain compelling forces. However, the new generation of younger, well-educated and ambitious MPs has shown a desire to act not merely as 'lobby fodder' but to exercise genuine control and scrutiny powers. A system of fourteen

Select Committees, involving 156 backbenchers, was thus established by the Conservative government in 1979 to act as watchdogs to investigate the activities of ministers and their departments. An earlier, less well thought out, system had been tried without great success in the 1960s. The current committees (see Table 2) enjoy the right to send for 'persons, papers and records' from both within

**Table 1  Government Defeats in Parliament, 1970–83**
*Number of Defeats*

| | | HOUSE OF COMMONS | | HOUSE OF LORDS |
| | | Caused by Government Backbench Revolt | Caused by Opposition Combination | |
| Government | Term | | | |
| Heath | 1970–4 | 6 | 0 | 25 |
| Wilson | 1974 | 0 | 17 | 15 |
| Wilson/Callaghan | 1974–9 | 23 | 19 | 347 |
| Thatcher | 1979–83 | 1 | 0 | 45 |

**Table 2  House of Commons Departmental Select Committees in 1986**

| Committee | Chairman | Members |
| --- | --- | --- |
| Agriculture | John Spence (Con.) | 11 |
| Defence | Sir Humphrey Atkins (Con.) | 11 |
| Education | Sir William van Straubenzee (Con.) | 11 |
| Employment | Ron Leighton (Lab.) | 11 |
| Energy | Ian Lloyd (Con.) | 11 |
| Environment | Sir Hugh Rossi (Con.) | 11 |
| Foreign Affairs | Sir Anthony Kershaw (Con.) | 11 |
| (Sub-committee) | Vacant | — |
| Home Affairs | Sir Edward Gardner (Con.) | 11 |
| (Sub-committee) | John Wheeler (Con.) | 5 |
| Trade & Industry | Kenneth Warren (Con.) | 11 |
| Scottish Affairs | David Lambie (Lab.) | 13 |
| Social Services | Renee Short (Lab.) | 11 |
| Transport | Harry Cowans (Lab.) | 11 |
| Treasury | Terence Higgins (Con.) | 11 |
| (Sub-committee) | Austin Mitchell (Lab.) | 5 |
| Welsh Affairs | Gareth Wardell (Lab.) | 11 |

and outside Parliament and to choose their own subjects for investigation. However, although the new Select Committees have gained a reputation for industry and expertise[1], they remain only advisory bodies, whose reports and recommendations are by no

[1] During the 1979–83 Parliament the House of Commons' Select Committees held 2,140 meetings to collect evidence and deliberate and issued 193 reports.

means binding on the government of the day. By the standards of US Congressional Standing and Investigative Committees they remain weak bodies. They do, nevertheless, represent a small step in the direction of the reassertion of the independent authority of members of the legislature.

A second check on the actions of the executive is imposed by the House of Lords, which has the power to delay non-financial bills for one year and is able to scrutinise the lower house's legislation and make sensible improvements.

This chamber, composed of 790 hereditary peers and peeresses, 350 life peers and peeresses, 20 Law Lords and 26 Lords Spiritual (Church of England Archbishops and Bishops), is, however, unelected and remains wary of exerting its powers to the full in case the Commons reacts by further clipping its wings or even abolishing it. Among the regular attenders in the Lords, it has been calculated that 49% support the Conservatives, 16% Labour, 10% the Alliance and 25% are independent 'crossbenchers'. This gives a moderate right-of-centre bias to the chamber which caused problems for both Labour and Conservative administrations during the years between 1974 and 1986 (see Table 1). During recent years, as the proportion of specially created life peers has increased, the House of Lords has become a more professional and influential body, including within its ranks (see Table 3) experienced figures from the political, industrial, academic and trade union spheres. Between 1960 and 1984 average daily attendance more than doubled from 142 to 322 members, the number of sitting hours per annum increased from 600 to 1195 and ad hoc Select Committees began to be employed to consider the implications of Bills presented.

**Table 3    The Occupational Background of Peers in 1981**

| | % of Total in Category | |
| | Hereditary | Created |
| Occupation | Peers | Life Peers |
| --- | --- | --- |
| Trade Union Officials | — | 4.9% |
| Civil/Diplomatic Service | 6.2% | 16.1% |
| Legal Profession | 5.9% | 18.3% |
| Banking/Insurance | 11.6% | 7.8% |
| Engineers | 1.6% | 3.2% |
| Accountants/Economists | 1.9% | 2.4% |
| Scientists | 0.4% | 1.5% |
| Medical Profession | 0.6% | 3.4% |
| Academic Profession | 3.4% | 18.8% |
| Industrialists | 15.6% | 21.5% |
| Politicians | 3.0% | 34.9% |

A third potential check upon the executive's actions are the residual powers retained by the monarchy, which stands at the apex of the British political system. However, while the monarchy remains a popular and unifying institution, it has become a mere rubber stamp for the executive machine. Only if there is a constitutional crisis or impasse, for example a 'hung parliament', is it likely to play an influential role in political affairs.

A fourth and more important check is exercised by the judiciary, which retains a significant independence from the executive and legislative machine and a considerable interpretative scope. The leading judicial officers are appointed by the Crown on the advice of the Prime Minister, with other judges being appointed by the Lord Chancellor. However, being appointed for life, judges retain great autonomy and their rulings can only be overridden by referral to the most senior judges, in the House of Lords, or by new legislation.

The institutions and laws of the European Community, including the still embryonic European Parliament, constitute a fifth constraint.

It is, however, the verdict of the ballot box exercised at least every five years that remains the ultimate check in the British system of representative government, as the electorate determines to which party effective sovereignty shall be transferred.

## The Party System: the Politics of Class

Britain, lacking the ethnic diversity of the United States or, outside Northern Ireland, the religious cleavages of many continental powers, has become the home for secular, class-based politics built around two competing, antagonistic and ideologically rooted major parties. This two-party division has passed through many cycles—the Royalists versus the Parliamentarians; the Whigs (later Liberals) representing commerce and industry, versus the Tories, representing landed interests; and finally Labour, representing the working community, versus the Conservatives, representing capital.

The chamber of the House of Commons reflects and reinforces this two party division, with the government ranged on one side of the long narrow chamber and the opposition on the other. Unlike the House of Lords, where there is provision for crossbenchers, members of minority parties are obliged to share one side of the

House of Commons with the official opposition. The acknowledgement within the constitution of an official opposition, whose leader is paid from public funds, and the House's procedural rules for debate and committee membership underline this demarcation. There are, for example, 17 debating days set aside for the official opposition and only three for the third largest party, the Liberals, and no select committee has a minor party chairman.

At the electoral level, however, while two parties did dominate politics prior to 1906 and during the years between 1945 and 1970, collecting between 87% and 97% of the votes cast, the periods between 1906 and 1939 and since 1970 have seen three-party politics in terms of electoral support. Only between 70% and 80% of the total votes cast have been given to the Conservative and Labour parties during the last decade, as first Scottish and Welsh Nationalists and latterly, and more solidly, the Liberal-SDP Alliance have risen to challenge their paramountcy. Two-party dominance has, however, persisted in Parliament as a result of the 'first-past-the-post' voting system, combined with the varying geographical spread of support for Labour and the Conservatives. (See Tables 4 and 6.)

**Table 4   Party Share of Commons Vote and Seats, 1945–87**

|  | Conservative Votes | Seats | Labour Votes | Seats | Lib/Alliance Votes | Seats | Total Votes | Turnout | Total Seats |
|---|---|---|---|---|---|---|---|---|---|
| 1945 | 9.6m (40%) | 213 | 11.6m (48%) | 393 | 2.2m (9%) | 12 | 24.1m | 73% | 640 |
| 1950 | 12.5m (43%) | 299 | 13.3m (46%) | 315 | 2.6m (9%) | 9 | 28.8m | 84% | 625 |
| 1951 | 13.7m (48%) | 321 | 13.9m (49%) | 295 | 0.7m (2%) | 6 | 28.6m | 82% | 625 |
| 1955 | 13.3m (50%) | 345 | 12.4m (46%) | 277 | 0.7m (3%) | 6 | 26.8m | 77% | 630 |
| 1959 | 13.7m (49%) | 365 | 12.2m (44%) | 258 | 1.6m (6%) | 6 | 27.9m | 79% | 630 |
| 1964 | 12.0m (43%) | 304 | 12.2m (44%) | 317 | 3.1m (11%) | 9 | 27.7m | 77% | 630 |
| 1966 | 11.4m (42%) | 253 | 13.1m (48%) | 363 | 2.3m (8%) | 12 | 27.3m | 76% | 630 |
| 1970 | 13.1m (46%) | 330 | 12.2m (43%) | 288 | 2.1m (7%) | 6 | 28.3m | 72% | 630 |
| 1974a | 11.9m (38%) | 297 | 11.6m (37%) | 301 | 6.1m (19%) | 14 | 31.3m | 78% | 635 |
| 1974b | 10.5m (36%) | 277 | 11.5m (39%) | 319 | 6.3m (18%) | 13 | 29.2m | 73% | 635 |
| 1979 | 13.7m (44%) | 339 | 11.5m (37%) | 269 | 4.3m (14%) | 11 | 31.2m | 76% | 635 |
| 1983 | 13.0m (42%) | 397 | 8.5m (28%) | 209 | 7.8m (25%) | 23 | 30.7m | 73% | 650 |
| 1987 | 13.8m (42%) | 376 | 10.0m (31%) | 229 | 7.3m (23%) | 22 | 32.6m | 75% | 650 |

The Conservative Party has proved to be the most resilient, skilled and adaptable. Once the party of the landed aristocracy, it accepted the Liberals' mid-19th century social reforms and courted the commercial-industrial middle classes and the skilled working class vote during the late 19th century, under the leadership of Benjamin Disraeli. Later during the 1920s, 1930s and 1950s the party, particularly when led by Baldwin and Macmillan, came to terms with further Liberal and Labour social reforms and established itself as a pragmatic and consensual 'one nation' body. The party has shown, in the words of Lord Salisbury, a 'preposition against change', but has nevertheless moved with the times and accepted the inevitable.

The Conservatives have always been in the forefront in terms of organisation and finance. During the late 19th century, under the direction of John Gorst and Captain Middleton, theirs was the first party to set up a network of local political agents and during the 1980s it pioneered the skilled use of advertising agencies and computerised direct mailing. In terms of publicity and finance, it has consistently maintained an edge over its rivals, being supported today by three-quarters of the national press and able to draw in substantial funds from business groups and smaller, constituency level, donations. Thus in a normal year the constituency branches, with a membership of 1.2 million, raise around £10 million and a further £4 million is provided by, predominantly business, donations. This compares with a Labour Party—national and local—annual income of below £4.5 million per annum and a combined Liberal and SDP Alliance income of below £2 million. The Conservatives can also boast a network of 360 full-time agents, compared with a Labour total of 62 and the Liberals' 22.

The party, with its cautious, free-market, individualist, low tax, strong defence philosophy, draws its support predominantly from middle class and white collar groups and from the more affluent regions of the Southeast, Southwest, East Anglia and the Midlands, particularly from suburban and small town localities. (See Tables 5 and 6.) It has also, however, been able to win support from the upwardly mobile, skilled working class and from lower income groups who share its social values. Within Parliament the party's transition from a landed to a commercial and business base has been reflected in the changed character of its MPs. Its parliamentary membership is still, however, elitist in nature, being

Table 5    Party Share of Votes by Social Groups (June 1987 Election)[1]

| Social Group | Conservative | Labour | Lib-SDP Alliance |
|---|---|---|---|
| Professional/Managerial (AB) | 57% | 14% | 26% |
| Office/Clerical (C1) | 51% | 21% | 26% |
| Skilled Manual (C2) | 40% | 36% | 22% |
| Semi/Unskilled (DE) | 30% | 48% | 20% |

[1] Based on Mori sample of 23,396.

Table 6    Party Share of Votes by Regions (June 1987 Election)

|  | Conservative | Labour | Lib-SDP Alliance | Nat |
|---|---|---|---|---|
| Scotland | 24.0% | 42.4% | 19.2% | 14.0% |
| Wales | 29.5% | 45.1% | 17.9% | 7.3% |
| England North/Northeast | 32.3% | 46.4% | 21.0% | — |
| Northwest | 38.0% | 41.2% | 20.6% | — |
| Yorks & Humberside | 37.4% | 40.6% | 21.7% | — |
| West Midlands | 45.5% | 33.3% | 20.8% | — |
| East Midlands | 48.6% | 30.0% | 21.0% | — |
| East Anglia | 52.1% | 21.7% | 25.8% | — |
| Southwest | 50.6% | 16.8% | 33.1% | — |
| Southeast | 55.6% | 16.8% | 27.2% | — |
| Greater London | 46.5% | 31.5% | 21.3% | — |

dominated today by those educated at public schools (forming 71% of its 1986 total) and those drawn from business (36%) and from the legal profession (21%).

The Conservative Party has always been noted for its cohesion and discipline and exhibits an organisational structure that remains more autocratic, in terms of selection procedures and policy making, than those of other contemporary parties. Within the parliamentary party there exist, however, a number of different ideologically-based factions. These include the once liberal and Disraelian Bow Group (formed in 1956 by Geoffrey Howe and boasting its own journal 'Crossbow'); the progressive Tory Reform Group (established in September 1975 by Peter Walker, which boasts today an extra-parliamentary membership of 1000 and a journal 'Reformer'); the centrist 36-MPs One Nation group (formed in 1950 and chaired today by Bill Benyon); the 'Old Right' Monday Club (established in 1961 to oppose rapid decolonisation in Africa and which today boasts the support of 12 MPs) and Selsdon Group (formed in 1973); and the left-of-centre Charter Movement, which has sought greater democratisation of the party's structure. Under Margaret Thatcher the party has veered away from its traditional pragmatism and consensus and re-adopted a 19th century, Manchester School liberal approach, whose roots can be traced to Sir Robert Peel. This widened the latent internal fissures and spawned a number of reactive ginger groups, most notably Sir Ian Gilmour's 'Inside Left', Francis Pym's 1985–7 'Centre Forward', Tim Yeo's 'Third Term Group' and Jim Lester's 120-MPs Conservative Action for Revival of Employment (CARE). On the radical right of the party, George Gardiner and John Carlisle's 80-MPs '92 Club' (formed in 1965) has pressed for an intensification of the Thatcher government's economic liberalisation programme and strongly opposed the imposition of sanctions against South Africa, while two influential 'New Right' dining clubs, 'The Blue Chips' and 'The St Andrews' Group' have been formed by the parliamentary intakes of 1979 and 1983 respectively.

The Labour Party's origins are much more recent, having emerged during the late 19th and early 20th century as voting rights were extended and as the trade union movement developed to represent the new industrial working classes. It first eclipsed the Liberal Party, briefly tasting power as a minority government in 1923–4 and 1929–31, before establishing itself as a major force in the postwar period, laying down the foundations of the welfare state during the years between 1945 and 1951.

The party has always drawn the bulk of its support from the industrial and manual working classes and particularly from trade union members, to which organisation it has remained umbilically tied. It is most deeply rooted in the traditional industrial regions of South Wales, Central Scotland and Northeastern and Northwestern England (see Table 6) and in the inner cities, and has always espoused an egalitarian and redistributionist policy programme. However, to gain electoral majorities during the 1940s and 1960s it also had to win over a substantial portion of the white collar, middle class vote. This it was able to do through moderating its policy programme and by projecting an attractive, just and progressive image.

The mass membership of the Labour Party is low in comparison to that of the Conservatives, standing at less than 270 000 today. However, it enjoys the affiliation of more than five million trade unionists, who provide 75% of its total funds and sponsor a quarter of its present MPs. Many of its leading parliamentarians have traditionally been drawn from middle class and public school backgrounds, such as Attlee, Cripps, Dalton, Gaitskell, Benn and Foot, and comprised 14% of its 1986 parliamentary total. However, during recent years the party has become dominated by trade unionists and radical white collar educationalists: a sector which provides a quarter of its present MPs.

There have long been strong ideological divisions within the ranks of the Labour Party. During the 1920s the three main factions were the gradualists, ranked around Ramsay MacDonald, the centrist trade unionists, grouped around Ernest Bevin, and the radical Independent Labour Party (ILP) socialists, led by James Maxton, with the first and last groups seceding from the rump of the party in 1931–2. More recently, strong right, centre and left-wing factions have persisted in a movement which has remained tolerant of opinion and notably democratic in its organisational structure.

The oldest groupings within Labour have remained the right-wing Fabian Society and the 'soft left' Tribune Group, both of which publish magazines and papers. The Tribune Group has become a dominating body in the Parliamentary Labour Party (PLP), spawning its two most recent leaders, Michael Foot and Neil Kinnock. It was, however, the right wing which dominated during the 1950s and 1960s. Indeed, it appeared possible at one stage, that, under the leadership of the late Hugh Gaitskell, Labour might radically remould itself along the lines of the moderate German Social Democrats (SPD), by abolishing Clause Four of its constitution and committing itself to a pragmatic, mixed economy approach. During the 1970s, however, the strength of the party's left wing, comprising trade unionists and middle class intellectuals, increased significantly and, centring itself around Tony Benn, pressed for a radical alternative economic strategy, involving widescale nationalisation, price and import controls, withdrawal from the European Economic Community (EEC) and compulsory planning agreements. To see these policies put into effect they called for a fundamental reform of the party's constitution which would increase the influence of committed activists and trade union leaders; make Labour MPs directly accountable to local members; and make conference decisions binding on the parliamentary leadership. They formed the Campaign for Labour Party Democracy (CLPD) in June 1973 and were supported on the fringes by even more radical bodies, including the Labour Co-ordinating Committee (LCC), the Socialist Campaign for Labour Victory (SCLV), the Rank and File Mobilising Committee (RFMC) and the 'Militant Tendency'. The right wing of the party attempted to block or modify these changes and established, in response, the Manifesto Group in December 1974 (later called Campaign for Labour Victory in February 1977) and the Solidarity Group in 1981. However, the left triumphed, with many of its reforms being passed at the 1979–81 conferences. This persuaded many right wingers to defect and establish the new Social Democatic Party (SDP).

Thus the Labour Party today has a clear left-of-centre balance and is composed of three broad bodies—the 84 MP 'soft left' Tribune Group; the 57 MP 'hard left' Campaign Group; and the 88 MP right-of-centre Solidarity Group. On the fringe of the party, a number of its leading figures having been expelled, lies the 7000 member 'party within a party', the Trotskyite 'Militant Tendency' (officially known as the Revolutionary Socialist League) and a number of London-based Trotskyite groups based around the newspapers 'Labour Herald', 'Labour Briefing' and 'Socialist Organiser'. Labour thus remains an unwieldy 'broad church' alliance and the most difficult party to lead and control.

During the last two decades the class-based, post war, two-party system has come under increasing pressure as a result of changing economic and social forces. Of particular importance have been the steady decline in the proportion of the workforce employed in the manual and manufacturing sector, from a peak of 40% in 1950 to only 25% in 1983, and the rise in the number employed in the white collar and service sector, from 43% to 65%, during the corresponding period. Secondly, the electorate has become progressively younger, more affluent, better educated and more mobile—the numbers travelling abroad on holidays, for example, doubled during the 1970s. These economic and social changes have weakened the class loyalties binding voters to the Labour and Conservative parties and have led instead to their shopping around at election time in a hard-nosed fashion and listening to and being influenced by the opinions and images projected by the mass media.

During the 1950s and 1960s this weakening of traditional voting patterns was camouflaged as the policies of the two main parties slowly converged in a 'Butskellite' fashion, enabling them to emerge as broad 'catch all' parties during a period of steady economic growth. However, this two-party system crumbled during the troubled 1970s as electors searched for more successful alternatives. Membership of the Conservative Party declined between 1970 and 1983 from 1.5 million to 1.2 million and that of Labour from 700000 to a mere 274000[1]; electoral swings became more pronounced; and by 1979 opinion polls showed only 20% of the electorate identifying closely with one of these two major parties. Decline was less serious for the Conservatives since it was to the right of centre rather than to the left that the electorate began to move. People became more affluent and bourgeois in outlook, many moving away from the inner cities and traditional industrial regions towards the suburbs, shire towns and the south and east of England and increasingly becoming home owners, even on council estates. These 'new middle classes' became satisfied with the existing welfare state and the mixed economy and were concerned

[1] In 1953 Conservative Party membership totalled 2.8m; Labour 1.3 million.

to resist any further extension of the public sector. They were disturbed by the increasing remoteness of centralised government and the movement towards large monopoly companies and standardised produce. These anxieties were reflected in the growth of the nationalist movement in Scotland and Wales; the emergence of the consumer lobby and environmental movement; and campaigns for real ale and wholesome food and the assertion that 'small is beautiful'.

At the electoral level these grassroots movements coincided with a revival in the fortunes of Britain's second oldest party, the Liberals, which, in alliance with the newly formed Social Democratic Party, threatened to 'break the mould' of the British political system. The Liberal Party, acted as the pioneers of social reform in the years between 1857 and 1914, gathering together the support of factory owners, skilled artisans and non-conformists around an almost Thatcherite programme of free-trade, fiscal probity and self improvement. The party, under the promptings of David Lloyd George, became more radical and interventionist during the 1900s, introducing old age pensions and national insurance, for example, and engaging in electoral alliances with the emerging Labour Party.

The Liberals were, however, squeezed out of power by the class based Conservative and Labour parties during the half-century between 1920 and 1970 and were forced back towards their Celtic and non-conformist fringes in Scotland and Southwestern England. The party, stressing individualism and decentralisation, remained weakly organised and became the home for eccentric and maverick figures. However, under the leadership of first Jo Grimond (1956–67) and Jeremy Thorpe (1967–76), it began to re-assert itself as a significant centrist force and captured white collar and middle class votes during the early 1970s. Support for the party dramatically tripled in 1974, when it won 6 million votes (19% of the total cast), as a result of substantial Conservative defections. Under the leadership of David Steel it has become more professional and hard-headed. It briefly shared power, during 1977–8, and joined forces in 1981 with the Social Democrats in a moderate, left-of-centre Alliance. This has won over many former Labour voters and given the two parties a unique and even spread of support across social groups and geographical areas. (See Tables 5 and 6).

Much of the following of the Alliance remains fickle and often negative, representing the protest votes cast alternately by disenchanted Conservative and Labour electors. The Alliance parties have, however, tried to establish a coherent centrist policy programme on the model of the SPD of West Germany. This involves commitment to the European Community and NATO, to the mixed economy and to a decentralised, participative approach to government. They reject the Labour Party's dogmatic adherence (in Clause Four) to further nationalisation, but share its concern for a more equitable distribution of wealth, following the tenets of Beveridge and Keynes. They share with the Conservative Party the desire to see the trade union movement reformed and democratised, but seek also to democratise industry through the establishment of workers' participation in industrial management. The Social Democrats are more 'socialist' in outlook than the Liberals and are more tightly and centrally organised. The Liberal Party remains, in contrast, a diffuse body and contains a number of diverse factions which include the radical left-wing National League of Young Liberals, the local-issue orientated 'Community Liberals', who are forcefully represented by Tony Greaves' Association of Liberal Councillors (ALC), and a declining and ageing coterie of right-wing Gladstonian individualists. In general, however, divisions within the Party remain less obvious, than those within the two major parties.

The revival of the Liberals and the emergence of the SDP, drawing support from new white collar, service sector and 'post industrial' groups, became one of the most significant features of British politics during the last decade as the pages which follow demonstrate. This emergence has been assisted by a polarisation in outlook among the Conservative and Labour parties, enabling them to create a centrist wedge of support among between 20% and 30% of the electorate and build up a combined membership of 160000 during the 1983–6 period. The Alliance anticipated further increasing this level of support to a threshold level of 30–35% in the 1987 election which would have enabled it to hold the 'balance of power' and play a key role in the determination of subsequent government policies. Such a 'breakthrough' would have had far-reaching consequences for the British constitution, promising to lead to a thoroughgoing reform of the parliamentary and electoral system, involving the introduction of proportional representation, reform of the House of Lords, a devolution and decentralisation of administrative power and the inauguration of a more open era of government. However, a recovery in the fortunes of the Labour Party under the centre-left leadership of Neil Kinnock and a solidifying of support for the Conservatives in the June 1987 election frustrated such a breakthrough, squeezing the Alliance into a clear, minority third position. This was a major and unexpected blow to its post-1970 advance as a 'Third Force'. It created a crisis in strategy for the left and centre-left in British politics, raising the prospects of continued Conservative hegemony in the manner of the 1920s and 1930s. Of equal significance for British politics, the re-election of the Thatcher administration for a third term removed from the immediate agenda any question of significant reform of the central governmental or electoral system.

# Part Two

# BACKGROUND TO THE CALLAGHAN AND THATCHER ERAS: 1945-76

## The Decline from Greatness: the 1945-74 Background

### 1945-51: A 'New Deal' for Britain

In the July 1945 general election, held just two months after the formal ending of hostilities in the Second World War, the Labour Party achieved an unexpected victory against the wartime premier and Conservative leader Winston Churchill, capturing 47.8% of the national vote compared with the Tories' 39.8%, thus achieving their first-ever parliamentary majority by the landslide margin of 146 seats. The Labour triumph of July 1945 reflected the shift in public attitudes away from self-help individualism towards socially concerned co-operatism that had resulted from the experience of more than four years of national coalition government, large scale state control and interventionism. It was a consequence, similarly, of the enforced radicalisation and intermixing of British society that had resulted from the 'total war' experience of 1939-45, with its mass conscription, service education, 'all-poor-together' rationing and city to countryside evacuee movements. These social changes had such an impact on the nation's previously cosseted middle classes that the Labour Party was, in July 1945, to win seats in the Tory shire counties of Southeastern England in a manner that was never to be replicated during the postwar era. Above all, the Labour victory of July 1945 resulted from the party's promise of a 'New Deal' for Britain and its pledge to construct a more just and equitable society than had existed during the unemployment-riven 1930s and to create the 'land fit for heroes' that had been proffered by Lloyd George in 1918, but had failed to materialise.

The new Labour government, led by the quietly efficient Clement Attlee and including the wartime coalition figures of Ernest Bevin

(Foreign Secretary 1945–51), Herbert Morrison (Deputy Prime Minister 1945–51), Hugh Dalton (Chancellor 1945–7) and Stafford Cripps (Board of Trade 1945–7, Chancellor 1947–50), was an experienced, high-powered body. Its promised programme, 'Let Us Face the Future', was ambitious and far-reaching. Building upon the initiatives of the wartime national coalition, including the December 1942 Beveridge Report on social security, R A Butler's 1944 Education Act and the 1945 Family Allowances Act, the Attlee administration placed top priority on social reform, aimed at effecting a substantial redistribution of income towards the poorer sections of society and establishing a new 'Welfare State' which would guarantee an acceptable minimum standard of living for all social groups. These aims were substantially achieved through the passage of the National Insurance and Health Service Acts of 1946, which established the principle of 'universality' as opposed to means-tested selectivity in the grant of sickness, unemployment and pension benefits, and the creation of a new National Health Service (NHS) to provide free health care for all, regardless of background or wealth.

The Attlee government, secondly, adopted a radically new approach to the conduct of economic policy which, accepting the recommendation of the 1944 White Paper on Employment, acknowledged it to be the responsibility of government to seek to maintain a 'high and stable level of employment'. This was to be achieved through a Keynesian 'demand-management' fiscal policy and the adoption of a measure of 'indicative planning' to establish a coherent national framework for resource use. In addition, the government decided to take into public ownership key strategic and monopolistic enterprises, including the Bank of England and civil aviation (1946), coal, cables and wireless (1947), rail and road transport and electricity (1946), gas (1949) and iron and steel (1951), so that the state could exert control over the 'commanding heights' of the economy. The form of public control adopted by nationalisation supremo Herbert Morrison was the sober and conservative 'public corporation' model, based on a board of government-appointed managers whose task it was to break even on an annual basis. This had already been used for the Central Electricity Board (1926), BBC (1927) and BOAC (1939) during the interwar period.

Finally, in the foreign policy sphere, the new Labour government began, with the grant of independence to India (1947), Ceylon (Sri Lanka–1948), Burma (1948) and Palestine (1948) and the creation of the 'New Commonwealth', a slow, painful process of decolonisation which was to be an important backdrop to British political history during the ensuing decades. At the same time, under the insistent promptings of Foreign Secretary Bevin, the Attlee administration played a key role in ensuring the maintenance of close American economic and military ties to Europe and sanctioned work on the development of an independent British nuclear deterrent.

The Labour government's achievements were such that the 1945–51 period represented, in hindsight, a major turning point for British politics and society. A new welfare state 'security net' was established, necessitating a sharp increase in government spending as a proportion of GNP from an interwar level of below 25% to a 1951 level of 36%. In addition, with a fifth of the economy being transferred to public ownership, a new Keynesian form private-public 'mixed economy' was framed. Both these changes led to a significant extension in the role and operations of central government and necessitated the creation of a new breed of technocrat administrators. Above all, however, the Attlee era saw a broader and more forward-looking transfiguration of political and public attitudes, with a new 'social democratic' consensus being gradually established on key welfare and economic management issues, as well as foreign policy. This consensus was broadly to persist through the ensuing two decades.

Both domestically and externally, however, the Attlee administration was faced with tremendous problems bequeathed by the costly and destructive Second World War. Constant currency and balance of payments crises forced the retention of price controls and rationing, while abroad the nation became embroiled, as part of the United Nations' forces, in the 1950–3 Korean War. The constant belt-tightening austerity of the postwar quinquennium, coupled with left-wing disappointment at the alleged conservatism of a number of the government's domestic and overseas initiatives, resulted in a reaction against the Labour Party in the general election of 1950. Faced by a Conservative Party, whose organisational structure had been radically re-organised and whose policy outlook modernised to come to terms with and accept the welfare reforms and many of the nationalisation measures of 1945–50, Labour's majority was reduced to only five seats. A year later, riven by internal policy dissensions over the decision by the new Chancellor, Hugh Gaitskell, to raise taxes and charge NHS patients for spectacles and dentures (that precipitated the resignation of Health Secretary, Aneurin Bevan), the party, although raising its share of the vote to a record level of 48.8% and topping the national poll (see Table 4), lost its parliamentary majority to the Conservatives in a new general election.

## 1951–9: The Years of Conservative Hegemony

The new Conservative government was led by Winston Churchill, now 77 years old and included Sir Anthony Eden as Deputy Premier and Foreign Secretary and R A Butler as Chancellor. Churchill ran and organised the cabinet on 1940–5 wartime lines, devolving considerable power to a select group of individual ministers who acted as policy 'overlords' in broad spheres. The Prime Minister's own views on economic management and welfare questions had failed to catch up with the 1945–51 advances of the Attlee era. However, domestic policy making was entrusted to the progressivist duumvirate of 'Rab' Butler (1902–81) and Harold Macmillan (Housing Minister), who proceeded to accept and build upon the achievements of their Labour predecessors, although giving greater emphasis to private initiatives in the new 'mixed economy' approach. Thus the iron and steel and road haulage industries were denationalised in 1953, private housebuilding was encouraged with special incentives, and the remaining price and rationing controls were fully removed, in 1953–4. In broader terms, however, the Churchill government continued to provide funding for the health and welfare sector and pursued a 'stop-go' Keynesian fiscal policy with such vigour that the term 'Butskellism' (combining the names of the two Labour and Conservative Chancellors of 1950–5) was coined to describe the new-found postwar policy consensus.

The Conservative Party assumed power during an era of strong growth in the international economy following the depression of 1945–51. This economic upswing, coupled with the ending of hostilities in Korea, provided the springboard for a landslide Conservative victory in the general election of May 1955 : the party's vote rising to 49.7% and its parliamentary majority increasing from 17 to 58 seats. The party was led into this election by Sir Anthony Eden (1897–1977), who had replaced the ailing Churchill as Prime Minister after the latter's retirement in April 1955. Eden, an impressively successful Foreign Secretary between 1951–5, proved to be an unfortunate choice as the new national leader and was to remain in office for barely twenty months. An excellent deputy, he lacked the skill and confidence for prime ministerial leadership. His constant interference in minor departmental matters earned him the enmity of senior colleagues, while exhibiting a reckless lack of judgment in his own policy initiatives. The most serious of these, his October 1956 decision to join with France and Israel in an abortive invasion of the Suez Canal, which had recently been nationalised by the new Egyptian President, Gamal Abdel Nasser—a bête noire of the British Prime Minister—precipitated an international crisis and forced a humiliating policy climbdown. It was to be followed in January 1957 by Eden's resignation on health grounds.

The 'Suez crisis' was to emerge as a turning point in British foreign policy, highlighting the nation's diminished world status and influence and ushering in an era of rapid decolonisation in Africa and Asia. Its impact on British domestic politics proved, however, to be only transitory. Harold Macmillan (1894–1987), the popular and successful Housing Minister between 1951–4 and Chancellor between 1955–7, was selected by Tory grandees to replace Eden as party leader and thus Prime Minister. He proceeded swiftly to repair the damage inflicted by the Suez fiasco by skilled diplomacy overseas and the adoption of a confident, decisive, media-orientated leadership style at home. In addition, Macmillan, working in tandem with Chancellor Heathcoat Amory, succeeded, through deliberate tax-cutting measures, in fuelling a strong domestic consumer boom during 1958–9 which provided the basis for a third successive Conservative general election victory in October 1959: the party capturing 49.4% of the national vote to Labour's 43.8% and increasing its parliamentary majority to 100 seats.

The 1950s were an era characterised by buoyant economic growth, Conservative dominance and political stability, with popular satisfaction with incumbent parties evidenced at national and local levels. They were also years which saw the apogee of Conservative-Labour two-party politics.

The Liberals, who had fielded candidates in more than three quarters (475) of the country's constituencies in the 1945 and 1950 general elections and captured more than two million votes, became a mere appendage to the political system. Their national vote slumped to below one million and hundreds of local constituency branches were boarded up as the party began to put up only 100–200 candidates in the 1951 and 1955 general elections. Ineffectually led since 1945 by Clement Davies, they failed to establish any clear, new or electorally appealing themes to prevent the defection of their former supporters to the ranks of the Conservatives or Labour. Thus during the elections between 1951-9 the Liberals garnered, on average, barely 3.7% of the national vote compared with the Conservatives' 49.0% and Labour's 46.3%.

The Labour Party's overall share of the vote stood, during the 1950s, at an historically high level when compared with its pre-war 30-35%. It enjoyed a solid base of manual and skilled worker support from the 40% of the labour force who were employed in the manufacturing sector, but also had the backing of a significant portion of the middle class electorate, thus enabling it to capture, for example, 126 of the 343 seats in Southern England and the Midlands in May 1955. Despite this growth in popular support, the party's prospects of rapidly regaining power were frustrated by serious and growing divisions within its ranks, as many of the senior figures of the 1945-51 administration, such as Attlee (1883-1967), Bevin (1881-1951), and Cripps (1889-1952), retired or died. In their stead, a new generation of, more radical, left-wingers, who included Michael Foot (1913- ) and Ian Mikardo (1909- ), as well as the more moderate Harold Wilson (1916- ), Barbara Castle (1911- ) and Richard Crossman (1907-74), rose to prominence under the leadership of the fiery Welsh orator Aneurin Bevan (1897-1960). This 'Bevanite faction' pressed for further nationalisation and welfare reforms and, siding with the recently (1958) formed peace pressure group, the Campaign for Nuclear Disarmament (CND), firmly opposed the development of an independent British nuclear deterrent. They remained outnumbered, however, by the party's centre-right majority led by party leader (since December 1955) Hugh Gaitskell (1906-63) and comprising Dalton (1887-1962), Morrison (1888-1965), James Callaghan (1912- ) and the young 'revisionists' Denis Healey (1917- ), Roy Jenkins (1920- ) and Tony Crosland (1919-77). This majority grouping was committed to an Atlanticist and nuclear-based defence policy and, drawing upon Crosland's seminal treatise 'The Future of Socialism' (1956), placed stress on improved welfare provision and income redistribution in a growth-orientated mixed economy, rather than on further nation-alisation. They enjoyed the firm 'block vote' backing of the majority of trade union leaders and were thus able to control the annual party conference. However, debates grew increasingly rancorous and divisive.

### 1959–64: A Period of Reckoning

October 1959 marked the highpoint of the postwar growth era and the stable, national two-party system. The ensuing decades were to see mounting economic difficulties and political and social instability, characterised by the growing realisation that Britain was failing to maintain its position in the world and undergoing a sharp and painful period of relative economic decline.

Evidence of the nation's decline could be traced as far back as the late 19th century when it began to lag behind Germany and the United States in the 'new wave' of steel, chemical and electrical industries. During the 1930s, however, Britain had continued to dominate the world economy, being responsible for 35% of world trade and presiding over a vast multiracial empire, which embraced a quarter of the world's population and land surface. The destruction wrought to Europe and global trading during the Second World War and its immediate aftermath enabled America to steal a march during the next decade and emerge as the new, paramount economic power. During the 1950s, as European trade expanded and Britain decolonised, the country's continental neighbours began to catch up rapidly and close the gap in terms of living standards, registering 'miracle' rates of economic growth. Thus, while in 1950 Britain's share of world trade had stood at 25%, by 1962 it had shrunk to a mere 15%. Per capita living standards increased substantially during the 'affluent' 1950s and unemployment remained at well below 2%, compared with the pre-war level of 10%, but the nation's diminishing ability to face up to sharpening overseas competition in a growing range of new industrial sectors was of mounting public concern and led to talk of a 'British disease'.

Discussion of this national malaise increased during the 1960s as the growth rate slumped to below 2% per annum during a period when rates of between 5–13% were registered in the United States, West Germany, Italy, France and Japan. At the start of the decade, following the engineered boom of 1958–9, a sharp deflationary 'stop' squeeze was applied by Chancellors Heathcoat-Amory and Selwyn Lloyd, between 1960–1. This led to a sudden stalling in industrial growth and the first serious recession since 1951, with the level of unemployment rising sharply to 800 000 in 1963 and the balance of payments seriously deteriorating. The Macmillan government responded by attempting to impose a 2.5% pay ceiling on public sector wage increases. This only served, however, to fuel a series of debilitating strikes by railway workers, postmen and nurses and to lead to a marked fall in the popular rating of the Conservative administration.

The prime beneficiary of the 1961–3 slump in government support was not, however, the Labour Party, which was riven by internal dissent over Hugh Gaitskell's attempt to restructure the party's programme by dropping adherence to Clause IV[1], but rather the revivified Liberals. Under the dynamic new leadership of Jo Grimond (1913– ), the party had, since September 1956, developed a fresh and distinctive new policy programme based on support for entry into the European Economic Community (EEC), calls for a radical reappraisal of Britain's costly world role and the advocacy of a more co-operative industrial policy of workers' participation and profit-sharing. The Liberal revival became strikingly apparent in March 1962 when, in a parliamentary by-election in the Kent commuter suburb of Orpington, the party dramatically overturned a Conservative majority of 14760. During the ensuing weeks national opinion polls were to show all three political parties neck and neck at 29–30%, in sharp contradistinction to the two-party 1950s.

Prime Minister Macmillan reacted to this sudden decline in government support by adopting a new Liberal-tinged foreign policy, founded upon support for more rapid decolonisation and the creation of a streamlined, non-conscripted, medium-power army. This was buttressed by the Nassau agreement with President Kennedy in December 1962 for Britain's purchase of the new Polaris nuclear missile system. Macmillan also continued to press forward Britain's application, which had been formally made in July 1961, to join the EEC, but was to be rebuffed by the French President, Charles de Gaulle, who was concerned with Britain's close 'special relationship' links with the United States. In the domestic economic sphere, a second, and equally significant, policy change was made in July 1962 by Macmillan's sacking a third of his cabinet, including Chancellor Selwyn Lloyd, in what became known as the 'Night of the Long Knives'. The flexible Reginald Maudling (1917–79) was appointed Chancellor and a more interventionist economic strategy was embarked upon. This had already been signalled by the creation of the National Economic and Development Council (NEDC), bringing together government,

---

[1] The commitment in the Party's 1918 constitution to bring into public ownership the means of production, distribution and exchange.

industrialists and trade union leaders to discuss growth targets in an 'indicative' manner, and was further emphasised by the appointment in 1963 of Lord Hailsham (1907– ) as Minister with Special Responsibility for the north east and Edward Heath (1916– ) as Minister for Industry, Trade and Regional Development.

The domestic policy changes of the Macmillan administration in 1962–3 were precursors to a more corporatist, planned approach to policy-making that was subsequently to be seen during the mid and later 1960s. The measures failed, however, in the short term, to revive either the fortunes of the economy or the administration's opinion poll rating. A depressing 'fin de siecle' atmosphere began to pervade the government during 1962–3, as it was rocked by spy and sex scandals, involving the Admiralty clerk, William Vassall, and the Minister for War, John Profumo. In the midst of these difficulties Harold Macmillan was rushed to hospital in October 1963 for a prostate operation. Faced with the prospect of a period of enforced convalescence and incapacitatation, the Prime Minister tendered his resignation. He was replaced, in November, following a backstage intra-party contest, by the 60-year-old former peer and Foreign Secretary, Sir Alec Douglas Home.

The replacement of the flamboyant and popular Macmillan by the awkward, aristocratic Home was a serious blow for the Conservative Party as it prepared to fight a new general election in 1964. Home had been a compromise choice, selected by the party's 'inner circle', who had been equally divided in their sympathies between the alternatives of Butler, Hailsham and Maudling. His selection, however, served to open up latent divisions within the Conservative Party, with the younger figures of Enoch Powell (1912– ) and Iain Macleod (1913–70) refusing to accept office in his new cabinet. It also proved suicidal in what was emerging as a new age of television electioneering.[1] His Labour opponent, Harold Wilson, who had been elected party leader following Gaitskell's sudden death from pleurisy in January 1963[2], constantly embarrassed Home both inside and outside Parliament with his debating and presentational skills. Thirteen years younger, and a grammar school and Oxford University-educated meritocrat, who combined a fine grasp of economic issues with a down-to-

---

[1] Television ownership had spread rapidly during the early 1960s, there being 12 million television licences in 1964 compared with only 4.5 million in 1955, and with 85% of householdings with TVs.

[2] Wilson had been challenged by the right-wingers George Brown and James Callaghan, defeating the former by 144 to 103 PLP votes in a 'run off' second ballot.

earth populist manner, Wilson cut a sharply contrasting figure to the Eton-educated Scottish aristocrat who joked about counting with matchsticks. Wilson succeeded in uniting the left and right wings of his party around a forward-looking economic strategy, based on planning and the harnessing of modern technology in a socialist manner, utilising the slogan, 'the white heat of the technological revolution'. With a manifesto entitled, 'The New Britain', and a leader who was marketed in a Kennedyesque fashion, Labour sought to establish itself as the party most in touch with the rising new postwar generation, pledged to introduce new, radical economic, educational, technological and social reforms to take the country forward, following what it termed 'thirteen wasted years' of Conservative rule.

This electoral strategy proved to be strikingly successful and when polling took place in October 1964 a marked 3.4% national swing towards Labour was recorded, turning the Conservative majority of 100 into a slender Labour majority of four seats. The Conservative vote slumped by 1.7 million to its lowest proportionate level since 1950, while support for the Liberals (fielding candidates in more than half the country's constituencies for the first time since 1950) climbed markedly by 1.5 million to a postwar high of 11%, as many Tory voters transferred support in a protest fashion.

## 1964–70: The Wilson Technocratic Era

With the election of the Wilson Labour government of October 1964, the first concerted attempt was made to address the problems of the so-called 'British disease', through a thoroughgoing programme of institutional and economic reform. A series of academic studies of Britain's economic problems had pin-pointed a number of factors which required remedy if the country was to regain a leading position in the world economic race. Industry needed to raise its productivity through investment in new technology and machinery and by reforming labour practices. In addition, it needed to improve the quality of its output and distribution through better design, better management and more aggressive marketing. The educational system needed to be remoulded to remove its bias towards the City and the professions and to produce a much needed new generation of well-trained engineers, technicians and managers. The country needed to adjust itself to a diminished world role, reducing its proportionately high level of defence expenditure and re-orientating itself towards the growing European market. The Treasury needed to give greater emphasis to domestic, as opposed to external, commercial considerations in its fiscal strategy. The civil service needed to open itself up and recruit from a broader spectrum of talent, with a wider range of ideas. Finally, Parliament needed to modernise and reform its ancient practices to adjust to an era of mounting legislative and administrative demands.

The Wilson team, concurring with much of this analysis, put forward a radically ambitious policy programme designed to reverse the cycle of decline. At the heart of this programme was, building upon the work of the Macmillan-Home administrations of 1962-4, the adoption of a more interventionist economic strategy, involving 'indicative planning', state investment support for industry, education and research, and the creation of a closer, corporatist partnership between government, industry and the trade unions. The early centrepieces of this programme were the creation of a special new planning and co-ordinating Department of Economic Affairs (DEA), headed by party deputy leader, George Brown, which was designed to counteract the strong, short-term, financier-based Treasury influence of the new Chancellor, James Callaghan, and the establishment of a Ministry of Technology, headed by the former TGWU trade union leader Frank Cousins. The DEA drew up, in 1965, a plan for 25% growth in industrial output between 1965-70, placing stress on improved industrial training, creating new Industrial Training Boards and increasing investment and rationalisation. To help achieve these aims, a new body, the Industrial Reorganisation Corporation (IRC), was established in January 1966 as a government-supported investment bank to provide funds to help finance merger operations, for example the amalgamation of Leyland and the British Motor Corporation (BMC). The object was to foster the creation of a new category of 'super firms', powerful enough to compete with American, German, French and Japanese conglomerates. In addition, in an effort to make such interventionist planning work without leading to wage inflation, a voluntary agreement was signed with trade union leaders in November 1964 which would relate new wage increases to improvements in productivity. An independent National Board for Prices and Incomes (NBPI) was also set up to monitor wages and prices movements. The framework for this new policy strategy was established during the

Wilson government's first year in office. With the re-election of the government, with a greatly increased majority of 96 seats in the March 1966 general election, the stage was set for the practical testing of the programme.

The new interventionist policy approach, which was combined, working on the recommendations of the 1963 Robbins Report, with a major expansion of the higher and tertiary educational sector, was well intentioned, being modelled to a considerable degree on the 'miracle' blueprints of West Germany, France and Japan. It ultimately failed, however, because of irresolution in its implementation, internal cabinet wrangles, the opposition of trade union leaders and adverse external economic conditions. Thus during 1965–6 serious policy differences emerged between George Brown at the DEA and Chancellor Callaghan over fiscal strategy following a period of balance of payments crises. Brown favoured an early currency devaluation, but Callaghan, influenced by Treasury opinion, chose instead to pursue a deflationary course. He was supported in this view by Prime Minister Wilson, resulting in the transfer of Brown to the Foreign Office in August 1966. A temporary and legally binding wage freeze was introduced as part of this deflationary programme, but it only succeeded in provoking a series of industrial stoppages. During 1967, following the outbreak of war in the Middle East and the temporary closing of the Suez Canal, economic conditions worsened, but it was not until November 1967 that the sharp (14%), inevitable, but belated, devaluation of sterling took place.

Straitened economic conditions forced sharp budgetary cutbacks by the new Chancellor, Roy Jenkins, who had replaced Callaghan in late November 1967, and many of the planning ideas of 1964–6 were abandoned. The Wilson government concentrated instead on a more conservative, managerialist approach to economic affairs. Policy-making moved increasingly into the hands of the Prime Minister himself, supported by a powerful 'kitchen cabinet' team, comprising his personal secretary Marcia Williams, later Lady Falkender, defence adviser George Wigg, the economic professors Nicholas Kaldor and Thomas Balogh and the rising politicians Gerald Kaufman and Peter Shore, who ran the DEA on Wilson's behalf from August 1967. The Labour leader, lacking the commitment to engage in major structural economic reform, concentrated instead on attempting to engineer a successful and orthodox economic recovery in time for fresh elections in 1970–1.

Similarly, in the sphere of institutional reform, the Wilson government failed, as a result of a combination of intra-party and external opposition, to push through meaningful changes. The government's proposal to reform the House of Lords, seeking to take away voting rights from second generation hereditary peers and those over the age of 72, had to be abandoned as a result of the combined opposition of Conservatives and Labour left-wingers in the House of Commons in February 1969. Secondly, and more seriously, its White Paper plan, 'In Place of Strife', for trade union reform, which aimed to force ballots before strikes and to withdraw the immunity of unofficial strikers from legal sanctions, was abandoned during its early stages as a result of the strong antipathy voiced by trade union linked MPs, including Home Secretary James Callaghan, within and outside the cabinet. Only three minor and diluted measures of reform to the political system were thus achieved between 1964–70: a re-organisation of the civil service, on more professional and specialised lines, following the recommendations of the Fulton Commission (1966–8); the establishment, by Leader of the House Richard Crossman, of a number of specialist, backbencher staffed, select committees; and the creation of the office of Ombudsman (Parliamentary Commissioner), in 1967.

In the foreign policy sphere, the Wilson administration also shied away from the full implementation of many of the manifesto proposals of 1964 or the decisions of its Party's conference and adopted, instead, a stance which was similar in large degree to that of its Conservative predecessor. It came to accept the need for a British independent nuclear deterrent and maintained close relations with the Johnson administration (1963–8) in the United States, publicly supporting America's involvement in Vietnam. It tried, but failed, as a result of a further French veto, to negotiate the country's entry into the EEC in 1967. Economic sanctions against the Smith UDI government in Rhodesia (Zimbabwe) were imposed, but a trade embargo against South Africa was refused. Finally, after an initial period of active funding, the flow of overseas development aid to the Third World was proportionately reduced, between 1966–70. The Wilson government, following the Prime Minister's declaration in 1960 that, 'Britain is a world power, a world influence or she is nothing', failed, above all, to wake up to the need to adjust to a substantially diminished world role. Not until January 1968, when economic necessity forced swingeing budgetary cutbacks, was a major re-appraisal of defence spending made, with the momentous decision to phase out the country's overseas commitments east of Suez and to concentrate instead on performing a more narrowly-based Atlantic and European defence role.

The Wilson years were not, however, completely barren of achievement. In the social sphere important measures were passed which served to update legislation in accordance with changed social patterns and opinions and to reduce social and class differences in what, during the 1950s, had remained a still divided nation. Into this category fell the lowering of the voting age and age of majority to 18, in 1969; the creation of a Race Relations Board, in 1965, to deal with complaints of harassment and discrimination; and the increased momentum given to the movement away from selective to comprehensive education.[1] Many other important social reforms were passed on an all-party basis through the use of Private Members' Bills. These included the abolition of capital punishment (1965); the legalising of homosexual practices between consenting adults and of abortion within guidelines (1967); the termination of the censorship of stage plays (1968); and the relaxation of the rules for divorce (1969).

However, despite such achievements in modernising and humanising society, the overall record of the 1964–70 Wilson government was one of considerable disappointment, particularly for supporters on the left. This disillusionment, following the high hopes of a 'new course' entertained in 1964, had considerable consequences both inside and outside Parliament, resulting in a lasting and fundamental change in the nature of British politics during the 1960s.

Inside the Commons, the Labour government was to find itself subject to an unprecedented number of backbench rebellions from the party's increasingly influential left wing, who were appalled by the conservative nature of many of the policy decisions of the right-wing-dominated Wilson Cabinet. Such revolts occurred primarily on defence and foreign policy issues, but also on trade union reform, spending economies and immigration law proposals. They were to be the precursor of the growing level of backbench instability which was to be evident within both major political parties during the 1970s[2] as a crop of divisive, cross-party

---

[1] By 1970 a third of the secondary school population was being educated in comprehensives.

[2] Divisions were, however, to be stronger within the Labour Party as a result of the party's left-right cleavage and the ability of its locally entrenched trade union sponsored MPs to defy the central Party headquarters.

issues—for example EEC entry and immigration control—began to enter the political agenda.

Outside Parliament the fall in voting levels in successive general elections, from 77% of the electorate in October 1964 to 72% in June 1970, and of party membership (see page 9), reflected the public's growing political disenchantment. In addition, the incumbent government began during these years to experience an unprecedented number of by-election defeats. During the 1945–51 and 1951–64 Labour and Conservative administrations the incumbent party had been defeated in by-elections on only one and ten occasions respectively. By contrast, the 1966–70 Labour administration lost 16 (52%) of its 31 contests. An additional feature of these reverses was the disproportionate number of successes achieved by minor parties, as the two-party dominance of the postwar era continued to decline. The Liberal Party, which had been under the leadership of Jeremy Thorpe since Jo Grimond's resignation after the 1966 election and which was only slowly adjusting to the era of Labour governance, failed to improve its standing significantly between 1966–70. It was, instead, the minor nationalist parties in Wales (Plaid Cymru) and Scotland (the Scottish Nationalist Party —SNP), which had been operating without success since 1925 and 1928 respectively, that now suddenly rose to prominence by achieving startling by-election successes in the Labour seats of Carmarthen (1966) and Hamilton (1967). These victories resulted primarily from the large-scale defections of disillusioned former Labour supporters. They were also, however, an indication of a growing regionalist antipathy to the actions of the remote government in London.

Of equal note were the actions outside Parliament of pressure groups and radicals. Trade unionists, opposed to the wage restraint policies introduced from July 1966, engaged in industrial action to a heightened degree, the number of working days lost as a result of labour disputes rising from a figure of 2.7 million in 1967 to 6.8 million in 1969. On the university campuses and streets of London radical student groups, influenced by the anti-Vietnam War movement sweeping across America, by the 'May events' in Paris during 1968 and by the spread of a 'New Left' political ideology, engaged in sit-in protests and spontaneous demonstrations. Thirdly, and most seriously, in Northern Ireland, the emergence, influenced again by similar developments in the United States, of a Catholic civil rights movement during 1968–9, which culminated in the election of the Irish republican student Bernadette Devlin to

Parliament in the Mid-Ulster by-election of April 1969, resulted in major civil turmoil and the forced despatch of British troops to the province in August 1969. This initiated an 'Ulster crisis' which was to defy solution during the ensuing two decades.

The deepest trough of unpopularity and by-election reverses experienced by the Wilson government occurred between 1967–9. During 1969–70, however, economic indicators began to improve and the opinion poll fortunes of the party dramatically revived. In July 1969 the Conservatives had led Labour by 19 points in national polls. Less than a year later, Labour, having performed well in recent borough elections, enjoyed a comfortable lead. A general election was thus called nine months ahead of schedule by Prime Minister Wilson, the date being set for June 1970. The party was faced by an unpopular and untelegenic Conservative leader, Edward Heath, who had already experienced defeat once in March 1966, and by a Liberal Party which was at a low ebb in its fortunes. Labour thus played up the leadership qualities of its skilled and populist tactician Harold Wilson, running an unprecedentedly presidential style campaign. With opinion polls on the very eve of polling day, 18 June, showing the party heading for a comfortable third successive victory, this strategy appeared to have been successful. However, when the nation's votes were finally cast, a stunning last-minute transfer of support took place among the increasingly volatile electorate and the Conservatives, on a national swing of 4.7%, gained a surprising victory, securing an overall parliamentary majority of 30 seats. Labour's claims to have established themselves as the new 'natural party of government' lay in shreds and the nation turned to a new market-based experiment at economic regeneration under the leadership of a radically reformed and re-organised Conservative Party.

## 1970–4: Heath and the 'New Conservatism'

During the 1950s the Conservative Party had established itself as the strongest national level political force in Britain and enjoyed a broadening social base of support. The parliamentary party remained dominated, however, by a narrow, upper class, public school educated elite, with organisational control vested in a mysteriously opaque clique of grandee power brokers. 87% of the members of the 1963 Home cabinet had enjoyed a public school education, while, more extraordinarily, 37% of the 85 members of the 1958 Macmillan government were actually related to the Prime Minister by marriage. Of the party's 304 MPs elected in 1964, 75% were public school educated, with 32% of the total being drawn from Eton alone. The anachronism of the narrow social background from which the party's national level representatives were drawn became increasingly recognised by party officials during the early 1960s and a reform movement was gradually set in train, aimed at broadening the base of the parliamentary ranks, democratising its power structure, restructuring its organisation and updating its image. This movement gained momentum from 1965 with the appointment, in January, of Edward du Cann as the party's new chairman and in July, following Home's resignation, of Edward Heath as the new leader. Heath, as a result of rule changes adopted in February 1965, was the first Conservative leader to be elected by a ballot of the parliamentary party, defeating Maudling and Powell by the margin of 150:133:15 votes respectively. In addition, in contrast to his predecessors, he came from a relatively lowly, meritocrat background, being the grammar school and Oxford University-educated son of a Kent-based middle class carpenter-businessmen. He had distinguished himself as an artillery major during the Second World War and had briefly worked in the civil service, before gaining election to Parliament in 1950 and serving in a variety of influential cabinet posts between 1955–64.

The new duumvirate of Heath and du Cann set about revamping the party: streamlining Central Office, improving the salaries and skills of constituency agents, encouraging the selection of parliamentary candidates from professional backgrounds, and promoting into the shadow cabinet a new generation of similar meritocrats. Most fundamental, however, was the reformulation of the party's policies away from Macmillan's consensual 'Middle Way' to a more radical market-orientated approach, coupled to a concern for major institutional reform. Party thinkers now began to argue against the detrimental effects on the private sector of the ever-rising level of government expenditure and favour a shift away from universality to selectivity, in social welfare provision, targeting resources to the poorest and most needy in a means-tested manner. In addition, they called for major reductions in the level of direct taxation, so as to restore personal incentives; for the removal of many state controls; for the denationalisation of non strategic industrial undertakings so as to 'roll back the frontiers' of the state; and, above all, for the radical reform of trade union laws, so as to make union leaders more accountable to their members and to end

31

the practice of shop steward called unofficial stoppages. Such proposals in the economic sphere drew on contemporary 'New Right' Republican Party thinking in the United States and were influenced by the Christian Democratic Union's successful 'social market' economy strategy that had been pursued during the 1950s and 1960s in West Germany. Combined with calls for fundamental institutional reform, so as to make central and local government more efficient and rational, they were all set out in the policy document framed by the shadow cabinet in January 1970 at the Selsdon Park Hotel in Croydon, which was later to be dubbed the 'Selsdon Manifesto'. The party's new leader, Edward Heath, having enjoyed a reputation as a close associate of Harold Macmillan during the 1950s and as a liberal on many social issues, was, in a number of respects, a curious advocate of such a radical change in policies. Heath firmly believed, however, that, following the experience of 1962–70, a major change to restructure the British economy and to make its industries efficient once more on the world stage was desperately required in this era of rapid, relative economic decline.

Once in office, Prime Minister Heath proved to be remarkably successful in effecting significant institutional reform. A new Central Policy Review Staff (CPRS), headed by Lord Rothschild, was established and attached to the Cabinet Office, with the intention of providing an alternative input of advice from academic experts on policy issues for cabinet members to set alongside the advice given by departmental civil servants. Two new 'super departments', Trade and Industry (merging together the Ministry of Technology and the Board of Trade) and Environment, combining the Ministry of Housing and Local Government, the Ministry of Transport and the Ministry of Building and Works, were created. A new two-tier system of local government, consisting of county and district councils, and, in large cities, metropolitan county and metropolitan district councils, was legislated for in 1972–3, coming into effect in 1974–5. Finally, in what was the most fundamental institutional reform of the postwar era, the Heath administration secured entry into the EEC, in January 1973. The French government, headed since June 1969 by President Georges Pompidou, decided not to veto the British application and the entry Bill was passed by Parliament in 1972.

Heath's record in the economic sphere, as he sought to implement the radical Selsdon Programme, proved, by contrast, to be a bitter failure. The new government began by rapidly announcing a series of controversial measures designed to signal its determination to effect significant economic change. First, the NBPI was disbanded and free collective bargaining restored; second, significant reductions in the level of income tax were announced to be balanced by cuts in social programmes, with the ending of free school milk and the raising of prescription and dental charges, while a new Family Income Supplement (FIS) was introduced to provide special funds to poor families with children; third, it was announced that the government would sell off to the private sector the state-owned travel company Thomas Cook and Son and the hotel section of British Rail and abolish the IRC. Within months of assuming office, however, the Heath administration was forced by adverse market circumstances to depart significantly from this new 'hands off' strategy and to inject funds into the aerospace-giant Rolls Royce, which had fallen into financial difficulties over a fixed-price contract to supply RB 11 engines to Lockheed, before taking it into public ownership in February 1971.[1]

The Rolls Royce 'bale out' was viewed at the time as an exceptional case and the government continued with its market orientated reform programme by introducing its central and most controversial domestic policy measure, the trade union reforming Industrial Relations Act.[2] It required the compulsory registration of unions if they were to retain their legal immunities and the adherence to a series of rules designed at preventing unofficial and ballotless stoppages. A National Industrial Relations Court (NIRC) and a system of tribunals were established to ensure rules were adhered to and members' rights respected. The Act was given the royal assent in August 1971. It was bitterly opposed, however, by trade unionists and served to sour industrial and trade union-government relations. A series of one-day stoppages was called, during 1971–2, to register opposition. More than thirty unions were suspended for refusing to officially register and a major dock strike was called in July-August 1972 as a result of the arrest of three dockers who, after picketing a container depot, had refused to appear before the NIRC.

[1] During the same year the government was also compelled to take over the Upper Clyde Shipyards which had gone into liquidation in June 1971.

[2] The Act was similar in some respects to the preceding Wilson government's abandoned 'In Place of Strife', but had taken little note of the Donovan Royal Commission Report on trade unions of 1968.

The rising level of industrial unrest, the number of working days lost as a result of stoppages reaching the figure of 23.9 million in 1972, generated by the Industrial Relations Act, occurred during a period of gathering economic recession. The unemployment figure rose sharply towards the one million mark in early 1972 and the inflation rate shot up from a level of below 6% between 1968–70 to one of almost 9% between 1970–3, as a result of excessive wage demands, world commodity price inflation, the switch to floating exchange rates, in June 1972, and the sudden oil price hike by the Organisation for Petroleum Exporting Countries (OPEC), following the October 1973 Arab-Israeli war. The novel phenomenon of 'stagflation', rising prices coupled with declining industrial production and mounting unemployment, thus now emerged between 1972–4 and forced a major 'U-turn' in the Heath government's economic approach. In March 1972 the Chancellor, Anthony Barber, introduced a major tax-cutting and credit loosening reflationary budget with the aim of engineering a growth rate of 5% per annum. The shift in budgetary policy was buttressed by the passage of a new Industry Act which established an Industrial Development Executive under Christopher Chataway, enjoying substantial interventionary powers, and by the government's appeal to the TUC and CBI for the adoption of voluntary pay restraint. The TUC, however, still bitter about the passage of the Industrial Relations Act, refused to enter into such an agreement and so, in November 1982, a statutory 90-day prices and wages freeze was imposed. This was followed, in January 1973, by the creation of a Price Commission and a Pay Board whose task was to monitor pay rises, imposing a maximum limit of £1 a week plus 4%, and outlawing pay strikes.

Not unnaturally, the imposed pay policy of 1972–4 was fiercely opposed by the trade union movement which was now in a strong and confident mood. In particular, to circumvent government legislation, resort was made to overtime bans and 'work to rules'. The most serious challenge came from the powerful and united National Union of Mineworkers (NUM), which had already, in January-February 1972, embarrassed the government by forcing a major pay increase following a six-week national strike. In November 1973, taking advantage of the energy crisis caused by the Arab-Israeli war, the NUM began a national overtime ban, which was supported by train drivers who also began a work to rule, rapidly reducing factory and power station coal stocks. Electricity power workers also joined the dispute by refusing to undertake out-of-hours work. The government responded by declaring a 'State of Emergency' on 13 November 1973, to ensure fuel economies, and eventually imposed a three-day working week on industry in January 1974, by restricting the supply of electric power. The Prime Minister, determined not to give in to the NUM's exorbitant wage demands on a second occasion, rejected a TUC compromise proposal to allow the miners to be treated as a special case. Deadlock thus appeared to be reached on 2 February 1974 when, following a national ballot supported by an 81% majority, the NUM Executive declared its intention to commence an all-out strike on 9 February. The Prime Minister responded on 7 February by announcing that a general election would be held on 28 February to seek renewal of his mandate and to decide the issue of, 'Who Governs Britain ?'.

# Who Governs Britain? 1974–6

## The February 1974 General Election

The last months of the Heath administration were a period of widening social divisions and mounting unrest during a premiership that had witnessed turmoil at home and in adjoining Northern Ireland[1], unprecedented during the postwar era. Political scientists began to seriously put forward the question, 'Is Britain Ungovernable?', and speculate on a possible sudden authoritarian lurch to the right or to the left in a desperate attempt to re-impose order on chaos. The February 1974 election, which was called 18 months ahead of Parliament's normal life, was designed to give voters the opportunity to make their democratic voice heard in the midst of this crisis. The election, however, in many respects, was called by Edward Heath out of a sense of powerless frustration, without any guarantee that a victory would materially help to resolve the pit dispute. When Parliament was dissolved the Conservatives were leading Labour in the opinion polls by 4%. The margin was slender and followed three years of consistent Labour leads. The government's prospects of being returned to power were somewhat enhanced, however, by the divisions that had emerged within Labour's ranks since June 1970.

[1] In Northern Ireland 20000 British troops remained installed in a peace keeping capacity and direct rule from London was established between April 1972 and January 1974. During 1972 468 people were killed as a result of terrorist violence, primarily by the Irish Republican Army (IRA), and bombings also spread to targets in England between 1971–4.

Ideological and personal fissures develop, by tradition, within the Labour Party during periods in opposition. They arose again between 1970–4 as leading figures within the party began to re-assess the record of 1964–70 and speculate on the reasons for the defeat of June 1970. The party's left wing, which had been growing in strength during the later 1960s and early 1970s, took the lead in this introspective debate. At the same time, a new generation of radical trade union leaders, such as Hugh Scanlon of the AUEW (1967–8) and Jack Jones of the TGWU (1969–78), assumed power and an influx of middle class 'New Left' activists entered the ranks of the local constituency parties. In addition, with the left's influence at national conference level and within the party's National Executive Committee (NEC)[1] mounting, policy decisions began increasingly to go in a direction contrary to the wishes of the centre-right majority within the Parliamentary Labour Party (PLP). Under the leadership of Tony Benn (1925– ), a longstanding supporter of CND and opponent of EEC entry, who became Party Chairman between 1971–2, the left began to press for the adoption of a radical new policy programme and for organisational reforms. These would increase the authority of the Party Conference and constituency branches to ensure that the programme would be adhered to once re-elected to government. New working parties were established to debate proposed rule changes and NEC documents produced during 1972–3, firmly supporting a radical new programme of nationalisation. These moves presaged a decade of an intra-party policy struggle which was to culminate in an eventual left-right fission in 1981. At the time of the February 1974 election, however, the left's power still remained circumscribed with its leading members excluded from the vital policy-framing bodies within the PLP and Shadow Cabinet executive.

Of greater short-term significance for the Labour Party were the even sharper divisions opened up within the PLP by the Heath government's decision to join the EEC in 1973. During the 1964–70 period the Wilson administration had favoured entry, starting formal negotiations with the member nations in 1967 and 1970. Once in opposition, however, the party's annual conference, in

---

[1] The NEC comprises 29 members—12 are chosen by the trade unions, 7 by constituency labour parties (CLPs), 5 women and 1 treasurer by the annual conference, 1 by the Young Socialists' conference. The party's leader and deputy leader are reserved places. It determines policy between conferences and has final sanction over candidate selection.

October 1971, largely as a result of the AUEW and TGWU's block votes, came out firmly against entry on the terms acceded to by the Heath government. Harold Wilson accepted this decision and pledged the party to seek a thorough re-negotiation of the membership terms. However, in the House of Commons vote of October 1971 69 Labour MPs, including deputy leader Roy Jenkins, defied a party three-line whip and a further 20 abstained. Six months later the shadow cabinet's support for the call for a referendum on EEC membership prompted Jenkins to resign the deputy leadership.

These policy divisions, combined with the resignation of the moderate, pro-Europe MP for Lincoln, Dick Taverne, in October 1972 as a result of conflicts with his CLP and his re-election as an Independent in March 1973, tarnished the party's public image during 1972 and 1973 and led to a narrowing of its lead over the Conservatives in national opinion polls. However, the skilful and consensual leadership of Harold Wilson, during 1973–4, succeeded in repairing much of the damage in time for the forthcoming general election. In February 1973 Wilson negotiated a 'Social Contract' of voluntary pay restraint with the TUC if returned to power. This served to heal the rift that had developed between Labour and the unions between 1966–70 and re-establish the party's reputation for enjoying a special co-operative relationship with the labour barons. Several months later the party leader succeeded in blurring the NEC's call for the nationalisation of 25 of the country's largest companies by achieving agreement instead on a more nebulous commitment in principle to a broad extension of public ownership under a National Enterprise Board (NEB). Wilson also secured Roy Jenkins' return to the shadow cabinet in November 1973 by devising an agreement that the party, if elected to power, would seek first to renegotiate the entry terms and then put the issue before the electorate in a general election or referendum. Through such dexterous means Labour was successfully re-united in readiness for the February 1974 election. It faced, however, strong competition from resurgent minor parties which had performed unusually well between 1971–3.

In Scotland, with the discovery of substantial quantities of offshore oil[1], a striking resurgence of SNP support was registered in by-elections during 1973. The party sliced into both the Labour and Conservative votes and captured the Glasgow Govan constituency

---

[1] Oil was first struck in the North Sea in 1970 and began to come 'on stream' in Scotland in 1975.

from Labour in October 1973. In England, the issues of EEC entry and the moderate stance adopted by the Heath government towards the immigration issue, saw the emergence on the political stage in a number of urban areas of the far-right National Front. It was, however, the Liberal Party which was to register the strongest growth in support between 1972–3, securing by-election victories at Rochdale (October 1972), Sutton and Cheam (December 1972), Ripon (July 1973), the Isle of Ely (July 1973) and Berwick-on-Tweed (November 1973), and achieving significant advances at local government level. Part of the Liberals' advances, at the local level in particular, could be ascribed to its adoption of a new form of radical, voter-orientated 'community politics', the prime example being the advance of the party in Liverpool, where it emerged as the largest bloc on the council in 1973, under the leadership of Trevor Jones. The principal reason for its surge in by-election support, (achieving more votes than any other party in such contests during 1973) was, however, the transfer of support by former Conservative supporters disillusioned with the record of the Heath administration. During the middle of 1973 opinion polls showed the Liberals' national level standing at an Orpington-like level of 20%, making their prospects of achieving significant electoral advances in February 1974 most promising.

The Conservative Party entered the February 1974 campaign superficially in a united condition, determined to stand up to the threat of blackmail from what they saw as a communist dominated NUM. Prime Minister Heath had been swayed into calling an early election by right wingers within the party's parliamentary and constituency level ranks and as a result of advice from party chairman, Lord Carrington. Below the surface, however, serious divisions had emerged during the Heath years, both as a result of the Prime Minister's policy decisions and his leadership style. For example, the decision to enter the EEC had been fiercely opposed by a vocal minority within the party, 39 Conservatives voting against the government and two abstaining on the entry vote in October 1971. A three-line whip had not been imposed on the government side. The issues of the immigration of Asians from Uganda (January 1973), sanctions against Rhodesia (November 1972) and the resort, contrary to 1970 manifesto promises, to a statutory pay policy between 1972–4, also precipitated revolts by the party's far right. The leader of this opposition was invariably the West Midlands' MP, Enoch Powell, who remained a controversially implacable opponent of immigration and membership of the EEC and who was to resign his seat and call on his supporters in the country to vote Labour in February 1974 so as to force a referendum on EEC membership. Many other Conservative MPs were less than satisfied with Prime Minister Heath's secretive, aloof and self-righteous leadership style, his failure to maintain close links with backbenchers, and his unwillingness to use his office and honour-granting patronage powers to mollify potential rebels. Much of this opposition remained muted, however, during 1974 as the party concentrated on attempting to secure re-election for a second term.

Heath determined at the outset to centre the party's February 1974 campaign on the constitutional question of 'Who Governs Britain?', declaring during a television broadcast on 12 February, 'The challenge is to the will of Parliament and a democratically elected government'. The party's manifesto, 'Firm Action for a Fair Britain', key sections of which had been drafted by the young backroom economic adviser, Nigel Lawson, combined calls for firmness against trade union extremism, by seeking to end social security for strikers and their families, with a willingness to show flexibility and compassion, by agreeing to amend the Industrial Relations Act so that a stage of conciliation would be introduced prior to legal proceedings, and promising to review pensions at twice-yearly instead of annual intervals, and to allow council houses to be purchased by their tenants. In addition, the party made great play of the growing radicalism of the post-1970 Labour Party, claiming that it had been taken over by left-wing extremists and would be a threat to democratic government.

The Labour manifesto, 'Let us work together—Labour's way out of the crisis', was indeed the party's most radical document since 1945. It included calls for substantially increased public ownership under the aegis of a specially established NEB, including public involvement in oil exploration and development in the North Sea; a commitment to fundamentally renegotiate the country's EEC terms and place the issue before the public in a national referendum; the establishment of a Royal Commission on Income Distribution and Wealth; the imposition of strict price controls; and, as its centrepiece, the return to voluntary wage control with the TUC under the newly framed 'Social Contract', with the unions' agreeing to negotiate responsibly in return for the government's pledge to repeal the 1971 Industrial Relations Act, introduce a new conciliation and arbitration service (ACAS) and implement a package of radical social spending pledges which would establish a new, minimum 'social wage'. In more general terms, the manifesto promised swingeing wealth taxes on groups who had prospered as a result of the 1970–4 Heath government income tax cuts and declared the party's determination to effect, 'a fundamental and irreversible shift in the balance of power and wealth in favour of working people and their families'. Despite these radical pledges, however, the central theme in the February 1974 Labour campaign became the experience of the party's popular shadow cabinet team and its ability to govern and to heal widening social divisions. The campaign managers argued persuasively that Labour had rescued the country from the mess of 1962–7, leaving its finances in a strong and stable condition in 1970. It was ready, drawing on its special relationship with the trade unions, to take on the same thankless task again in 1974.

This theme, and Labour's ability to shift the campaign agenda away from the pit dispute and towards broader economic and social issues, paid dividends for the opposition party as the contest entered its final week. A series of adverse trade reports and an off-the-record remark by the CBI Director-General, Campbell Adamson, that the 1971 Industrial Relations Act had been a grave mistake which had sullied manager-employee relations, served seriously to erode the Conservatives' opinion poll lead. Thus when electors' votes were finally cast on 28 February 1974 the Conservative majority of 1970 vanished and a 'hung Parliament', in which no single party dominated, resulted for the first time since 1929. Despite an increased turnout of 78.1%, helped by the adoption of a new register only weeks before polling day, both principal parties lost votes. The Conservatives' share of the vote fell by 1.2 million (8.3%) and Labour's by 0.5 million (5.8%)[1]. It was the minor parties which emerged the real victors of February 1974 (see Table 7). Fielding an unprecedented number of 517 candidates, in what was a record year for overall nominations (2135 compared with, for example, 1868 in 1950), the Liberals secured a postwar high 19% share of the national vote and 14 seats. They had campaigned on a manifesto, 'Change the Face of Britain. Take power and vote Liberal', which had stressed the themes of

---

[1] Conservative support slumped in particular in the West Midlands, in large measure as a result of Enoch Powell's injunctions, a swing of 5–10% being registered to Labour in this region. The Labour vote fell most markedly in southern England where there was a major surge to the Liberals, who took first or second place in 51 of the 76 south coast county seats. Labour's decline in the south was to become a permanent feature of the post-1974 period.

decentralisation, workers' participation and profit-sharing in industry and, helped by the flamboyant leadership of Jeremy Thorpe,
had succeeded in projecting a fresh, anti-party and anti-interest
group image, which reflected the anti-Westminster mood of much
of the nation in 1974. The SNP, fielding 70 candidates, also
performed well, securing a 22% share of the Scottish vote and the
election of 7 MPs. Plaid Cymru, with 36 candidates, captured 11%
of the Welsh vote and 2 seats and the National Front achieved an
average 3% of the vote in the 54 seats it contested. The minor
parties secured, in particular, a substantial breakthrough in the
fringe regions of south western England, North Wales and northern
Scotland, drawing away votes in particular from the Conservatives.
Their 23 seats, combined with the 11 Ulster Unionists, who had
split away from the Conservative whip as a result of opposition to
the Sunningdale power-sharing agreement, and one Northern
Ireland Catholic Social Democratic and Labour Party (SDLP) MP
(Gerry Fitt) and two Labour Independents, proved to be of unusual
value, holding the balance as they did in the 'hung Parliament' of
1974.

Table 7    The General Election of February 1974

| Party | Votes Gained | % of Total Vote | Average Vote Per MP | Number of MPs |
|---|---|---|---|---|
| Conservative | 11.869m | 37.9 | 39,963 | 297 |
| Labour | 11.639m | 37.1 | 38,669 | 301 |
| Liberal | 6.063m | 19.3 | 433,105 | 14 |
| SNP | 0.632m | 2.0 | 90,290 | 7 |
| Plaid Cymru | 0.171m | 0.6 | 85,682 | 2 |
| Others (GB) | 0.241m | 0.8 | — | 2[1] |
| Others (NI) | 0.718m | 2.3 | — | 12 |
| Total | 31.333m | 100.0 | 49,344 | 635 |

[1] These comprised the two independent, former Labour, MPs: Dick Taverne
(Lincoln) and Eddie Milne (Blyth).

## The February–October 1974 Wilson Government

In the immediate wake of the February 1974 election, Edward
Heath, as leader of the party which had received the largest
national backing, attempted to put together a coalition government
with Liberal Party and Ulster Unionist support. He held a two-hour
meeting with Jeremy Thorpe on Saturday 2 March and sent a

telegram to Harry West, leader of seven dissident Ulster Unionist MPs, on 3 March. Heath offered the Liberals full participation in a coalition government and agreed to establish a Speaker's Conference to discuss the desirability of electoral reform. However, when the Liberals' 14 MPs met to discuss this offer on Monday 4 March, they unanimously rejected any idea of a formal coalition, preferring instead the establishment of either an all-party government of national unity or providing backbench support to a minority government on an 'agreed but limited programme'. Liberal party workers were even more firmly committed against any accommodation with the Conservatives, which, if entered into, might have provoked a serious internal split. Lacking the prospect of establishing an effective coalition from amongst the remaining, and hostile, minority groupings, Heath thus went to Buckingham Palace during the early evening of 4 March to tender his resignation as Prime Minister. The Queen turned to Harold Wilson, leader of the largest single parliamentary grouping, who agreed to form a minority government.

Remembering the party's bitter experience in 1931, Harold Wilson determined from the very outset in February 1974 not to entertain any thoughts of forming a coalition government with the potential allies that may have existed within the ranks of the Liberal, SDLP, SNP and PC parties. He decided instead to govern as if possessing a majority, refusing to compromise on manifesto pledges, thus putting the challenge to his opponents to bring down the government and take the blame for forcing a fresh election. Wilson was buttressed in this strategy by the knowledge that neither the increasingly divided Conservatives nor the financially strapped Liberals were anxious for an early contest.

The new Prime Minister put together a powerful cabinet team which included many who had served in the 1964–70 administrations and which was carefully balanced between right and left and between pro- and anti-marketeers. The party's centre-right still held a clear majority within the full cabinet, but two of the most prominent left wingers, Tony Benn and Michael Foot, were given the key posts of Industry and Employment respectively. Prime Minister Wilson inherited the CPRS headed by Lord Rothschild and established his own new Policy Unit[1], directed by Bernard Donoughue, a senior lecturer from the LSE, to work alongside his private office headed by Marcia Williams and press secretary Joe

[1] Similar Policy Units were also established by departmental ministers to provide an additional and party-orientated source of advice.

Haines. Harold Wilson was now to govern in a more detached manner than between 1964–70, devolving considerable decision-making authority to his individual ministers and taking on the role, in his own footballing analogy, of that of 'sweeper' rather than 'centre forward'.

The new government inherited an economy in tatters, inflation standing at 15%, the balance of payments deficit in excess of £3 billion and industrial production and per capita incomes in decline, and a bitterly divided nation. It rapidly, however, made its presence felt during its first week in office by negotiating a settlement to the coal strike, granting miners pay increases of 29%, and thus an end to the three-day week and 'State of Emergency'. In addition, an immediate freeze on rents was announced, a major rise in pensions promised and strict price controls imposed. Three months later, in June 1974, the Heath government's policy (Stage 3) of compulsory wage constraint was brought to an end, the Pay Board abolished and the new 'Social Contract' of voluntary agreement introduced. Finally, in July 1974 the Trade Union and Labour Relations Act, which abolished the Heath administration's Industrial Relations Act, was given the royal assent and a special 'mini budget' announced by Chancellor Denis Healey, in which the rate of VAT was reduced from 10% to 8%.

These practical measures were accompanied by the introduction of a series of eye-catching White and Green Papers which set out the government's future legislative objectives and were designed very much with a view to the possibility of calling an early election in the autumn. The Chancellor and the Prices and Consumer Protection Secretary, Shirley Williams (1930– ), geared their actions during these months towards effecting a sharp short-term reduction in the inflation rate and a temporary improvement in living standards. This they succeeded in doing, with price rises being held to a figure of 8% between March and October 1974 while wages increased by more than 16%. A mild improvement in the level of real disposable income was thus generated, providing a helpful background for the fighting of a new election. In such circumstances and concerned with the increasing frequency of legislative reversals within Parliament and the narrowing of Labour's lead over the Conservatives in national opinion polls, Harold Wilson tendered the government's resignation to the Queen on 18 June 1974 and asked for fresh elections. The Queen was not constitutionally obliged to agree immediately to such a dissolution. However, the events of 1–4 March 1974 had shown that no

Conservative-Liberal coalition alternative existed. Thus a dissolution was granted and elections were announced for 10 October 1974.

## The October 1974 General Election

The March-September 1974 Parliament had been the shortest on record since 1681 and voters were forced, on old registers, to recommence the process of choosing a new government for the second occasion within eight months. The odds in this follow-up election favoured Labour who had solved the coal strike and introduced a number of populist social spending measures. Prime Minister Wilson thus hoped to repeat his success of the March 1966 'follow-up election' and secure a comfortable working majority. The outcome of the October 1974 general election remained, however, very much open to doubt as a result of the continuing divisions within the Labour Party and the public disquiet about a number of the more radical measures within its manifesto. The still high level of support that was being recorded by the Liberals in rural and suburban England and by the SNP in Scotland also threatened Labour's success.

Awareness of the growing imminence of a fresh election served to concentrate minds within the Labour Party during the months between March and October and enabled an image of surface unity to be presented to the electorate. However, within the party, strong divisions still existed over the EEC issue, prompting the defection of Christopher Mayhew (Woolwich East) to the Liberal Party in July 1974, and over Industry Minister Tony Benn's radical nationalisation plans. Home Secretary Roy Jenkins, Prices Secretary Shirley Williams and Education Secretary Reg Prentice were particularly vocal critics of the latter's proposals. The party's manifesto, launched under the slogan 'Britain will win with Labour', was similar in substance to that of February 1974. The major innovation was its conversion to the need for devolution, proposing the creation of directly elected assemblies for Scotland and Wales 'as soon as possible' in the life of the new Parliament and the creation of a new development agency for Scotland. These ideas drew heavily on the neglected findings of the 1969–73 Kilbrandon Commission on the Constitution and were prompted in large measure by party pollsters' findings that without the grant of devolution Labour stood to lose a possible 13 seats in Scotland at the forthcoming election. To show the government's commitment to such a reform, a White Paper, 'Democracy and Devolution: Proposals for Scotland and Wales', was published in September 1974, on the very eve of the dissolution of Parliament.

The Conservative Party had been numbed by its unexpected defeat in February 1974 but succeeded in maintaining a show of unity during the following spring and summer. However, the decision of three prominent ministers, Sir Alec Douglas Home, Anthony Barber and Christopher Chataway to step down from active politics at the October election did little to improve the party's image or confidence. In addition, the free-thinking former Social Services Secretary, Sir Keith Joseph, refused to serve in the new shadow cabinet and established, instead, his own Centre for Policy Studies, with the aim of examining new ways of 'increasing the efficiency of capitalism' and of re-examining Conservative ideas. Joseph rapidly emerged as the leading dissident voice within the right wing of the party, making a powerful and well-publicised speech at Preston on 5 September 1974 in which he totally rejected the Keynesian demand management system adopted by postwar governments and declared that the only means of conquering inflation was through the adoption of strict monetary control, even though this might lead to a sharp transitional rise in the unemployment level.[1] Joseph's speech, which foreshadowed the party's post-Heath commitment to monetarism, proved deeply damaging, enabling the opposition to label the Conservatives once more as 'the party of unemployment'.

The Conservatives did, however, revamp their organisation during the months preceding the October election. The popular former Northern Ireland and later Employment Secretary, William Whitelaw, was appointed the new Party Chairman in June 1974 and the 'Heathites' Ian Gilmour and Chris Patten were brought in respectively as chairman and director of the Conservatives' Research Department, being given the brief to prepare a draft of the new manifesto. This document, titled 'Putting Britain First', was sombre in tone, laying stress on the gravity of the continuing economic crisis and on the need to give top priority to the fight against inflation. It included, however, a number of significant departures from the manifesto of February 1974. The party offered,

---

[1] The other principal Tory dissident, Enoch Powell, joined the Ulster Unionists in October 1974, being accepted as parliamentary candidate for the South Down constituency.

for example, if elected to government, to establish indirectly elected assemblies for Scotland and Wales, although enjoying fewer powers than those proposed by Labour. In addition, it abandoned any idea of re-introducing the Industrial Relations Act and came out in favour of a policy of voluntary rather than statutory wage control. The programme put forward was thus in many respects Macmillanite in tone, being a throwback to the manifestos of 1959 and 1964. Its major theme was one of caution and reconciliation, putting forward the idea of the formation of a government of national unity, even if returned with a full majority, as a means of trying to wean back voters who had defected to the Liberals in February 1974.

The outcome of the October 1974 election depended in large measure upon how well the votes for the Liberals and nationalist minor parties would hold in comparison with the February levels. The Liberals were thus subjected to close media scrutiny during the spring and summer months of 1974 and their leaders' opinion sought on the choice the party would make if a second 'hung parliament' was returned in a new election. Inside Parliament the party's chief whip, David Steel, and its national leader, Jeremy Thorpe, supported the idea of participating in a 'recovery coalition', particularly with Labour, if no clear majority emerged. However, the broader membership of the party remained wary of such talk of coalitions. This served to create uncertainty in the minds of the electorate as to the Liberals' likely future decision and had an adverse effect on the party's national opinion poll standing.

Labour's campaign of September-October 1974 stressed the three themes of the experience of its leadership team; its ability to keep its promises when in government; and the sense and competence of its policies to see the country through a difficult future era. The Conservatives, aware of the unpopularity of their leader Edward Heath, sought to soften his public image and project other members of his shadow cabinet team. Once again, however, it was the animated figure of Jeremy Thorpe, embarking on a novel, hovercraft-based, campaign, who made the greatest and most favourable public impression. The campaign was short, lasting only three weeks, and more low-key than the divisive contest of February 1974. A number of 'smear stories' concerning leading Labour Party figures temporarily raised the political temperature, but when polling day arrived, on 10 October, the total turnout, on an ageing register, slumped by more than two million from the February 1974 level. There was a national swing of 2.2% towards

Labour. However, the movement was stronger in the Labour's urban strongholds than in suburban marginal seats and the party was thus only able to achieve a slender parliamentary majority of three seats. Labour broadly maintained the absolute level of its February 1974 vote (see Tables 7 and 8) and raised its proportional share to 39.2%. The Conservatives experienced a further haemorrhage of 1.4 million votes and recorded, at 35.9%, their lowest share of the national total since 1935. The Liberals held strong at 18.3%, but, despite fielding a record 619 candidates, failed to achieve a breakthrough to a new, higher level of support. It was the SNP which recorded the greatest success in October 1974, succeeding in increasing its share of the vote in Scotland to 30% and its number of seats to 11, and, in the process, reducing the Conservatives to third-party status, in vote terms, north of the border.[1] The far-right National Front, which was fielding 90 candidates, also made a number of minor regional advances, capturing more than 6% of the vote in a number of East London constituencies. The election served, above all, however, to confirm the growth of regional support for the nation's two principal parties, the Liberals having replaced Labour as the principal opposition party in the southern half of the country, and the Conservatives having been reduced to a rump in the industrial north and Scotland.[2]

Table 8   The General Election of October 1974

| Party | Votes Gained | % of Vote | Average vote per MP | Number of MPs |
|---|---|---|---|---|
| Labour | 11.457m | 39.2 | 35,916 | 319 |
| Conservative | 10.465m | 35.9 | 37,779 | 277 |
| Liberal | 5.347m | 18.3 | 411,209 | 13 |
| SNP | 0.840m | 2.9 | 76,329 | 11 |
| Plaid Cymru | 0.166m | 0.6 | 55,340 | 3 |
| Others (GB) | 0.212m | 0.7 | — | * |
| Others (NI) | 0.702m | 2.4 | — | 12 |
| Total | 29.189m | 100.0 | 45,967 | 635 |

* The Labour rebels Dick Taverne (Lincoln), Eddie Milne (Blyth) and Eddie Griffiths (Sheffield Brightside) were all defeated by official Labour Party candidates in this election.

[1] Plaid Cymru increased its representation in Wales to three seats, but its share of the Welsh vote, 10.8%, was the same as in February 1974.

[2] For example, the Conservatives in October 1974 boasted only 16 MPs from Scotland compared to 36 in 1955 and 13 MPs from Lancashire compared to 22 in 1964. Two-thirds of its MPs were now drawn from the South and East of England.

## The October 1974—March 1976 Wilson Government

The new Wilson government of October 1974 boasted an absolute majority of only three seats over all the opposition parties combined. This majority, being more slender than that of 1964–6, significantly enhanced the bargaining power of backbenchers on the Commons' Standing Committees and on the floor of the House. It also encouraged the House of Lords to assert itself more vigorously (see Table 1) as a constitutional check on a government which had been elected on the smallest share of the vote (excluding February 1974) recorded during the postwar period. Labour did boast, however, a 42-seat advantage over the Conservatives and could look for sympathetic support from the 28 Plaid Cymru, SNP, Liberal and SDLP MPs on many of its economic and social policy measures. In such circumstances Harold Wilson determined that his party would accept office with a view to implementing a full parliamentary programme, ruling out the possibility of holding a further new election.

The Prime Minister re-assembled the cabinet team of February-October 1974 and immediately set about putting into effect the measures that had appeared in White Paper form during the summer months of 1974. Two of the these central early reforms were the Industry and the Employment Protection Acts of 1975. The former measure, which was substantially drafted and piloted through the Commons by Industry Secretary Tony Benn, established the National Enterprise Board (NEB) as a new state holding company in charge of the administration of government share interests in private companies and which was empowered to acquire further holdings and to extend financial aid to troubled concerns. The NEB, which was granted initial funds of £1 billion, was envisaged by those on the left of the party as a means of extending state control over strategic private sector industries and of introducing new forms of industrial democracy. The Industry Act thus included a call for key private firms to sign planning agreements with the government, while an investigative committee, inquiring into the subject of workers' participation and management, was now established by Prime Minister Wilson, under the chairmanship of Lord Bullock. The government's second important early measure, the Employment Protection Act, served to complement the 1974 Trade Union and Labour Relations Act by significantly extending employee rights, granting workers redress against unfair dismissal and establishing new regulations in the fields of redundancy pay, maternity rights and the minimum period of notice.

1975 was, however, a year of considerable difficulty for the government as it was forced to address itself to the thorny and divisive problem of renegotiating the country's EEC membership and of coming to grips with what was a rapidly deteriorating economic situation.

## The EEC Referendum

The October 1974 Labour Party election manifesto had committed the party, if re-elected, to radically re-negotiating Britain's entry terms to the European Community and putting the results, with a government recommendation in either direction, to the public in a national referendum within one year of assuming power. Such a re-negotiation was duly effected by Prime Minister Wilson and Foreign Secretary James Callaghan during the closing months of 1974, with an agreement on new membership terms being signed at the EEC's Dublin Summit in March 1975. This included a number of minor concessions over sugar, beef and New Zealand dairy produce and the establishment of a new system for re-imbursing members' budget contributions on the basis of their levels of GNP and rates of economic growth. Many of these concessions were largely cosmetic and the new agreement fell far short of the 'fundamental changes' demanded by Labour during its period in opposition. However, when the question of membership was put before the cabinet a 16:7 majority in favour of continuation was obtained.[1] The government thus informed the Commons on 18 March 1975 that it had decided to recommend a 'Yes' vote for the national referendum on membership whose date was set for 5 June 1975.

The Labour Party's sharp divisions over the EEC issue continued to be evident between March and June 1975, however, both in votes within the Commons and at party meetings outside. When the government's pro-Market White Paper was voted on in the House in April the party split 138:145 between those in favour and

---

[1] The seven cabinet opponents were Tony Benn (Industry Secretary), Michael Foot (Employment), Peter Shore (Trade), Barbara Castle (Social Services), Eric Varley (Energy), John Silkin (Planning and Local Government) and William Ross (Scotland).

those opposed, with 32 Labour MPs abstentions. The motion was thus only carried as a result of Conservative and Liberal Party support. In addition, at a special party conference convened by the NEC on 26 April an overwhelming vote of 2:1 in favour of withdrawal was registered. Prime Minister Wilson thus agreed to the unusual precedent of waiving collective ministerial responsibility for statements made outside the House of Commons on the EEC issue during the months leading up to the referendum vote. This enabled the anti-Marketeers Tony Benn and Michael Foot to play a vocal role in leading a 'Britain out' movement which crossed party lines, embracing a number of trade union leaders and members from the SNP, Plaid Cymru, as well as Enoch Powell from the far right. This movement ('The National Referendum Campaign') found itself overwhelmed, however, both in financial and numerical terms, by the broad, opposing pro-European coalition ('Britain in Europe') which embraced the popular, cross-party figures of Roy Jenkins, William Whitelaw and David Steel and enjoyed substantial backing from the Whitehall establishment, big business and the national press. When votes were finally cast in the country's first national referendum, the pro-European lobby comfortably triumphed, securing, in reply to the question, 'Do you think that the United Kingdom should stay in the European Community?', 17.38 million (67%) votes in favour against 8.47 million (33%) opposed.[1] The turnout was surprisingly high, at 64.5%, and all UK regions, with the exception of the Shetland and Western Isles, registered a majority in favour of continued membership.

Harold Wilson's flexible tactics during 1974–5 over the EEC issue succeeded in forestalling a major party rupture. The moderate EEC supporters within the cabinet remained in office, satisfied with the outcome of the June 1975 vote, while anti-marketeers on the left were forced to accept the people's wishes as registered in a referendum for which they had fervently campaigned between 1972–4. The time devoted to the referendum campaign during 1975 had, however, had adverse consequences for other aspects of government policy, distracting attention, in particular, from the rapidly deteriorating domestic economic situation.

[1] By the end of the campaign, when the £125,000 provided to each side by the taxpayer is included, the pro-European lobby had spent £1.48 million and the anti-EEC grouping £0.13 million on publicity and advertising.

## From 'Social Contract' to Wage Control

During the spring and summer of 1974 a temporary consumer upturn had been stimulated by the electioneering measures of Chancellor Healey, but almost immediately on resuming office in October 1974 new sets of adverse trade, industrial growth and inflation figures emerged, showing the economy to be heading into a sharp, downward, economic spiral. The inflation rate rapidly moved to above 20%, reaching a high of 26% in July 1975; the balance of payments deficit, primarily as a result of an additional £2.9 billion incurred in importing dearer oil, had reached the record level of £3.5 billion during 1974; the unemployment level sharply increased to a figure of 0.68 million, or 3% of the workforce, in January 1975; and industrial production began to decline. Prime Minister Wilson recognised the gravity of the economic situation, in his immediate post-election victory speech to party workers at Transport House on 11 October 1974, describing it as 'the gravest economic crisis since the war'. The government believed, however, that they could escape from the downward spiral by determinedly pursuing a bold five-point economic strategy. First, they would finance the immediate balance of payments deficit through large-scale borrowing on the international money market, instead of giving in to Treasury pressure to introduce a more orthodox deflationary squeeze. Second, they would attempt to forestall a serious contraction in the level of world trade by, through the institution of world economic summits, persuading other major OECD nations, in particular the United States, West Germany and Japan, to pursue more expansionary, growth-orientated fiscal policies. Third, they would reduce the yawning trade gap by giving top priority to investment in export industries, through the aegis of the NEB. Fourth, and most crucially, they would seek to contain 'wage inflation' through the new innovation of the 'social contract', in which trade union leaders pledged to undertake 'sensible' wage bargaining in return for the government agreeing to introduce favourable trade union and social reforms. This agreement, which mirrored in many respects the successful contemporary West German 'concerted action' system, was viewed by leading ministers as the key to solving the postwar British disease of poor labour relations, low productivity and rampant wage inflation and was to form the centrepiece of the 1974–9 Labour government's economic pro-gramme. Fifth, the government envisaged funding much of its

'social contract' welfare spending programmme through redistributing income from high earners to the poor through sharply
raising income tax at its upper level.

During the winter months of 1974 and spring of 1975 the Wilson
government remained optimistic that this bullish strategy could
break the economy out of the stagflationary spiral that had gripped
it since 1973. Chancellor Healey, having introduced a reflationary
'mini budget' in July 1974, followed this with a more neutral
package after the election in November 1974, but continued to
raise social spending in line with the 'Social Contract' commitment.
The government looked optimistically to an improvement in world
trade and a recycling of the world oil surpluses, borrowing back
funds from the Middle East to maintain demand in Western Europe.
Unfortunately, however, the other leading Western economies
continued to pursue a more cautious policy line and a sharp
contraction in world trade was registered between 1975-7. As a
consequence, British GDP fell sharply during 1975, the balance of
payments remained fragile, inflation continued to rise and the UK
unemployment total leapt above the one million barrier to a figure
of 1.13 million in December 1975, or 5% of the workforce.

In such a worsening economic situation it became evident to the
government's leading ministers that the 1974-5 policy package was
failing to work, proving to be dangerously contradictory in many of
its effects. For example, the increase in the Public Sector Borrowing
Requirement (PSBR), which had resulted from enhanced social
spending and state industrial investment, had served both to push
up interest rates, thus discouraging private industrial investment,
and to lead to further falls in the exchange rate, hence making
imports dearer and fuelling the domestic inflation rate. It was also
found that the voluntary wage restraint promised by trade union
leaders as part of the 'Social Contract' had failed to materialise,
wage rises averaging 27% during 1975 and continuing to outstrip
the inflation rate (see Table 9). As a consequence, therefore, a
major change in policy was embarked upon from the late spring of
1975. In April 1975 Chancellor Healey introduced an 'austerity
budget' in which there were substantial increases in both income
tax, the standard rate rising 2p to 35p, and VAT on luxury items.
Public spending for the ensuing fiscal year was slashed by £900
million, the principal economies occurring in defence spending
and through the removal of many nationalised industry price
subsidies. This harsh and deflationary budget was followed in June
1975 by the announcement by Prime Minister Wilson that the

free-spending and interventionist Industry Secretary Tony Benn was being moved to head Energy and would be replaced at Industry by the more cautious and pliable Eric Varley. Benn's transfer was ostensibly carried out as a consequence of his vocal opposition to continuing EEC membership. It represented, however, an abandonment of the radical left wing, state-led ' new industrial strategy'.

**Table 9    Economic Indicators 1974–9**

| | Real Disposable Income | Weekly Earnings | Retail Prices | Av % of Workforce unemployed |
|---|---|---|---|---|
| 1974 | NA | +17% | +16% | 2.6 |
| 1975 | +0.6% | +27% | +24% | 3.9 |
| 1976 | −0.4% | +16% | +17% | 5.3 |
| 1977 | −1.9% | +10% | +16% | 5.7 |
| 1978 | +6.2% | +13% | +8% | 5.7 |
| 1979 | +9.8% | +18% | +13% | 5.1 |

| | Working days lost in stoppages | GDP | Money Supply Growth | Balance of Payments (£m) | Av. Exchange Rate (US$) |
|---|---|---|---|---|---|
| 1974 | 14.75m | +0.2% | NA | −3565 | 2.34 |
| 1975 | 6.01m | −1.6% | +8.6% | −1671 | 2.22 |
| 1976 | 3.31m | +2.3% | +8.5% | −1404 | 1.76 |
| 1977 | 10.14m | +0.9% | +8.1% | +154 | 1.74 |
| 1978 | 9.28m | +3.4% | +14.6% | +254 | 1.92 |
| 1979 | 31.19m | +2.2% | +11.2% | −902 | 2.13 |

Under the new Industry Secretary, while the public sector continued to be substantially extended with the nationalisation of British Leyland (1975) and the shipbuilding and aerospace industries (1977), the NEB increasingly concentrated upon rescuing declining 'lame duck' industries rather than investing in new and prosperous 'sunrise' concerns. In addition, the 1974–5 commitment to imposing compulsory planning agreements on key, strategic private firms was abandoned and replaced with purely voluntary consultation, as the Labour government began to woo the CBI and the private industrial sector during the years after 1975. The third clear indication of a change in policy course occurred in July 1975, with the negotiation with the TUC of Stage One of a policy of formal pay restraint. An across-the-board £6-a-week limit on wage increases was announced, which represented a 10% rise for those on average earnings, while the pay of those earning in excess of £8,500 per annum was frozen. These limits contained an egalitarian bias towards those on lower pay, designed to placate potential opponents on the left. In addition, the pay policy remained voluntary, no legal sanctions existing against individual unions which breached the guidelines. Firms were, however, to be deterred from passing on excessive wage increases in their price schedules as a result of the sanction powers that were granted to the government's Pay Board.

The policy U-turn of April-July 1975 was accepted as necessary by the centre-right majority that existed within the Cabinet and PLP and was acquiesced to in the short-term by the majority of trade union leaders. It served slowly to bring the inflation rate down to below 20% during the winter of 1975 and spring of 1976, as wage rises began to lag behind prices and living standards were depressed (see Table 9). This belt-tightening succeeded also in narrowing the trade deficit and maintaining the value of sterling. Its consequences were, however, a sharp rise in unemployment during the closing months of 1975 and the re-opening of the latent left-right divisions that existed within the Labour Party. Claiming betrayal, the left succeeded in ousting Denis Healey from the NEC in September 1975 and their leader, Tony Benn, remained vocal in his criticism of recent policy decisions. Against such a background, and having just survived a confidence vote in the House of Commons, Harold Wilson surprised the nation, on 16 March 1976, by announcing that he had decided to retire in mid-term to give a new leader, with a fresh and open mind, the opportunity to take charge and seek solutions to new problems confronting the government during the second half of the 1970s.

## All Change at the Top: the New Party Leaders

Harold Wilson's resignation stunned the political world, marking the end of a political career that had spanned three decades and had included almost eight years as Prime Minister. Commentators speculated that Wilson had been 'forced out' as a result of an impending scandal, while others, prompted by cryptic comments from Number 10, suggested that he had been a victim of MI5 intelligence service plotting. It later transpired, however, that his retirement, shortly after his sixtieth birthday, had been planned several years in advance and was primarily the result of the toll taken on Wilson's health as a consequence of the demands of party and national leadership. Wilson had given prior warning of his intentions to his private office staff as early as February 1974. None of his close ministerial colleagues were made aware of this decision, however, until several days in advance. Six candidates thus hastily gathered to contest the succession in a ballot of the PLP: Roy Jenkins (56), Denis Healey (59), Tony Crosland (57) and James Callaghan (64), from the right and centre and Michael Foot (62) and Tony Benn (51) from its left wing. On the first ballot, held on 22 March, Michael Foot narrowly topped the poll ahead of James Callaghan.[1] In the second poll a week later, Callaghan, Foot and Healey remained in the contest, garnering 141, 133 and 38 votes respectively. Finally, on 5 April, in what was a centre-right versus 'soft left' showdown, James Callaghan emerged triumphant, capturing 176 PLP votes to Michael Foot's 137.

A change in leadership also took place in the country's other two parties during the eighteen months between February 1975 and July 1976.

The Conservatives had been the first to seek a new captain in the wake of their twin electoral defeats in 1974. Edward Heath, the party's first leader to be selected under the new election rules of 1965, had remained throughout his term at the helm a most controversial choice. He had built up strong and loyal support among a coterie of younger, often lower middle class, Tory MPs, dubbed the 'Heathites', but had alienated many others through his arrogant, autocratic and distant style of leadership, and through the faulty tactics that had contributed to the party's loss of three out of the last four general elections. In addition, a small, but vocal and expanding, grouping began to voice increasing criticism of the former Prime Minister's U-turns during 1972–4 and his failure to push through the radical 'new right' monetarist and individualist counter-revolution which had been promised at Selsdon Park in 1970.

The leader of such opposition to Heathite Conservatism was Sir Keith Joseph (57), the high-spending, but innovative, former Social Security minister and controversial apostle of a 'New Conservatism', propounded in his speech at Preston in September 1974. His views were founded on the teachings of the gurus of monetarist economics, Friedrich von Hayek and Milton Friedman. It was not,

---

[1] Foot captured 90 of the first ballot votes, Callaghan 84, Jenkins 56, Benn 37, Healey 30 and Crosland 17. Healey and Jenkins, who had promised to be Callaghan's most serious rivals from the centre-right, polled poorly as a result of hostility to Healey's recent record as Chancellor and Jenkins' divisive stance on the EEC issue.

however, Joseph who challenged for the leadership in February 1975, when Heath eventually put himself forward for re-election.[1] Joseph recognised that he lacked the personality to become a viable national leader. He therefore supported, instead, Margaret Thatcher (50), a likeminded and apparently malleable former Education Secretary who had recently gained broader recognition within the party's ranks by promising low cost 9% house mortgages during the October 1974 election campaign and for skilfully opposing the government's Finance Bill during the 1974 parliamentary session. There were other, more likely, alternatives to Edward Heath in 1975, William Whitelaw (56), in particular, James Prior (47), and Sir Geoffrey Howe (48), but they remained loyal and did not contest the first ballot. This enabled Margaret Thatcher to defeat Heath surprisingly by 130 to 119 when Conservative MPs cast their votes on 4 February 1975. The other contestant, Hugh Fraser, MP for Stafford and Stone, received 16 votes, while 11 MPs abstained. Deeply wounded by this vote of no-confidence, Heath immediately tendered his resignation as party leader. This left Margaret Thatcher as the new front-runner and such was the momentum behind her candidature, in a campaign adeptly managed by Airey Neave (1916–79), that by the time Whitelaw, Prior and Howe had announced their intentions to enter the contest it was too late. In the second ballot on 11 February 1975 Thatcher won a decisive majority of 146 out of 279 votes leaving Whitelaw (79 votes), Prior (19) and Howe (19) trailing in her wake.[2] In what was later to be termed the backbench 'peasants' revolt' of February 1975, the party of conservatism had elected the country's first female party leader and had vaulted to centre-stage a figure who was to emerge as the dominating influence on British politics during the ensuing decade.

Months later rumours of an unsavoury affair centring around the Liberals' extrovert leader, Jeremy Thorpe, threatened to lead to an enforced change in leadership of a third political party. Matters came to a head early in 1976 when, during court proceedings against Norman Scott for defrauding the Department of Health and Social Security, an allegation was made that Scott, a former male model, had had a homosexual relationship with Thorpe. This

---

[1] Heath stood for re-election as a result of pressure exerted by the backbench 1922 Committee, chaired by Edward Du Cann, and the recommendation of the hastily convened Home Committee on party procedure that there should be annual leadership elections.

[2] 11 votes, in addition, went to the outsider candidate John Peyton.

scandal dragged on for months and involved accusations of blackmail and conspiracy to murder Scott in a desperate 'cover up' operation.[1] With support for the party slumping in national opinion polls and at contemporary by-elections, Thorpe eventually accepted the inevitable and resigned, on 10 May 1976. Jo Grimond agreed to return as interim party leader while a new election procedure (involving direct voting, by constituency party members in a fashion weighted in accordance with regional electoral strength, for candidates who had been nominated with the backing of a quarter of the party's MPs) was drafted and agreed upon at a hastily convened special Liberal Assembly held in Manchester on 12 June 1976. With the new selection system in place two sharply contrasting figures emerged to contest the vacant leadership: John Pardoe, the aggressive North Cornwall MP and party treasury spokesman, and David Steel, the shrewd and cool 38-year-old Scots MP for Roxburgh and 1970–6 chief whip.[2] After a surprisingly robust campaign, Steel emerged a convincing 2:1 (12,541 to 7,032 votes) victor on 7 July 1976. He was the first party leader to be elected by his national, rather than parliamentary, party.

[1] The 'Scott scandal' rumbled on throughout 1976–9, climaxing in May-June 1979 in the trial of Thorpe and three friends on conspiracy to murder charges. They were fully acquitted on all charges on 22 June 1979.

[2] Steel, born in March 1938, was the son of a Church of Scotland minister who carried out missionary work in Kenya during the 1950s. He won a scholarship to George Watson's College, gained a general MA and law degree at Edinburgh University and worked for six months as a BBC Scotland reporter/presenter before winning the Roxburgh, Selkirk and Peebles seat in a March 1965 by-election.

# Part Three

# THE CALLAGHAN ADMINISTRATION: 1976–79

## The Prime Minister Who Nearly Never Was

### The Making of 'Sunny Jim'

Leonard James Callaghan, entered No. 10 Downing Street with impressive credentials, having, uniquely, held all the great offices of state, Chancellor of the Exchequer, Home Secretary and Foreign Secretary, except Prime Minister. He came from a lower middle class background, his father having been a naval chief petty officer of Irish descent who died in 1920, and, as a non-smoking, chapel-going tee-totaller, had been instilled from an early age with the need for self-discipline and hard work. Callaghan was also unusual among postwar Prime Ministers in not having enjoyed a university education. He left secondary school at Portsmouth during the late 1920s with the School Certificate, equivalent to contemporary 'O' Levels, and became first a tax officer and then a trade union organiser for the Inland Revenue Staff Federation. After war service in the Royal Navy, where he reached the rank of lieutenant, he came under the wing of Hugh Dalton and, at the age of 33, was elected to the House of Commons in the momentous election of 1945 for the constituency of Cardiff South-East.

Callaghan's rise up the party hierarchy during the 1950s and 1960s had been less spectacular than that of his contemporary, Harold Wilson. He had succeeded in building up, however, a strong personal following on the centre-right of the party and among older union leaders, and had established a reputation as a solid, pragmatic, non-ideological, intuitive politician concerned, above all, with improving the material conditions of the poor and underprivileged. Calllaghan's period as Chancellor of the Exchequer between 1964–7 was an unhappy one, culminating in the enforced devaluation of sterling in November 1967 and his replacement by the more successful Roy Jenkins. As Home Secretary (1967–70), however, he showed firmness in dealing with the Irish crisis of 1969 coupled with a liberal flexibility in his approach to domestic social issues. Following the February 1974 election he was appointed to the prestigious post of Foreign Secretary and emerged as a popular and successful figure, finding his forte as a world statesman who was keen to foster continued detente and who successfully re-negotiated Britain's EEC entry terms. This background and experience made Callaghan, although aged 64, the natural choice to succeed Harold Wilson in March 1976.

However, with Wilson apparently destined to serve another three years in office, Callaghan had not expected to be elevated any higher. He thus assumed the leadership in a relaxed, but ebullient, mood. He inherited Wilson's Number 10 Policy Unit, headed by Bernard Donoughue, and brought in his own personal advisers Tom McNally (Political Secretary), Gavyn Davies (Economic Adviser) and Tom McCaffrey (Press Officer), but did not establish a presidentialist 'kitchen cabinet' in the manner of his predecessor. Callaghan, instead, presided over the new administration in the manner of a wise elder statesman, allowing extensive policy debate within cabinet and delegating considerable authority to his individual ministers, while weaving together the agreed threads into a broader and coherent framework.[1] This style conflicted with the personal interventionism of the 1964–74 Wilson-Heath era, but represented a continuation of the more detached governing style of the third and fourth Wilson governments (1974–6). It suited the outward character of the new leader, who projected the reassuring and avuncular image of 'Sunny Jim', the favourite uncle of the nation, although privately he tended to be a pessimist. It reflected also the Prime Minister's predilection for concentrating his attention on the 'big issues' of politics, such as foreign affairs and the fight against inflation, where he did take a more high-profile and aggressive lead, rather than on becoming involved with the narrow policy details. Callaghan would, however, need all his charm and every ounce of luck if he was to lead his party successfully to and through the next election. He had inherited a very slender

---

[1] On some controversial issues, however, for example, the decision to go ahead with the Chevaline programme to upgrade the Polaris nuclear missile system, Callaghan acted in a more narrowly circumspect manner, avoiding debate within the full cabinet by hiving off decision-making to secret sub-committees.

parliamentary majority, which was decreasing with every by-election; an economy in turmoil; and a Labour movement which was being torn apart by a damaging left-right cleavage.

## The Callaghan Team and Style

Callaghan was bequeathed a strong cabinet team by Wilson, but felt it necessary to make a number of changes in April 1976 in order to assert his early authority (see Table 10). He thus moved out of the cabinet Barbara Castle (64), a bitter personal opponent, William Ross (65), Edward Short (63) and Robert Mellish (63) and brought in Albert Booth (47), Edmund Dell (54), David Ennals (53) and Bruce Millan (48). Within a year a number of other significant changes were made, with the replacement of Roy Jenkins, who left to become the EEC's new Commissioner in Brussels in January 1977, with Merlyn Rees, as Home Secretary; of Tony Crosland, who died suddenly in February 1977, with the 38-year-old Dr David Owen as Foreign Secretary; and the induction of Roy Hattersley (44) as Prices Secretary, Shirley Williams (46) moving to Education. A year later, John Smith (39), a young Scots barrister, replaced Edmund Dell as Trade Secretary.[1] These changes retained a strong right-of-centre bias in a cabinet which contained only four left-wingers: Benn, Foot, Booth and Silkin. The Callaghan team planned to press on along the 1975–6 path of solid, consensual economic recovery built around the 'Social Contract' incomes policy to overcome what was now seen as the prime enemy of double-digit inflation. They aimed also to pilot through legislation for Welsh and Scottish devolution, in order to protect the party's flanks against the mounting nationalist challenge, and to add to this a dash of adventure abroad, with an ambitious peace initiative in Rhodesia, and of social reformism at home under the aegis of the new Education and Health Secretaries. These plans were abruptly disturbed, however, by a gathering financial crisis.

---

[1] The other changes made during the September 1976 and February 1977 re-shuffles were the moving of Roy Mason to Northern Ireland, Fred Mulley to Defence, Fred Peart to the Lords, as the party's new upper chamber leader, and John Silkin to Agriculture. The Overseas Development and Planning Departments left the Cabinet, but the posts of Transport Secretary (William Rodgers), Social Security Minister (Stanley Orme) and Chief Secretary to the Treasury (Joel Barnett) were added to an expanded Cabinet of 24.

Table 10   The Callaghan Cabinet of April 1976

| | |
|---|---|
| Prime Minister | —James Callaghan |
| Chancellor of the Exchequer | —Denis Healey |
| Foreign Secretary | —Tony Crosland |
| Home Secretary | —Roy Jenkins |
| Defence Secretary | —Roy Mason |
| Environment Secretary | —Peter Shore |
| Industry Secretary | —Eric Varley |
| Energy Secretary | —Tony Benn |
| Employment Secretary | —Albert Booth |
| Trade Secretary | —Edmond Dell |
| Social Services Secretary | —David Ennals |
| Leader of the Commons | —Michael Foot |
| Agriculture Secretary | —Frederick Peart |
| Education Secretary | —Fred Mulley |
| Prices Secretary | —Shirley Williams |
| Northern Ireland Secretary | —Merlyn Rees |
| Scottish Secretary | —Bruce Millan |
| Welsh Secretary | —John Morris |
| Overseas Development Minister | —Reg Prentice |
| Minister for Local Govt/Planning | —John Silkin |
| Lord Chancellor | —Ld Elwyn-Jones |
| Chllr of the Duchy of Lancaster | —Harold Lever |
| Lord Privy Seal/Leader of the Lords | —Lord Shepherd |

# The Art of the Possible: 1976–8

## The IMF Crisis

When he assumed office in April 1976 James Callaghan was not to know that within six months he would be faced with the greatest economic and political crisis confronting a Labour Prime Minister since 1931. The problem he inherited had been slowly developing between 1973 and 1976. Public spending and the level of wage increases had been kept under reasonable control during the last quarter of 1975 and the first quarter of 1976 and the size of the contemporary balance of payments deficit was not unduly worrying. However, there were fears that there were insufficient currency reserves to protect the pound should there be a run on it. Early in 1976 the Treasury, under its Keynesian Permanent Secretary Sir Douglas Wass (53), sought to obtain a controlled devaluation of sterling to assist exports and thus ease the balance of payments situation. They had in mind the successful devaluation by Roy Jenkins nine years earlier. The new Prime Minister, who tended to view a strong pound as a symbol of national vitality and strength, entertained personal doubts about allowing the pound to fall below the $2 rate. However, rumours of the Treasury's intentions spread through the City and led to a rapid slide in the value of sterling which the nation's currency reserves proved insufficient to halt. Thus within weeks of taking high office Callaghan faced a crisis recalling that which had confronted him in 1966–7. This time, however, it was Denis Healey's turn to attempt to placate the financial markets.

Chancellor Healey's immediate response was to introduce in, April 1976, a 'responsible', neutral budget which was specifically designed to restore the city's confidence in the government's fiscal prudence. The budget included a promise of tax cuts if the unions showed further moderation in their negotiation of wage settlements and was followed in May 1976 by the hammering out of a new 'Stage Two' of the 'Social Contract' incomes policy with the TUC and CBI, based on a 4.5% ceiling on new pay increases. The Chancellor's failure, however, to effect a significant reduction in the level of the PSBR caused unease among the foreign exchange markets. The pound thus continued to slip in international value, falling to $1.70 by May 1976, and foreign reserves were rapidly exhausted as desperate efforts were made to halt its slide.

By the early summer it was clear that the government would need an injection of outside funds to tide over this temporary financial crisis. However, it did not wish to apply to the International Monetary Fund (IMF) and have to subject itself to outside policy constraints. Harold Lever, the cabinet's currency expert, thus suggested taking out a six month $5.3 billion standby credit from American and West European central banks, while announcing, at the same time, a £1 billion cut in public expenditure for 1977–8.

The mention, however, of spending cuts, following on the heels of the social service economies that had already been introduced during 1975–6, alarmed both left and right wingers in the party and cabinet. Those on the far left, led by Tony Benn, recalled the crisis of 1929–31 and mistrusted Treasury-suggested 'financier solutions'. They commended instead a new 'alternative economic strategy', which was being developed by the Cambridge Economic Policy Group (CEPG) and Benn's economic adviser Stuart Holland, and proposed a radical programme of import controls, greater public industrial investment and planning to deal with what they termed this 'capitalist crisis'. Those on the 'revisionist right', led by Tony Crosland, the only professional economist in the Cabinet, also opposed spending cuts, feeling that that the government should keep its nerve and try to ride out what they saw as only a temporary crisis. A third, middle, view, articulated by the Wilsonite, Peter Shore, favoured selective import controls. The Treasury was equally divided, between Keynesians and monetarists, over the need to reduce the PSBR. In the end, however, a £1 billion reduction in public spending was agreed and Chancellor Healey managed to raise another £1 billion through a 2% increase in employers' national insurance contributions. In addition, interest rates were increased to new record levels.

The 'July package', as the spending cuts and contribution increases became known, signalled an abandonment of the postwar Keynesian attempt to foster full-employment through government 'pump-priming' and marked the start of a new era of strict 'cash limits' public expenditure control. In the short term, however, the measures proved inadequate to win over the financial markets, while the new national insurance surcharges were greeted with dismay by industrialists, being termed a 'tax on jobs'. Chancellor Healey had thus ended up with the worst of all worlds. He had succeeded in more or less permanently alienating the left wing of his party, thus ending any future hope of his succeeding to the leadership; he had upset industry; and he had failed to restore confidence in the pound.

Matters reached a head at the Labour Party's conference in Blackpool in September 1976. The left, with NEC support, forced through a radical policy resolution, 'Labour's Programme 1976', which called for the nationalisation of banks and insurance companies, compulsory planning agreements and the introduction of an extensive range of new welfare benefits. It was James Callaghan, however, who dominated proceedings, delivering a courageous, if sullenly received, watershed speech in which he called for a 'New Realism' in the party's approach to economic policy. Having already decided to apply to the IMF on 29 September, Callaghan proceeded to castigate the failure of Keynesian policies during the preceding six years, which, in his view, had weakened sterling, stoked up inflation and added to unemployment. He stated forcefully: 'We used to think that you could spend your way out of a recession and increase employment by cutting taxes and boosting government spending. I tell you in all candour that that option no longer exists, and that, in so far as it ever did exist, it only worked on each occasion since the war by injecting a bigger dose of inflation into the economy, followed by a higher level of unemployment as the next step. Higher inflation followed by higher unemployment—that is the history of the last twenty years.' This was the sort of assertion that was to be repeatedly made by the succeeding Thatcher government.

Outside the conference chamber the pound continued to fall in value, reaching $1.50 on 6 October 1976, and the minimum lending rate had to be raised to 15%. The currency reserves continued to melt away and it was clear that the government would be unable to repay its July standby loan without recourse to the IMF. In many respects the July loan had been a trap deliberately set by the US Treasury, possibly with the connivance of a number of monetarist civil servants within the UK Treasury, which was anxious to see Britain put its house in order and join other OECD nations in taking what was seen as a necessary dose of deflationary medicine. This American plot succeeded as bargaining commenced between the IMF and the Callaghan government during September-October 1976.

The IMF eventually agreed to provide a $3.9 billion loan to the UK but attached stringent policy strings, insisting that, in return, the government pledge itself to a £2.5 billion cut in the PSBR over two years, the sale of £500 million BP shares, and the strict control of the money supply. These terms engendered lengthy and bitter conflicts in the cabinet, with the left and Croslandites, who included Roy Hattersley, Shirley Williams and Harold Lever, speaking out against this 'meat axe' approach. At the vital moment, however. Crosland lost his nerve and pledged his grudging support with the words: 'This is nonsense, but we must do it'. The measure thus passed through cabinet, despite the left's opposition, and on 15 December 1976 Denis Healey presented the 'Letter of Intent' to the IMF to the House of Commons amid sounds of dismay from his own benches and shouts of derision from the Tory opposition.

It is interesting to speculate on how necessary recourse to the IMF had been (later Treasury figures, for example, showing the PSBR deficit to have been less than anticipated) and whether the 'alternative economic strategy', if followed wholeheartedly, would have worked. The left wing of the Labour Party believed that Healey had 'used' the IMF to impose the deflationary policies he wanted to pursue anyway. The humiliating IMF crisis also called into question the wisdom of the Treasury, whose devaluation strategy precipitated financial panic in 1976. In broader terms, the IMF crisis opened a debate on whether postwar Keynesian expansionism had finally been discredited or just temporarily destabilised by the sudden 1973–4 OPEC oil price hike and switch to floating exchange rates. Whatever conclusions a post-mortem might reach, it is clear that the IMF crisis had an important bearing on future relationships within the Labour Party and on the economic policies which subsequent administrations were to pursue, marking a shift from Keynesianism to a new, more parsimonious, monetarist approach.

## The Lib-Lab Pact

By January 1977, following the loss of three by-elections, at Woolwich West (June 1975), Workington (November 1976) and Walsall North (November 1976), the two most recent on swings of 13% and 22% to the Tories, Labour's overall parliamentary majority had been eroded. The party was in a minority of one if all the opposition parties combined together. The government was granted the support of the 14 Scottish and Welsh Nationalist MPs, as well as Gerry Fitt, the SDLP MP, during December 1976 and January 1977 to ensure the passage of many of its key legislative measures. However, such nationalist backing was suddenly withdrawn following the defeat of the 'guillotine' motion for the Scotland and Wales (Devolution) Bill in February 1977. The government was thus placed in an overall minority during the spring of 1977, with the situation exacerbated by defections of a clutch of Scottish MPs and dissident right-wingers[1] and by the knowledge that a number of the party's 80 Tribunite left-wingers, disillusioned with the IMF arrangements, could no longer be relied upon for consistent support in the division lobbies. The Labour leader declined, however, to seek an early election, realising that, with unfavourable opinion polls, the Conservatives at this time enjoying a 16-point national lead, he would almost certainly be defeated. He decided, instead, to seek out a novel working agreement with the thirteen Liberal MPs under the stewardship of David Steel.

Liberal leaders in the past, Jo Grimond in 1964–5, Jeremy Thorpe in 1974, had shown a desire to engage in governing alliances with each of the two major parties, but had been overruled by their colleagues and party at large. The Liberals' new leader, David Steel,

[1] Two Scottish MPs, Jim Sillars (Ayr) and John Robertson (Paisley) had refused the party whip in January 1976 and formed a breakaway Scottish Labour Party (SLP) to mark their opposition to what they saw as the timidity of the government's devolution reforms, while Reg Prentice, a maverick right-winger who was in conflict with his local CLP, resigned from the cabinet in December 1976 and was later to take the Conservative whip in October 1977.

who had gained a reputation as a prominent figure within the cross-party pro-EEC movement in 1975, as president of the all-party anti-apartheid movement and as the architect of the 1967 private members Abortion Bill, was an even firmer advocate of participation in government, viewing it as a means of re-establishing the party's electoral credibility, broadening its experience, transforming its members into harder-headed realists and securing the passage of cherished legislation. Thus in March 1977 when, following a defeat on the key Public Expenditure White Paper, Margaret Thatcher announced her intention to table a motion of 'no-confidence' in the government, he was receptive to the idea of a temporary Lib-Lab pact.

Cledwyn Hughes, Labour's PLP leader, and William Rodgers first sounded Steel out on 18 March and arranged a meeting between Steel and Callaghan at Chequers on 21 March, two days before the 'no-confidence' motion. This meeting was warm and cordial and was followed afterwards by Steel's gaining support for the idea of a pact from his parliamentary colleagues, who feared having to fight an election in the midst of the damaging and continuing Thorpe-Scott scandal and at a time when their national support rating stood at barely 9%.

Steel thus went away and drew up a formal, written list of six conditions for a pact which were put before Callaghan and his cabinet colleagues: the setting up of a joint consultative committee to review government policy in advance of its presentation to parliament; an early meeting between Chancellor Healey and his Liberal 'shadow', John Pardoe to confirm a sufficient identity of views on economic strategy; the introduction and commendation to the House of Commons of a Bill for direct elections to the European Parliament; the re-introduction of legislation on devolution for Scotland and Wales; no further nationalisation proposals; and the dropping of the Local Government Direct Labour Bill. In return, the Liberals would agree to support the government on any confidence issue until the end of the summer.

These terms seemed modest and acceptable to Callaghan and his colleagues, but when Steel went back to his parliamentary colleagues for their endorsement they argued that the elections to the European Parliament should be on the basis of proportional representation (PR). At first Callaghan disagreed and it seemed that the whole idea of a Lib-Lab pact might founder on this one point. Finally, however, the Labour leader offered to include both forms of voting in the European Elections Bill and allow a free, 'unwhipped', vote in Parliament, without the government expressing a preference for either system. He assured Steel, however, that he himself would vote for PR, and so the pact was agreed.

The Lib-Lab pact came successfully into effect, to the Tories' anger, at the end of the 23 March 1977 'no confidence' motion. It continued for another eighteen months, being formally renewed by the Liberal Party Assembly in September 1977 and January 1978, but was not always a happy arrangement. The public reacted against it in the May 1977 local government elections, with Labour taking control of only 18 out of 54 county councils, relinquishing its hold over the Greater London Council (GLC), and the Liberals losing three-quarters of their sitting councillors.[1] Inside Westminister, while Steel and Callaghan developed an unusually close and warm relationship, Healey and Pardoe had strong differences in policy and personality. David Steel and the Commons' Leader, Michael Foot, thus needed to exercise all their skills of conciliation and leadership to keep the pact intact.

The pact period saw the final abandonment of any attempts at radical reform by the Callaghan administration, David Steel stressing his party's determination to prevent any 'further expansion of socialism'. It brought, in addition, a number of minor, though significant, policy victories for the Liberals, for example, in the increased attention paid by the government to encouraging small businesses and industrial democracy, through workers co-partnerships, and Chancellor Healey's defeats in 1977–8 over plans to substantially raise the petrol excise duty and the level of employers' National Insurance Contributions. The centrepiece of the 'Lib-Lab Pact' era was, however, the re-introduction of legislation on devolution for Scotland and Wales.

## The 1976–9 Battle for Devolution

In the 1976–7 parliamentary session the government had introduced a combined Scotland and Wales Bill which envisaged the creation of separate Scottish and Welsh Assemblies to be elected by simple majorities on the basis of existing parliamentary constituencies and with their own executives drawn from the Assemblies. The Scottish Assembly was to enjoy extensive law-making powers in the

---

[1] In addition, Labour lost two by-elections to the Conservatives in late March and April 1977: Birmingham, Stechford and Ashfield.

fields of health, education, social services, housing, local government planning and roads, although the House of Commons would retain the ultimate right of veto. The Welsh Assembly, by contrast, would lack legislative authority, but would take over the executive functions of the Welsh Office and enjoy a number of powers in relation to specially delegated legislation. Both Assemblies would be financed by means of 'block grants' from Westminster and would not have the authority to levy their own taxes. These proposals fell far short of the demand for all-out separatism that had been contained in the SNP's 1974 election manifesto, but were supported by the nationalist parties as a useful 'first step' and warmly embraced by the pro-decentralisation Liberal Party. The Bill was thus approved by a majority of 45 during its second reading in December 1976. A combination of opposition from Conservatives, who under the new leadership of Margaret Thatcher had moved away from the support given to limited devolution in the party's October 1974 manifesto, and dissident Labour MPs, however, led to defeat of the motion on 22 February 1977 when the government attempted unsuccessfully to impose a 'guillotine' to expedite its passage through the committee stage.

In accordance with of the new 'Lib-Lab Pact' however, in 1977 devolution returned to the forefront of the political agenda. New and separate Bills for Scotland and Wales were introduced in the Commons in November 1977, similar in nature to that of 1976–7, but including the provision for referenda in Scotland and Wales before the measures, if passed, were to take effect. They were ruthlessly 'guillotined' to ensure their rapid passage on to the statute book and were given the royal assent on 31 July 1978. In the process, however, the government was forced to make a number of significant committee stage concessions. First, a clause was inserted under which any future bills not affecting Scottish interests which were given a Second Reading in the Commons as a result of the support of Scottish MPs would have to be confirmed by a second Commons vote within a fortnight. This was designed to deal with arguments concerning the equity of Scottish MPs, with their own Assembly in which Scottish laws were framed free of English interference, exerting a continuing and potentially decisive influence over English affairs. Second, an amendment was added to exclude the Orkney and Shetland Islands from the provisions of the Scotland Bill if a majority of islanders voted 'No' in the forthcoming referendum. Third and, as it proved to be, most crucially, on 25 January 1978 (Burns' Night), the opposition successfully inserted the provision into each Bill that they could only become law if the support of 40% of the electorate was received when the referendum was held. This meant that unless turnout was unusually high, far more than a simple majority would be required. This succeeded, as was intended, in wrecking the proposals when the referenda were held eventually on 1 March 1979. In Scotland 52% (1.23 million) of those casting a vote supported the devolution scheme, However, with the turnout at only 63.6%, this only corresponded to 33% of the total electorate. In Wales, where the turnout was even lower at 58.8%, only 20% (0.24 million) of those participating voted 'Yes'. This corresponded to a mere 12% of the electorate.

## The 'Economic Miracle'

In the longer term, the Devolution Bills of 1977–8 resulted in creating the conditions which brought the eventual downfall of the Callaghan administration. In the short term, however, the political and economic tide appeared to be slowly turning in the government's direction as the pact period progressed. In particular, the economy began to recover strongly from the trough of 1974–6 during 1977–8. A 'Stage Three' to the 'Social Contract' incomes policy, which had been agreed with the TUC in July 1977, was being broadly adhered to on the basis of a maximum earnings increase of 10%, and the pound had been freed to float upwards so that by the summer of 1977 it had recovered to just under $2. Inflation had fallen from the 1975 level of more than 25% to less than 10%; the numbers of days lost as a result of industrial stoppages was at a ten-year low; and unemployment, although at an unwelcome total of 1.6 million (6% of the national workforce) was displaying a falling trend. In addition, the balance of payments had moved from deficit to surplus and both visible and invisible earnings had been in surplus for four consecutive months. In such circumstances, Hugo Young, captured the new mood of optimism when he asked in a 'Sunday Times' article, 'Is this the Labour miracle?'.

This strong recovery continued throughout the autumn and spring and was further fuelled by reflationary budgets in October 1977 and April 1978, by the expansion of the production of North Sea oil and by the boost to world trade which was to follow the July 1978 Bonn economic summit. By the spring of 1978 the country was free from the constraints imposed by the IMF and set to make early repayments of its loan; unemployment had fallen to 1.4 million, inflation was continuing to decline; opinion polls were strongly recovering in the government's favour (see Table 11); and its run of by-election defeats was finally halted. With the passage of the Devolution Bills in July 1978 Gallup Polls showed Labour and the Conservatives neck and neck. In such circumstances speculation concerning the possible calling of an early election rapidly spread and it seemed so certain that James Callaghan would go to the electorate in the autumn of 1978 that the Conservative Party began to launch a £2 million poster publicity campaign in anticipation.

**Table 11  Gallup Poll Trends 1974–9 (% By Quarters)**

|  | 1974 | | 1975 | | | | 1976 | | | |
|---|---|---|---|---|---|---|---|---|---|---|
|  | III | IV | I | II | III | IV | I | II | III | IV |
| Con % lead over Labour | −3 | −10 | −3 | +2 | 0 | 0 | +2 | 0 | +1 | +20 |

|  | 1977 | | | | 1978 | | | | 1979 |
|---|---|---|---|---|---|---|---|---|---|
|  | I | II | III | IV | I | II | III | IV | I |
| Con % lead over Labour | +13 | +13 | +10 | +2 | +5 | +1 | +3 | −2 | +13 |

|  | 1974 | | 1975 | | | | 1976 | | | |
|---|---|---|---|---|---|---|---|---|---|---|
|  | III | IV | I | II | III | IV | I | II | III | IV |
| Liberal Poll Rating | 16 | 13 | 9 | 9 | 12 | 10 | 9 | 8 | 9 | 9 |

|  | 1977 | | | | 1978 | | | | 1979 |
|---|---|---|---|---|---|---|---|---|---|
|  | I | II | III | IV | I | II | III | IV | I |
| Liberal Poll Rating | 10 | 8 | 7 | 7 | 7 | 6 | 5 | 5 | 6 |

These hopes were confounded, however, by the Prime Minister, who was determined to push on with a 'Stage Four' of his anti-inflationary incomes policy crusade. This was first made clear in a radio interview in January 1978 when Callaghan floated the idea of 5% price and income increases: an idea which evolved not from the Treasury, but from conversations between Callaghan and the circumspect West German leader, Helmut Schmidt. The figure of 5% appeared to be plucked out of thin air, being simply, in Callaghan's words 'half 10%'. It was, however, to be bitterly opposed by many union leaders who saw it as unrealistically low and who were anxious to return to free collective bargaining. The TUC General Council rejected the 5% norm, but the Callaghan cabinet quietly accepted it in July 1978, since its members were certain that an election would be called before the autumn pay round got into full swing.

In September 1978 the Lib-Lab pact was formally ended by a Liberal Party which had become increasingly disillusioned after its failure to gain PR for the European Assembly elections in the January 1978 'free vote', the clause, for a regional list system, being defeated by a combination of Conservatives and rebel Labour MPs. There was mounting internal dissent under the leadership of the colourful figures of Cyril Smith (Rochdale) and David Penhaligon (Truro). This seemed to add force to the argument for an autumn election. But on 7 September Callaghan astonished his colleagues, with the exception of the likeminded Healey and Foot, by announcing his decision to battle on as a minority government and not call an election until 1979. This decision, taken in the belief that a further successful period of wage restraint and economic growth coupled with the successful enactment of Scottish devolution, would enable Labour to achieve a solid victory on a fresh register in the spring of 1979, was ill-judged and was to doom Labour to a decade in the electoral wilderness.

## A Serious Miscalculation: 1978–9

### The Winter of Discontent

Three years of pay restraint had served to depress living standards and narrow pay differentials, and, as a consequence, built up pressure among union leaders, particularly those in successful industries, to put in large, leap-frogging, claims in the new pay round. Matters were worsened in the winter of 1978–9 by the retirement of two key supporters of the Labour government's 'Social Contract' strategy, Jack Jones, head of the powerful transport workers union (TGWU) and the framer of the earlier £6 pay norm, and Hugh Scanlon of the engineers (AUEW), and their replacement by Moss Evans and Terry Duffy, both advocates of free collective bargaining. There was also a growing militancy in the new breed of public sector union leaders. Despite such rumblings and warning signs, however, James Callaghan continued to believe that his trade union allies would endure a further short period of self-sacrifice, in order to ensure the return of a Labour government with an effective new parliamentary majority. This was to prove to be a serious miscalculation.

On 2 October 1978 the Labour Party conference rejected the new 5% pay norm guidelines. More seriously, and surprisingly for the Prime Minister, a month later, on 4 November 1978, the TUC's general council rejected, by one vote, the proposed pay restraint package as pitched at a figure which was unrealistically low. This effectively gave sanction to member unions freely to begin bargaining for higher wage claims. This challenge was taken up by the AUEW, who, following a nine-week strike at the profitable Ford Motors, achieved a 15% pay increase in December 1979. Lorry and petrol tanker drivers belonging to the TGWU soon followed by announcing strike action in support of a 25% pay claim and during January-March the strike movement rapidly widened to include a rash of disputes involving low-paid government workers represented by the municipal workers' union (GMWU), health workers' (COHSE), civil servants' (CPSA) and public employees' (NUPE) unions. Such strikes, which were characterised by extensive 'secondary picketing', impinged directly upon the public and resulted in the breakdown of essential services, such as refuse collection, hospital supply and even the disposal of corpses. They were only to be brought to a halt in March 1979 by the grant of pay increases in the region of 10%. This anarchic and rancorous period, which was the worst in terms of industrial stoppages since 1926, was to gain the inglorious epithet the 'winter of discontent'. It left in tatters the government's anti-inflation strategy, brought to an end any successful Labour claims of enjoying a special and harmonious relationship with the union barons and led to a rapid slump in opinion poll support for Prime Minister Callaghan and the Labour Party (see Table 11) and a dramatic rise in Conservative and anti-union support.

This sudden change in the climate of opinion was disastrous for the government, which, lacking a parliamentary majority, was liable to be catapulted into a sudden election at any juncture. This is what happened in March 1979, when following the defeat of the 1 March referenda in Scotland and Wales, the disappointed eleven Scottish Nationalist MPs, in an action which Callaghan likened to 'turkeys voting for an early Christmas', withdrew the support which had maintained the Callaghan administration since September 1978. The government fell by a majority of one, 311:310, in a 'no-confidence' motion on 28 March, the first such defeat since Ramsay Macdonald's in 1924, and the date for a general election was set for 3 May 1979.[1]

## 1979 General Election

The Callaghan administration faced in 1979 a resurgent Conservative Party led by a novel female leader who presented to the electorate a radical manifesto entitled 'Time for a Change'. This document recalled Ted Heath's 'Selsdonite manifesto' of 1970. It broke with the party's postwar pragmatic paternalism and called instead for a radical 'counter revolution' to set the people free. It declared that the last two decades had seen an inexorable rise in government spending, accounting for 33% of the nation's GDP in 1959 and 41% in 1978; a dangerous growth in trade union power; a diminution in freedom of choice; and a decline in moral standards and law and order. It saw the ratchet shifting slowly but surely leftwards, with the country on the verge of becoming an Eastern European-style socialist state. The 1979 election was thus depicted as the 'last chance' to halt this movement and to restore the proper balance between the individual and the state.

This interpretation was supported by the growth of 'radical right' opinion during the 1970s and the intellectual shift away from liberalism and Keynesianism. In the economics profession monetarism gained increasing attention. It attracted converts who included Peter Jay (James Callaghan's son-in-law and ad hoc adviser) and Sam Brittan (the 'Financial Times' economics correspondent), while the work of Robert Bacon and Walter Eltis ('Britain's Economic Problem : Too Few Producers' (1976)), which suggested that the inexorable growth of the public sector had served to 'crowd out' private industrial investment, became highly influential. Elsewhere in academic circles Paul Johnson (the former editor of the 'New Statesman') and the historian Hugh Thomas became prominent converts to the 'New Right'. Within middle income circles there was a feeling that taxation had reached its limits and needed to be reduced to improve incentives and stem the growth of the 'black economy'. Among lower income groups

---

[1] One sick Labour MP, Sir Alfred Broughton, was unable to attend the division, while the two Northern Ireland Catholic MPs, Gerry Fitt and Frank Maguire, abstained. The government had, however, been supported by two Ulster MPs and the three Plaid Cymru MPs as a result of the introduction of legislation promising Northern Ireland extra parliamentary seats and a Bill to compensate Welsh slate-quarrymen suffering from lung disease.

the nationalist and racist National Front gained temporary popularity, boasting a membership of 25000 and capturing 9% of the vote in the seats it contested during local elections in 1976. Finally, among diverse groups, there was a reaction against the alleged adverse consequences of the 'permissive sixties' : rising divorce rates, increasing violence and pornography, personified by the campaigns of Mary Whitehouse's National Viewers' and Listeners' Association and Norris McWhirter's National Association for Freedom (NAFF).[1]

Such academic and populist views were drawn upon in the framing of the Conservative Party's 1979 manifesto, which concentrated on three areas. First, in dealing with the economy, the government placed top priority upon conquering inflation through a monetarist approach. This involved reducing government borrowing and spending by cutting out waste and inefficiency and through the selling off ('privatisation') of a number of state-owned firms. The party sought, in addition, to promote individual enterprise through reducing taxes and 'de-regulation' , getting government off people's backs. It aimed at widening home-ownership through the sale of council houses to tenants and creating a broader shareholding democracy. It vowed that it would adopt a laissez-faire approach to industry and not constantly prop up 'lame ducks' or involve itself in wages disputes in an incomes policy manner. Closely allied to this radical economic programme, was the party's determination to curb union power, vowing to reform and democratise them. It was believed that Labour's Employment Protection and Trades Unions and Labour Relations Acts of 1974–6, covering dismissal and redundancy rights and companies' disclosure of information, had gone too far and that union leaders had been allowed to become too powerful during the preceding decade. The Conservatives thus pledged to end the 'corporatist' dialogue with these 'barons' and to force through reforms on balloting and picketing which would return unions to their rank and file members. The manifesto also offered an improvement in law and order, pledging to increase spending on the police and to press for tougher sentences.

This manifesto was supported by the bulk of the popular press and backed up by a slick and well-financed advertising campaign planned by the recently hired Saatchi and Saatchi agency and

[1] These trends mirrored to some degree the contemporary revival of radical 'New Right' conservatism in the United States seen in the California taxpayers' revolt of 1978 and the growing support for religious fundamentalism.

directed by the party's new Director of Publicity, the successful television producer, Gordon Reece. It targeted 97 marginal seats and the skilled working class 'floating voter' for particular attention, launched a major poster campaign against unemployment under the slogan 'Labour Isn't Working' and carefully arranged television 'photo-opportunities' and stage-managed ticket-only rallies to display the leadership qualities of Margaret Thatcher to their maximum effect.[1]

James Callaghan and the Labour team attempted to counter the Conservatives' campaign by projecting an image of conciliation, competence and conservatism to contrast with the untried radicalism of their opponents. They vigorously defended their record in office, which, they argued, had seen them rescue the country from the crisis and 'State of Emergency' of 1973–4, steer a sensible course through the storms of the 1974–6 OPEC-induced recession and engineer a buoyant and controlled recovery. The party's moderate manifesto, which was largely drafted by James Callaghan and his private office team[2] declared, 'The Labour Way is the Better Way', and warned the electors that unemployment would sharply rise and the welfare state be endangered if a Conservative government was elected. It promised, instead, to continue the work of 1976–9, aiming at a reduction in the rate of inflation to 5% in 1982, a drive against unemployment, improving pensions and welfare benefits and the implementation of a newly signed 'Concordat' with the TUC to deal, on a voluntary basis, with the problems of secondary picketing, 'closed shops' and strikes without ballots. The Labour campaign was brilliantly led by the popular James Callaghan, dubbed by his opponents 'the best Conservative Prime Minister we have', and might have been successful if the election had been held seven months earlier. The 'Winter of Discontent' had, however, undermined the party's conciliatory image and had turned the public against the trade union movement. This feeling, combined with the collapse of the Liberal vote in the wake of the Thorpe scandal, enabled the Conservatives to gain a comfortable victory on polling day on 3 May.

[1] In what was, in real terms, the costliest general election campaign since 1964, the Conservatives spent £1.3 million on their central campaign, Labour £1 million and the Liberals £0.14 million.

[2] Labour Party Conference calls for the abolition of the House of Lords, compulsory planning powers, the abandonment of nuclear weapons, nationalisation of the four main banks and strict import controls were rejected by Callaghan as was an earlier and more radical NEC draft manifesto.

The swing to the Conservatives was 5.1%, the greatest of any election since 1945 and an indication of the increasing volatility of the electorate. The largest swing towards the party took place in rural Wales, the Midlands and the South, and among skilled, upwardly mobile, manual (C2) groups and new voters. The smallest swing was, surprisingly, among women and professionals, and, less surprisingly, in the north of the country. In Scotland, indeed, there was a net swing towards Labour as a result of the collapse of support for the radical, secessionist SNP, whose share of the Scottish vote slumped to 17% and who secured the return of only two MPs. Overall, the Labour Party managed to draw in 75000 more votes than in October 1974 (although the turnout was admittedly higher in 1979), but they were defeated by the switch of Liberal votes to the Conservatives as the nation experienced a temporary return to more polarised politics. The Conservatives gained 2.2 million more votes than in October 1974 and were left with an overall Commons majority of 43 seats. (See Table 12.)

**Table 12   The General Election of May 1979 (Turnout 76.2%)**

| Party | Votes Gained | % of Vote | Average vote per MP | Number of MPs |
|---|---|---|---|---|
| Conservatives | 13.697m | 43.9 | 40,407 | 339 |
| Labour | 11.532m | 36.9 | 42,870 | 269 |
| Liberal | 4.313m | 13.8 | 392,091 | 11[1] |
| SNP | 0.504m | 1.6 | 252,000 | 2 |
| Plaid Cymru[2] | 0.132m | 0.4 | 66,000 | 2 |
| Others (including N Ireland)[3] | 1.060m | 3.4 | — | 12 |
| Total | 31.221m | 100.0 | 49,167 | 635 |

[1] Three prominent Liberal MPs Jeremy Thorpe, John Pardoe and Emlyn Hooson lost their seats.

[2] Plaid Cymru secured 8.1% of the Welsh vote, its lowest share since 1966.

[3] The National Front, fielding a record number of 303 candidates, secured 0.19 million votes, averaging 1.4% of the vote in the seats in contested. The newly-formed Ecology Party put up 53 candidates and captured 0.04 million votes, an average 1.5% share in each constituency. The Communists, with 38 candidates, secured 0.02 million votes.

# An Evaluation of the Wilson-Callaghan Administration

The Wilson-Callaghan administration of 1974–9 was an extra-ordinary one. It assumed power in the aftermath of the 1973–4 coal strike and had to cope with the sharp recession of 1974–6. It held only a slim and diminishing majority and had to make both formal and informal pacts and deals with minority party politicians: Liberals, nationalists and Ulstermen. It saw the retirement of its leader in mid-term, the holding of two constitutional referenda and the introduction of 15 budget packages. It was forced to turn to the IMF for funds, obey its external wishes and make a fundamental change in economic strategy, and finally, it was engulfed in a bitter winter of industrial strife. Constitutionally, this was a fascinating and instructive period, with the Callaghan government being threatened by backbench rebellion on numerous occasions and experiencing the loss of 'cabinet sovereignty' and control over events to the IMF, minority parties and eventually to the trade unions. It was an era which experienced, with the 'Social Contract', both the apogee of postwar corporatism as well as a period of unusually weak executive control, with the British political system temporarily assuming the character of the US White House-Capitol Hill 'pork barrel' bargaining model.

The administration set out in 1974 apparently intending to implement a radical socialist economic programme which would effect 'a fundamental and irreversible shift of the balance of power and wealth'. The centrepiece of this programme was to be intervention in industry under the direction of the left-wing technocrat Tony Benn. The National Enterprise Board was established in 1975 with immediate funds of £700 million and the promise of £300 million more, and empowered to acquire shares in both healthy and ailing industries. Within months the troubled Harland and Wolff Shipyard, employing 12000 in Belfast; the British Leyland car giant; Alfred Herbert; and Ferranti Electronics had been nationalised. Benn also enthusiastically supported the workers' co-operatives set up at the bankrupt Norton Villiers Triumph motorcycle works at Meriden and at Kirkby Engineering. After his departure, in June 1975, financial aid of £162 million was extended to ailing Chrysler (December 1975). British Shipbuilders and British Aerospace were nationalised (March 1977) and the British National Oil Corporation (BNOC) established. In addition, substantial investment was made in the growing micro-technology industry through Inmos, Amersham International, ICL and Cable and Wireless. This represented a substantial expansion in the state sector. However, it did not satisfy those on the left who were disappointed that planning agreements with private industries had not been made compulsory and who saw the NEB being used more as a rescue service for 'troubled capitalism' rather than as a positive investment body.

It was, however, the change towards quasi-monetarist economic policies after 1976 that rankled with the party's growing left wing. It was signalled by the Treasury's switch from 'volume terms' public expenditure plans to 'cash limits', with the imposition of tight 'external finance limits' on nationalised industries and the setting of targets for monetary growth, the rejection of the radical 'alternative economic strategy' and the fudging of policies to meet the needs of the IMF and Liberals. To MPs such as Ian Mikardo, Dennis Skinner and Tony Benn these actions represented a betrayal of socialism. However, for centrists and the right wing of the party this shift in policy was inevitable in the circumstances of 1976–9. For them it was preferable for a Labour government to stay in power to prevent what they saw as the greater evil of untrammelled Conservatism. They argued that the party, while implementing painful measures, could at least mitigate their effects, defend the poor and elderly, and continue to push through a number of cherished social reforms, which included the Equal Opportunity Act, the phasing out of 'pay beds', the continued spread of comprehensive education and ending of selection, the establishment of a Police Complaints Board and the creation of a new Commission for Racial Equality. This shift from a transforming to a governing approach had considerable success and engineered an economic recovery between 1977 and 1979, through a combination of monetarism and Keynesianism. It fell apart, however, in the 'Winter of Discontent' and was to have dire consequences for the party as it moved into opposition.

# Part Four

# THE FIRST THATCHER ADMINISTRATION: 1979-83

## The Start of a New Era: 1979-82

### The First Female Prime Minister

Margaret Hilda Thatcher, the new Prime Minister, was born at Grantham, Lincolnshire in 1925, the daughter of Alfred Roberts who had a small, but fast-expanding, grocery business and was to become an Independent mayor of the town. As a girl, Margaret Roberts helped her parents in the shop over which the family lived, while working hard at Grantham High School, before going on to read chemistry at Somerville College, Oxford. This background and upbringing was to have an important influence on her later political life.

Although in office Margaret Thatcher has seemed dominant enough to merit Lord Shinwell's description of her as the only man in the cabinet, her attitudes and beliefs seem to have been acquired less from the development of original thought as from the influences of particular men. Her father was undoubtedly a powerful influence, while her mother was a shadowy, background figure. It was from Alfred Roberts, a strict teetotal Methodist and self-made man, that she inherited her appreciation of the virtues of thrift, enterprise and good housekeeping. These beliefs were strengthened by her marriage to another businessman, Denis Thatcher, a man ten years her senior and an inheritor of a paints firm, whose wealth enabled Margaret to train for the Bar and pursue an active political career. The third important influence has been Sir Keith Joseph, whose Centre for Policy Studies (CPS), set up in 1974 with Margaret Thatcher as its president, and the colourful former communist Alfred Sherman as its director, provided the intellectual gloss for what subsequently became known as 'Thatcherism'.

Margaret Thatcher has frequently described herself as a 'conviction politician' who has adhered to strong, instinctive beliefs. In addition, she has seen herself as a 'populist' leader, able to understand and identify with the ordinary man and woman. In 1979 this instinct suggested that lower middle and working class voters were more concerned about personal disposable income, rising crime, the abuse of union power and the inefficiency of state bureaucracies than with unemployment or welfare services.

Her childhood was spent in an environment where the qualities of frugality and hard labour in a competitive setting were self-evident and her academic training had taught her to think in a logical, lateral manner rather than in broad, historical and social terms. Thus when her political mentor, Sir Keith Joseph, exposed her to the simple, free-market economics of Hayek, Friedman and Ralph Harris, of the Institute of Economic Affairs (IEA), she felt as if a light had been turned on in that murky interface between economics and politics. Instead of the 'fudge' of balancing opinions and the 'fine tuning' of the economy, she was offered something which was more a creed than a branch of social science. In a sense, Adam Smith had said it all in 1776. The market should be allowed to rule and the task of government should be to create the framework within which private enterprise could flourish. Sound money and a minimum of state interference would guarantee prosperity. If Gladstone had been her contemporary Margaret Thatcher would have made him her first Chancellor.

Allied with this clear ideological vision was a determination not to lose her nerve and be brushed off course in a U-turn as occurred in 1972. Margaret Thatcher was willing to be cautious and pragmatic and accept small tactical rebuffs en route, but about her main strategy there was no doubt. As she was later proudly to tell her party conference, 'this lady's not for turning'.

## Thatcher's First Year

Margaret Thatcher had been forced to make only two major changes in the shadow cabinet she inherited from her predecessor, losing Peter Walker and Geoffrey Rippon, who had been staunch allies of Edward Heath and who had refused to join the new team. Walker, a grocer's son and astute self-made millionaire financier who had set up the new socially-conscious Tory Reform Group in September 1975, made his peace with her in 1978 and stepped into the cabinet in 1979. This cabinet (see Table 13) was dominated by

'Heathites', 18 of the 22 having served in the former leader's administration and it was characterised by landed and public school-educated, traditional Tories. Only a minority, Joseph, Howe, Biffen, Jenkin, Nott, Howell and Maude, could be regarded as firm personal supporters and an even smaller number were convinced monetarists. These committed supporters were placed in charge of the key economic ministries, but it was not until 1981 and 1983 that further changes tilted the balance towards the Thatcherites.

**Table 13    The Thatcher Cabinet of 1979**

| | |
|---|---|
| Prime Minister | —Margaret Thatcher |
| Chancellor of the Exchequer | —Sir Geoffrey Howe |
| Foreign Secretary | —Lord Carrington |
| Home Secretary | —William Whitelaw |
| Defence Secretary | —Francis Pym |
| Environment Secretary | —Michael Heseltine |
| Industry Secretary | —Sir Keith Joseph |
| Energy Secretary | —David Howell |
| Employment Secretary | —James Prior |
| Agriculture Secretary | —Peter Walker |
| Northern Ireland Secretary | —Humphrey Atkins |
| Scottish Secretary | —George Younger |
| Welsh Secretary | —Nicholas Edwards |
| Education Secretary | —Mark Carlisle |
| Social Services Secretary | —Patrick Jenkin |
| Trade Secretary | —John Nott |
| Paymaster-General | —Angus Maude |
| Lord Privy Seal | Sir Ian Gilmour |
| Lord Chancellor | —Lord Hailsham |
| Commons Leader | —St John-Stevas |
| Leader of Lords | —Lord Soames |
| Chief Secretary to Treasury | —John Biffen |

In other respects the early days of the new administration were similarly cautious. Thatcher seemed content to rely upon established civil service machinery and even reduced the size of the Number 10 Policy Unit used by her predecessors. This harmonious 'honeymoon' period was, however, short-lived. The civil servants working for her soon came to realise they were dealing with a different animal from the politicians they had become used to serving. This Prime Minister knew her own mind and was not shy in expressing it. It became her practice to write terse marginal comments on minutes sent for her consideration. If she disagreed with the views expressed or thought that they were imprecise, or not sufficiently forceful, she would scribble 'wet' and this epithet was rapidly extended to describe members of her cabinet or party who, in her view, were not as committed as she was to the radical policies she intended to pursue.

Through a combination of fortuity and design Thatcher was able, in a comparatively short time, to surround herself with people she felt able to trust. She brought with her Richard Ryder and David Wolfson as political aides and appointed, on the advice of Sir Keith Joseph, John Hoskyns, a 51-year-old ex-soldier who had founded a successful computer business, to head her Number Ten Policy Unit and Bernard Ingham (47), an abrasive Yorkshireman and former journalist and socialist, as her Chief Press Secretary. Professor Alan Walters was seconded from an assignment in America to provide economic advice and Terry Burns (36), an avowed monetarist from the London Business School, was inducted as Chief Economic Adviser to the Treasury. The Treasury's permanent secretary, Sir Douglas Wass, whose own predilections were Keynesian, was rapidly convinced that the new government was prepared to test monetarism to the point of destruction, if need be. His early relations with Mrs Thatcher and her Chancellor were thus uneasy, but he gradually won their confidence and remained in office until 1983. However, during the next six years, because many permanent secretaries were coming up for retirement, Mrs Thatcher was able to personally approve the appointment of 23 of the 27, or 85%, and promote likeminded servants. She also brought Sir Derek Rayner, from Marks and Spencer, back into temporary public service to head a waste cutting 'cost efficiency unit'.

It was in economic policy that the presence of the new government was most evident. This policy, 'Thatcherism', started from the premise of the supremacy of the market, went on to include a tight control of the money supply and of public sector spending, added a belief in the encouragement of enterprise through personal tax incentives and concluded with a determined attack on trade union power. It was all pervading, affecting every action considered by the government.

Many 'Heathites' and so-called 'wets' in the cabinet rejected this extreme and doctrinaire outlook. Mrs Thatcher thus kept the formulation and implementation of economic policy concentrated in the hands of a chosen few: herself, the Chancellor, Sir Geoffrey Howe (52), the Industry Secretary, Sir Keith Joseph (61), the Chief Secretary to the Treasury, John Biffen (48), and the Financial Secretary to the Treasury, Nigel Lawson (47). Economic policy was never deeply discussed in full cabinet, meetings of which were in any case restricted to one per week: fewer than would normally be expected. Political discussions of the economy were conducted mainly in the cabinet 'E' economic sub-committee. Although, this committee included James Prior (51) and Peter Walker (47), two acknowledged 'wets', it was well packed with monetarist hard-liners and was chaired by the Prime Minister herself. The policy decided was pushed through with diligence and obedience by Sir Geoffrey Howe, a liberal-minded barrister, with the senior 'Tory grandees', William Whitelaw (deputy leader), Lord Hailsham (Lord Chancellor) and Lord Carrington (Foreign Secretary), providing crucial, if grudging, support out of a deep sense of party duty.

In the event, the Thatcher administration's economic policy during its first year was little short of disastrous. Fulfilling a rash election promise to pick up the tabs for any public sector pay awards which arose from the reports of the Clegg Commission on pay comparability, the government was obliged to give pay increases of 15% to 30% to a wide band of public sector workers, including the teachers. Professor Clegg and his colleagues were dismissed at the earliest opportunity, but the damage had been done. This, coupled with the return to free collective bargaining, led to a sudden pay explosion across industry.

On top of this pay award came the first budget of Sir Geoffrey Howe in June 1979. Keen to put into practice the liberalising wisdom of Hayek and Friedman and to meet the party's manifesto commitments, he removed exchange, pay and price controls and substantially reduced the level of direct taxation, lowering the top rate from 83% to 60% and the lowest rate from 33% to 30% while at the same time raising tax thresholds. However, to pay for this, the burden of taxes on spending had to be raised, with VAT being almost doubled from 8% to 15%, and nationalised industry price supports being reduced. This directly added 6% to the inflation rate, further fuelling it. Interest rates were also soon raised to a record level of 17% in an attempt to control the money supply and the pound (now a petro-currency) was allowed to float up towards $2.40. These measures, carried out at a time when the world economy was about to be rocked by a quadrupling of OPEC oil prices, following the fall of the Shah in Iran, were disastrous for the British economy and British industry. They led to a sharp nose-dive into recession, with inflation rising from 10% to 22% and unemployment from 1.3 million to over 2 million within a year of the Thatcher government assuming office.

While the administration's hardline evangelicals had been given a free rein in economic matters, on the industrial front there was more patience and pragmatism. James Prior, the popular Employment Secretary, drawing a lesson from the Heath years, was convinced of the need to move slowly and seek to gain the consent of unions and, in particular their members, for changes made. He thus pursued a 'softly softly', incrementalist approach to union reform which proved to be most effective. His 'July Orders' of 1979 and Employment Act of 1980 represented the first and tentative steps in this reform process, giving employers the right to take legal action against secondary picketing, allowing new 'closed shops' only when approved by an 80% margin in a secret ballot, granting management more leeway in the question of dismissals and making available public funds for postal ballots of union members.

It was in the field of international affairs that Mrs Thatcher was least competent and therefore heavily reliant on her Foreign Secretary, Lord Carrington. It has been said that she tended to admire 'toffs' and the suave and sophisticated Carrington, an Eton-educated landowner and company director who had served as Defence Secretary during the 1970–4 Heath government, filled this role perfectly. In the summer of her first year she was to be called upon to attend her first summit of Commonwealth leaders, in Lusaka, and high on the agenda was the position of Rhodesia as a member of the Commonwealth. Her first inclination was to give recognition to the rather spurious, white-inspired, government of Bishop Muzorewa, and this would have turned the bulk of the Commonwealth against her. She even considered advising the Queen not to attend, but the subtle arguments of Carrington eventually prevailed. She arrived in Lusaka to demonstrations and protests and within a short time, following the Foreign Secretary's advice, had agreed to a constitutional conference to be attended by the two black guerrilla leaders, Robert Mugabe and Joshua Nkomo, and had completely captivated the Zambian president, Kenneth Kaunda.

The first impressions Thatcher made on the two most powerful West European leaders, Helmut Schmidt and Valery Giscard d'Estaing, were also highly favourable, but within months she had become embroiled in an unedifying row over the reduction of Britain's contribution to the European Community budget, a row which earned her a reputation for obstinacy and a lack of real commitment to the European ideal.

Margaret Thatcher's first year ended on a note of sourness and disappointment. She had certainly made her imprint on British politics, but in many respects it was a lost year. Her attempt to expose Britain to a sharp blast of economic reality had not produced the results she had hoped for. Inflation and unemployment had increased and output was declining. The prospects of her being more successful than her predecessors were not propitious.

### The Rhetoric and the Reality: Thatcherism 1981–2

As the Thatcher government entered its second year the right things were being said but the results were not evident. The Chancellor of the Duchy of Lancaster and Leader of the House, Norman St John-Stevas, had been heard to say: 'All is show: nothing is substance', and yet Margaret Thatcher was growing in confidence as she more firmly grasped the reins of office. She was already dominating her cabinet and her parliamentary performances were improving week by week. In particular, her rapport with Conservative backbenchers was better than anything her predecessors had achieved. She was realising how best to use the machinery of government, appointing political advisers whom she felt she could trust. She was largely dismissive of the CPRS 'think tank' created by Heath, preferring to draw upon the Centre for Policy Studies. She massaged the media through 'lobby leaks' and private handouts via her press office. She also realised the enormous powers of patronage which a Prime Minister can exercise and by November 1979 had reinstated the Wilsonian practice of awarding honours for political service. It was a practice she was to employ unashamedly during her succeeding years in office.

There was, however, a gap between rhetoric and performance, particularly in the field of economic policy. Here Sir Geoffrey Howe made the Medium Term Financial Strategy (MTFS) the centre-piece of his March 1980 budget. It had been largely devised by the Financial Secretary, Nigel Lawson, and Treasury Adviser, Terry Burns, and welded together monetarism with the new 'rational expectations' approach to economics. It set four-yearly targets for growth in the money supply (M3)[1] and envisaged a staged reduction in public expediture and the PSBR. This, it was believed, would lead to a progressive fall in the inflation rate and enable businessmen and union leaders to plan ahead their

---

[1] M3 was a measure of the money supply which included notes and coins in circulation plus bank deposits.

investment and wage-bargaining decisions. Unfortunately, however, the money supply proved difficult to both ascertain and control, while economists continued to dispute whether there was really an automatic link between the PSBR, interest rates and inflation. By January 1981, when Mrs Thatcher held a review meeting at Chequers, she was faced with a situation with the monetary indicators out of control, an inflated exchange rate of $2.40 and interest rates of 14%, which were squeezing small companies out of business.

The Prime Minister reacted to these mounting problems by carrying out her first cabinet reshuffle in January 1981. She sacked the roguish Leader of the Commons, Norman St John-Stevas, the man who had pushed through the introduction of the troublesome new Select Committees and who had light-heartedly variously termed his leader the 'Blessed Margaret', 'the Immaculate Misconception' and 'The Leaderene'. Angus Maude, one of her old friends and colleagues, who had been in charge of government information, chose to retire. Francis Pym, who at Defence had resisted spending cuts, was made the new Leader of the House. The reliable and compliant John Nott was moved from Trade to Defence. John Biffen was switched from the Treasury to Trade, his place being taken by Leon Brittan (41), the barrister brother of Sam of the 'Financial Times'. Norman Fowler, another reliable ally, was brought into the cabinet at the Department of Transport. This was not a major reshuffle, but it served to assert Mrs Thatcher's authority and strengthen her position.

Her dominance was evident at the cabinet meeting on 10 March 1981 when Sir Geoffrey Howe outlined the structure of his forthcoming budget. It came as a brutal shock to those ministers who were not fully confirmed Thatcherites. Despite rising unemployment and falling output, the Chancellor proposed taking a further £4.3 billion out of the economy and reducing the PSBR from £13.5 billion to £10.5 billion. Increases in a wide range of indirect taxes were also to be made and the index-linking of income tax bands to be temporarily suspended. Faced with a similar economic situation, Edward Heath would have reflated, however cautiously. Margaret Thatcher, in contrast, through her dutiful Chancellor, prescribed more of the same medicine, on the premise that the patient must get worse before he gets better. The potential cabinet dissenters, Walker, Prior, Gilmour, Pym and Soames, were presented with a stark choice: support the budget or resign. They conceded, marvelling at their leader's self-confidence and resolve.

Mrs Thatcher knew, however, that she would have greater difficulty in pushing through a similar budget in the future if her cabinet team remained the same, as, with Hailsham, Carrington, Heseltine and even Biffen and Nott, expressing doubts, in an open vote she would stand every chance of being defeated.

When the cabinet assembled on 21 July 1981 for its annual review of the economy the climate was bleak. Violent inner city riots had erupted in London (Brixton), Liverpool (Toxteth) and Manchester (Moss Side) and unemployment had risen to 2.7 million, with the Chancellor unable to promise an early reduction. When asked whether he thought it could go over the 3 million mark, he replied 'I'm afraid so'. He rejected, however, a Keynesian approach and said he wanted a further £5 billion taken out of the economy to continue the battle against inflation. This July meeting proved to be a test of Mrs Thatcher's leadership and the 'wets', unable to form a concerted front, capitulated, but the resentment remained. Even the Party Chairman, Lord Thorneycroft (71), who had resigned from Harold Macmillan's government in 1958 because he was refused the spending cuts he had wanted and who had been been Mrs Thatcher's personal selection to head the party machine in 1975, spoke out publicly against the policy of retrenchment. The Prime Minister took a holiday in Cornwall to prepare herself for what promised to be a difficult and challenging party conference in September.

She returned with her mind made up and acted with typical decisiveness. Lord Thorneycroft refused to stand down and so was dismissed together with Sir Ian Gilmour, Mark Carlisle and Lord Soames. James Prior was informed he was to be sent to Northern Ireland and initially refused to go. When told there was no other post for him he accepted. He was allowed, as a sop, to remain on the vital cabinet 'E' committee, but Margaret Thatcher knew that his duties in the Province would preclude his attending most of its meetings. Prior's backdown confirmed her view that she had nothing to fear from the 'wets' and could now consolidate her supremacy. Norman Tebbit (50), an abrasive former airline pilot and East London shop manager's son who had long been a close backstage adviser and tactician of the Prime Minister, was brought into the cabinet to replace Prior at Employment; Sir Keith Joseph was moved to Education after an agonising period as Industry Secretary; Cecil Parkinson (49), a Lancashire railwayman's son and self-made industrialist, became Party Chairman, with a seat in the cabinet; Nigel Lawson was promoted to become Energy Secretary;

Denis Howell was demoted to Transport; Patrick Jenkin (54), a barrister contemporary of the Prime Minister, was promoted to Industry; Norman Fowler (43) became Social Services Secretary; and Nicholas Ridley (53), an old Etonian and veteran monetarist strategist, became Financial Secretary to the Treasury. (See Table 14.)

**Table 14    The Thatcher Cabinet in October 1981**

| | |
|---|---|
| Prime Minister | —Margaret Thatcher |
| Chancellor of the Exchequer | —Sir Geoffrey Howe |
| Foreign Secretary | —Lord Carrington |
| Home Secretary | —William Whitelaw |
| Defence Secretary | —John Nott |
| Environment Secretary | —Michael Heseltine |
| Industry Secretary | —Patrick Jenkin |
| Energy Secretary | —Nigel Lawson |
| Employment Secretary | —Norman Tebbit |
| Education Secretary | —Sir Keith Joseph |
| Welsh Secretary | —Nicholas Edwards |
| Paymaster-General | —Cecil Parkinson |
| Transport Secretary | —David Howell |
| Agriculture Secretary | —Peter Walker |
| Trade Secretary | —John Biffen |
| Northern Ireland Secretary | —James Prior |
| Scottish Secretary | —George Younger |
| Social Services Secretary | —Norman Fowler |
| Lord Chancellor | —Lord Hailsham |
| Leader of Lords | —Baroness Young |
| Commons Leader | —Francis Pym |
| Lord Privy Seal | —Humphrey Atkins |
| Chief Secretary to Treasury | —Leon Brittan |

These changes brought into office younger and more loyal, new style, 'self made' Tories, who were convinced believers in the Thatcherite approach and who would be willing to press for substantial cuts in the spending budgets of their respective departments. They were a clear indication that the Prime Minister would not be deflected into performing a 'U-turn'. Instead, a new phase of more radical reform was launched. This was centred around the passage of a second Employment Act (1982) which outlawed secondary strikes, made unions liable for claims for damages caused by unlawful industrial actions and strengthened the rights of individuals against 'closed shops'. The proposals included, in addition, a tightening of control over the purse strings of local government as attempts were made to keep local spending in check, with the financial support provided from the centre now being based upon central estimates of local needs ('grant related expenditure') rather than on past spending records. Most radical of all, however, was the new impetus that was given to the programme of de-regulation and privatisation that had begun haltingly in 1979–80 with the sale of council houses and BP shares. A range of government-managed firms under the aegis of the NEB (which was subsequently to be dissolved and renamed the British Technology Group charged with co-ordinating industrial research) were now placed under the stewardship of bullish, market-orientated managers in readiness for flotation; greater competition was fostered with and among public sector services, seen, for example in the opening up of coach services to competition; and small businesses were encouraged through the establishment of the Business Expansion and Enterprise Allowance Schemes and the formation of low tax 'enterprise zones'.

The Prime Minister's new moves on the economic front were buttressed by major reforms of the civil service, which was increasingly being viewed by Thatcherites as an inefficient and frustrating barrier to radical change. A new 'management information system' (MINIS), devised by Michael Heseltine at the Environment Ministry, aimed at establishing clear policy priorities and achieving the more efficient use of manpower, was slowly tried in other departments, albeit with less obvious success, while Sir Ian Bancroft, head of the civil service, was retired, his Civil Service Department scrapped and the role of the loyal and efficient Cabinet Secretary, Sir Robert Armstrong (54), upgraded to that of de facto civil service supremo.

With the potential rebels within the cabinet and establishment routed, Margaret Thatcher went to the party conference in October 1981 in a more confident and determined frame of mind and, despite some mutterings, mainly at fringe meetings, it was a success. Opinion polls were registering her, with 'satisfaction ratings' of only 25–30%, as the most unpopular Prime Minister in memory. However, during the early months of 1982 her approval rating began to edge slowly upwards and by March 1982 the Prime Minister had established a significant lead over the curious new Labour leader, with the Conservative Party also remaining ahead in what was becoming a three-party race.

## The Opposition Parties 1979–82

The Labour Party had shown progressive signs of disintegration during the 1970s as a result of the widening cleavage and changing balance between its right and left wings. During the early 1970s an influx of young white collar middle class radicals (dubbed the 'polytariat'), a number of whom had been involved previously with radical, single-issue groups such as Shelter, Amnesty International and the Child Poverty Action Group (CPAG), combined with the demise of the traditional moderate working class activist, began to give what became known as the 'New Left' a majority on the constituency level committees, particularly on the 50–80 member General Management Committees (GMCs). In addition, the trade unions, who controlled 90% of the vote at the annual conference, became increasingly dominated by leftist leaders. These groups felt betrayed by the 1964–70 and 1974–9 parliamentary leadership and were determined in future to have a radical policy programme adopted and implemented by effecting far-reaching changes in the constitution.

The 'New Left' supported the radical 'Alternative Economic Strategy' of import controls, nationalisation, workers' democracy, greater state industrial investment and compulsory planning agreements to cover the private sector. Secondly, it continued to call for withdrawal from the European Community, since continued membership would prevent the full-scale implementation of the alternative economic programme. Thirdly, it aligned itself with the burgeoning peace movement, led by the Campaign for Nuclear Disarmament (CND), which was provoked into action by the November 1979 NATO decision to station Cruise and Pershing II medium-range nuclear missiles from the winter of 1983 and by the Conservative government's decision to replace Britain's Polaris system with the multiple warhead Trident system. It called for unilateral nuclear disarmament and withdrawal from NATO.

The rule changes the 'New Left' sought consisted of: granting activists and union leaders a direct role in the election of the party leadership; making sitting MPs regularly accountable to their constituency parties; and forcing the party leadership to put conference resolutions in the election manifesto. Demand for the last rule change was provoked by the actions of Harold Wilson and, in particular, James Callaghan in 1974 and 1979, who simply drew a line through the radical sections of the NEC's proposed programme.

The 'New Left' set up the Campaign for Labour Party Democracy (CLPD) in June 1973 to push forward with this 'democratisation' campaign. It sought to win over key unions and slowly gain control of constituency parties, working in close liaison with the policy-making Labour Co-ordinating Committee (LCC), set up in 1978 and including MPs such as Michael Meacher and Stuart Holland and the umbrella Rank and File Mobilising Committee (RFMC), established in 1980, which embraced, in addition, a number of far-left Trotskyist organisations. They put pressure on moderate MPs, managing to unseat Dick Taverne (Lincoln 1973), Eddie Milne (Blyth 1974), Eddie Griffiths (Sheffield Brightside 1974) and Reg Prentice (Newham North-East 1976–8), placed members on the NEC and won an increasing number of the party's annual conference resolutions.

The right wing of the party objected to the activities of this 'New Left' group and poured scorn on their 'democratisation' claims. In their view, an MP elected by the voting public was of greater democratic weight than the constituency party activists or 'block votes' wielded by union bosses and should not act as a mere delegate puppet. They made their first stand on the issue of the European Community, membership of which they fervently supported, revolting under the leadership of Roy Jenkins in 1971 and 1973 (see page 37). After 1975 the party's right wing became more organised, setting up the grassroots Social Democratic Alliance (SDA), run by the polytechnic lecturers Stephen Haseler and Douglas Eden and the editor of 'Socialist Commentary', Peter Stephenson, and the broader based Campaign for Labour Victory (CLV), which began in February 1977 as successor to the December 1974 established Manifesto Group and included Shirley Williams, David Owen, William Rodgers and John Cartwright, to fight against the leftward drift of the party.

These bodies lacked, however, the commitment and determination of the CLPD and RFMC. Thus the left continued to make steady gains. By 1974 a third of the PLP was sympathetic to its views and this included an even larger proportion of its younger members. Its most prominent allies were Joan Maynard, Jo Richardson, Dennis Skinner and Tony Benn. By 1979 they had gained control of the NEC, which began to turn a blind eye to the selection of controversial far-left prospective parliamentary candidates by local CLPs, and once in opposition they set about bitterly denouncing the party's 'failed' right-wing leadership and succeeded in winning a series of crucial rule change votes at the conferences between 1979–81.

At the October 1979 conference held at Brighton, majority support was given to motions giving it control of the next election manifesto, calling for the mandatory re-selection of MPs by their CLPs and for the establishment of a commission of inquiry to look into the party's finances, membership and method of electing its leader. A year later matters came to a head at the 1980 Blackpool conference. The previous year's manifesto motion was overturned and support given to continued membership of NATO. However, the need for regular re-selection of MPs was re-affirmed, majority backing was given to unilateral nuclear disarmament, the closing of all nuclear bases in Britain, and withdrawal from the EEC, and, most significantly, the conference accepted the need for a broader 'electoral college' selection procedure for choosing the party's leader. The exact details of this new selection system were left to be sorted out by a Special Rules Revision Conference to be held at Wembley in January 1981. In the meantime, James Callaghan, having vainly appealed to conference delegates to 'stop arguing, the public is crying out for unity', decided to resign on 15 October 1980 in the hope that the PLP would choose Denis Healey as his successor and thus fortify the party's right wing in the battle over rule changes. Surprisingly, however, despite the enormous public popularity of the colourful and rumbustious Healey, the PLP, its members under intensive constituency pressure, chose the 67-year-old Michael Foot, deputy leader since 1976, by 139 to 129 on the second ballot.[1] Foot was a radical, public school educated, left-wing Bevanite and long-time rebel against the party leadership, who had fervently opposed EEC membership and continued to campaign for unilateral nuclear disarmament. He enjoyed, however, close links with the union movement and having recently shown between 1974 and 1979, when first Employment Secretary and then Leader of the Commons, qualities of unification and compromise, was viewed as the man most likely to hold the party together during the difficult months ahead. Denis Healey (63) became deputy leader.

Michael Foot attempted to heal the rift in the party, calling for the creation of an 'electoral college' with a 50:25:25 balance between the PLP, trade unions and constituency parties. This would still have given the party's centre-right a dominant voice. The party's right wing, led by Owen and Rodgers, called instead for 'one man one vote' extended to the entire party membership. The party's left

[1] On the first ballot Healey gained 112 votes, Foot 83, John Silkin (the 'soft-left', anti-EEC former Agriculture Secretary) 38, Peter Shore (the centre-right, anti-EEC former Environment Secretary) 32. Tony Benn did not contest the leadership, arguing that the election should be deferred until the new 'electoral college' had been created. He gave his verbal backing, however, to Foot.

wing, including the NEC, countered with a demand for a 33:33:33 division of votes. In the end, after the union block votes had been cast, the moderate AUEW, which had sought a supra-50% allocation for the PLP, controversially abstaining, a 30:40:30 division was agreed, giving the trade unions predominating power.

This decision, coupled with the election of Michael Foot as leader represented the final straw for Labour's right wing. Roy Jenkins, the former Chancellor and Home Secretary who had left to become President of the EEC Commission in 1976, had already floated the idea of the formation of a new 'centre party', incorporating moderate Labourites and radical Liberals, in the televised Dimbleby lecture of November 1979. Jenkins, the cultured, Oxford University educated son of a Welsh miners' MP, who had served as a Royal Artillery captain during the Second World War and had subsequently held a succession of key ministerial offices as well as carving out a career as a respected historical biographer, was a powerful figure who had gathered around him a group of like-minded followers during his period in the Labour Party. He began a series of informal discussions with Owen, Rodgers and Williams, who had lost her Hitchin parliamentary seat in the May 1979 election, and with the Liberal leader David Steel, during the closing months of 1980.

Steel argued that the formation of a separate party, rather than a sudden merger with the Liberals, would have a greater publicity impact. Thus on Sunday 25 January 1981, the day after the Wembley Conference, Owen, Williams and Rodgers finally announced their intention to leave the Labour Party and, joined by Roy Jenkins and nine other Labour MPs, set up the Campaign for Social Democracy (CSD), calling for a realignment in British politics, the 'Limehouse Declaration'[1]. The CSD drew wide public support, which increased further when a half-page recruitment advertisement, 'The Declaration of a Hundred', in the 'Guardian', signed by dignitaries who included David Sainsbury (the supermarket magnate), Lord George Brown and Frank Chapple (General Secretary of the EEPTU electricians' union). On 26 March the new Social Democratic Party (SDP) was finally launched in a blaze of media attention and within ten days 40000 people had joined and paid their membership subscriptions

[1] Taking its name from David Owen's house in Narrow Street, Limehouse, London E14 where the 'Gang of Four' gathered to set out the aims of the new CSD.

The party rapidly agreed an organisational structure and constitution, based around area parties, and decision-making and elections on a one-man-one-vote basis, and made a series of electoral agreements with the Liberal Party. By the autumn of 1981 the SDP boasted 24 MPs (one of whom, Christopher Brocklebank-Fowler, from Norfolk North-West, was a former Conservative); a membership of 60000; an election fighting fund of £1 million; and was rapidly establishing a clear centrist philosophy, through the books published by its leading 'Gang of Four'. At the electoral level it was remarkably successful, Roy Jenkins almost topping the poll in the solid Labour constituency of Warrington in July 1981. William Pitt (Liberal), Williams and Jenkins eventually triumphed in Conservative constituencies in three successive by-elections in Croydon North-West (22 October 1981) Crosby (Merseyside: 26 November 1981) and Glasgow Hillhead (23 March 1982) during the six months between October 1981 and March 1982, while major gains were made in local council contests. With opinion polls during these months showing the two parties gathering the support of 30–40% of those questioned, the Liberal leader, David Steel, solemnly told party workers attending the packed and expectant annual assembly at Llandudno in September 1981, 'go back to your constituencies and prepare for government'.

During this period Labour party membership sharply decreased as a number of MPs, local councillors and grassroots supporters joined the SDP and as the party continued to be torn apart by internal conflicts. The most bitter of these disputes was the challenge made by Tony Benn, under the new rules, for the party's deputy leadership between April-September 1981. A number of left-wing Tribunite MPs, including Robin Cook and Jack Straw, attempted to dissuade Benn from standing on the grounds of party unity and, having failed, put forward John Silkin as a 'soft left' alternative. Benn, however, arguing that the issue was one of 'policies, not personalities', pressed forward with an energetic campaign, stumping around the country delivering rousing populist speeches which drew rapturous support from constituency party activists. He also secured the allegiance of a number of left-wing union leaders, including the important TGWU. Denis Healey remained, in contrast, the most popular Labour politician with the public at large and among the trade union rank-and-file, but, as a consequence of his period as Chancellor, was reviled by the party's left wing and treated with suspicion by a number of union bosses. His fight against Benn was rancorous and personal and ended at the Brighton conference, on 27 September 1981, with only a narrow victory for the incumbent Healey by 50.4% to 49.6%, after two recounts.[1]

In retrospect, the Wembley Special Conference and Tony Benn's challenge for the deputy leadership in 1981 marked the highpoint for the 'New Left'. The party's centre began to fight back after 1981 and found itself being helped by a swing to the right among crucial trade union leaders. A new Labour Solidarity Campaign was formed by 150 centre-right MPs pledged to fight for a 50:25:25 PLP-dominated formula for the 'electoral college' and at the Brighton conference of September 1981 they successfully defeated the motion calling for the party's manifesto to be drawn up by the NEC alone and won back a majority on it. Two weeks later the PLP voted Tony Benn out of the shadow cabinet and during the following two years Michael Foot set in train moves to investigate the 'entryist' activities of the Trotskyite 'Militant Tendency' (Revolutionary Socialist League) which had established a strong foothold in at least 50 CLPs, including Liverpool and Bradford.[2] However, despite this fightback, the events of 1979–81 had been deeply damaging for the party and had visibly shifted it leftwards. In addition, Labour was burdened with an elderly, stop-gap leader, who appeared to the public as weak, vacillating, dishevelled and disorganised. It was faced with a conference which continued to pass radical and controversial motions on defence, economic and EEC issues. Finally, it continued to be buffeted by controversies at the local level, caused by the extremist activities of its constituency branches and even its city councillors, after the 'New Left' had assumed control of the greater London Council (GLC), under the leadership of Ken Livingstone (1945– ), in 1981, and the 'Militant Left', led by Derek Hatton (1948– ), of Liverpool, in 1983.

## The Turn of the Tide

### Margaret Thatcher's South Seas Adventure

The divisions in the Opposition were of great value to the

[1] On the first Healey captured 45.3% of the party vote, Benn 36.6% and Silkin 18%. On the second ballot a number of leading Tribunites, including the party's future leader Neil Kinnock, who had previously supported Silkin, pointedly abstained, thus earning the undying enmity of the 'hard left'.

[2] These moves resulted in the expulsion, in February 1983, from the Labour Party of the five members of the editorial board of the 'Militant' newspaper: Ted Grant, Peter Teague, Clare Dobbs, Lyn Walsh and Keith Dickinson.

Conservative Party during 1981–2 as it passed through a deep trough of unpopularity. In September 1981 the party trailed third in the opinion polls, with a national rating of only 27%, compared with Labour's 33% and the Alliance's 37%, and then proceeded to lose a string of by-elections to the Alliance, as unemployment moved above 3 million. By March 1982, with inflation falling to 12%, there was a slight improvement in Conservative fortunes, as all three parties stood neck and neck in the low thirties. However, one event overseas dramatically transformed the position within the space of nine weeks: the Falklands War.

Mrs Thatcher was inexperienced in foreign affairs, but she held a number of firm, gut convictions. She abhorred the Soviet bloc and East-West detente, admired the United States and its free-enterprise system, disliked the subsidy-ridden European Community and was intensely nationalistic. This frequently brought her into conflict with the Foreign Office and its urbane permanent secretary, Sir Michael Palliser, and departmental minister Lord Carrington, both of whom favoured detente and an expanded role in Europe.[1] However, although Mrs Thatcher disliked the Foreign Office's 'fudged' diplomacy, she was willing to make concessions on issues ranging from Zimbabwe, EEC contributions and relations with Southern Ireland. It was always clear, however, in these negotiations that there was a 'bottom line' below which she was not prepared to go.

Such a sticking point was reached in April 1982 when she was faced with her gravest challenge: a dispute with Argentina over the tiny Falkland Islands, where sheep outnumbered the human population many times over, situated on the fringe of Antarctica, deep in the South Atlantic.

From the late 17th century onwards, several nations had disputed ownership of the Falkland Islands but since 1832, when a British naval squadron took formal possession of them, they had been a crown colony. Argentina had never been happy with this de facto annexation and in 1965 had formally notified the United Nations of its wish to acquire a transfer of sovereignty. It had been encouraged by the attitude of successive British governments. Harold Wilson's first government, for example, had not renounced the Argentinian claim in outright terms and Edward Heath's administration had signed a communication agreement which effectively gave

---

[1] It was notable that Palliser, unlike his five predecessors, was not awarded a life peerage when he retired in April 1982.

Argentina control over air access to the islands. Following this, the Buenos Aires government extended the Port Stanley airstrip, enabling tourists to visit it and islanders to make use of Argentinian schools and hospitals, in the hope that they would be sufficiently reassured to agree to a further closening of links. The passing of the British Nationality Act (1981) meant that the Falklanders were no longer British passport holders so that their ties with the home country seemed more sentimental than practical.

Low key negotiations on the Falklands' future continued between Britain and Argentina during the years after 1965, but the stumbling block was always London's insistence on the principle of 'self determination' for the islanders. However, in 1976, diplomatic links were severed after a brutal military junta assumed power. Such was the deterioration in relations between the two countries that in December 1977 a hunter-killer submarine had to be despatched to Port Stanley in response to a threatened invasion.

When the Conservative government returned to power, in 1979, the Foreign Office became anxious once more to press forward with a negotiated settlement and sent its junior minister, Nicholas Ridley, on a fact-finding tour of Latin America and the South Atlantic. They had in mind two options: condominium (joint sovereignty and rule) or 'leaseback' (transferring formal sovereignty to Argentina, who would, in turn, lease back the islands' administration to Britain). However, these were rejected when put before the Falkland Islanders themselves and were disliked by the Prime Minister. The Argentinians then offered the islanders what they termed 'most pampered region status': the guaranteed retention of their own democratic form of government, legal and education systems and local customs, in return for their acceptance of Argentinian sovereignty, but once again this was rejected.

Negotiations continued in 1981 and early 1982, but the Argentinians, ruled now by the more hard line junta led by General Leopoldo Galtieri, grew increasingly impatient. It became evident from press reports emanating from Buenos Aires that the junta were once more contemplating invasion: a fact underlined by the temporary raising of the Argentine flag on the uninhabited South Georgia dependency by a group of scrap metal merchants. Richard Luce, who had taken over Ridley's post in September 1981, alerted Lord Carrington to these developments, but it was decided that the situation was not serious enough to call a meeting of the cabinet's Overseas and Defence (OD) Committee to ask for the authority to take, what would be costly, deterrent action. However, the

Antarctic survey vessel, HMS Endurance, which had a 21-man crew of marines, was retained in the South Atlantic.

Later, on 29 March 1982, indications of Argentinian preparations for an invasion became firmer. It was thus decided to send a submarine with support ships from the Mediterranean to the South Atlantic and Mrs Thatcher called her first crisis cabinet meeting on the Falklands on 1 April. It was, however, too late. The next morning Port Stanley was invaded, the British marines overpowered and the islands placed under Argentine control.

Mrs Thatcher hastily convened a special cabinet meeting on 2 April and announced calmly and firmly: 'Gentlemen, we shall have to fight'. She reiterated this message to a packed emergency session of the House of Commons on Saturday 3 April 1982 and was supported by the leaders of all the opposition parties. A handful of Labour left-wingers dissented, but most speakers hoped that a negotiated settlement would be reached before the naval task force reached its 8000 mile destination.

Over the weekend, the Foreign Secretary, Lord Carrington, and his colleagues, Richard Luce and Humphrey Atkins, resigned, accepting responsibility for the failure to anticipate and avoid the invasion. John Nott, the Defence Secretary, who had made a poor speech to the House, also considered resignation, but was dissuaded by the Prime Minister. Francis Pym was appointed Foreign Secretary in a rapid reshuffle and Mrs Thatcher took central control over the 'Falklands campaign', chairing a sub-committee of the OD Committee (Overseas and Defence South Atlantic: ODSA) which, understandably, soon became known as the 'war cabinet'.[1] Its members were the Prime Minister, her deputy, William Whitelaw, Francis Pym, John Nott, and, surprisingly, the new chairman of the Conservative Party, Cecil Parkinson.

In military terms the subsequent 'Falklands campaign' proved to be an undoubted success but it raised a number of political questions, the chief being whether a peaceful solution could have been found before the real fighting began. The task force was assembled and despatched on Sunday 4 April and on 12 April a 200 mile maritime exclusion zone around the Falklands was announced, the Argentinians being warned that ships within the zone would be attacked, even though the only means of doing so was by the nuclear submarine which had been sent ahead of the

---

[1] In the reshuffle John Biffen became Leader of the Commons and Lord Cockfield, Trade Secretary.

main force. A fortnight later the first British surface ships were sailing south of Ascension Island aiming, initially, at the reoccupation of South Georgia. Meanwhile, discussions with the Argentinians continued, mainly through the US Secretary of State, Al Haig, and later the UN Secretary-General, Perez de Cuellar, of Peru. Francis Pym and Al Haig were busily shuttling across the Atlantic and Haig also visited Buenos Aires.

By late April Mrs Thatcher's advisers were warning that the southern winter was fast approaching and military operations could not be long delayed. On 27 April Al Haig published his final proposals for a settlement which were accepted by Britain and on 28 April John Nott announced that the exclusion zone would become total, covering air and sea operations. On 29 April the Argentinians made an equivocal response to the Haig proposals, neither accepting nor rejecting them. Haig interpreted their attitude as a rejection, although a Peruvian peace formula was still being put together, with the approval of the UN Secretary-General. On Friday 30 April the British war cabinet authorised two major air strikes on Port Stanley airfield for Saturday 1 May. Meantime, on 29 April, Argentinian naval vessels, including the elderly cruiser 'General Belgrano', left home waters with instructions not to enter the exclusion zone. The air raids on Port Stanley took place and then on Sunday 2 May the 'General Belgrano' was attacked and sunk. The conflict had begun in earnest. On 4 May the first British Sea Harrier was lost to enemy action and the destroyer 'Sheffield' was hit by an Exocet missile and subsequently sank, resulting in the death of twenty crew members. Before the conflict ended, with the Argentinian surrender on June 15, some 1000 men on both sides had lost their lives: more than half the normal population of the islands.

Critics of the government subsequently asked whether the sinking of the 'General Belgrano' had precipitated the conflict and destroyed the Peruvian peace initiative. Their suspicions were aroused because of the government's delay in reporting the action and because of some equivocation in parliamentary statements. The questioning, led by Labour MP Tam Dalyell, rumbled on for another two years until, on 16 July 1984, Clive Ponting, a senior civil servant in the Ministry of Defence, sent copies of a 'Top Secret' study of the events surrounding the sinking to Dalyell. Ponting was subsequently prosecuted under Section 2 the Official Secrets Act and, following a trial at the Old Bailey, acquitted.

The Falklands war also raised a question concerning the state of preparedness of Britain's armed forces, some critics arguing that had the Argentinians invaded a year later there might not have been adequate ships and equipment to defend or recapture them. Two inquiries into the Falklands were subsequently set up. The first, chaired by Lord Shackleton, who had also reported six years previously, looked for ways to regenerate its economy. He recommended the spending of £100 million over a five-year period on the development of an airfield, and the expansion of the fishing and tourist industries. In the meantime, it was necessary, to increase the permanent garrison at an estimated cost of £1.5 million for each of its 1800 inhabitants. A second inquiry, by Lord Franks, on the events leading to the invasion, concluded that 'the Government could neither have prevented nor foreseen Argentina's invasion of the Falklands'. Although its membership of six privy councillors was drawn from political parties on both sides of the Commons, it is difficult not to agree with Hugo Young's comment in the 'Sunday Times' of 23 January 1983: 'a state paper written by the establishment for the benefit of the establishment'.

## The 'Falklands Factor'

In the twelve months between the end of the Falklands conflict and the dissolution of Parliament, in May 1983, most of the economic indicators continued to be unfavourable. The one redeeming feature was the level of inflation and even that was falling at a lower rate than the average for EEC countries. Unemployment was still rising, at more than double the average EEC rate, and national income was lower than it had been when the Conservative government came into office in 1979. Output in the manufacturing, engineering, textiles, construction and consumer goods industries was falling markedly, again in stark contrast with most European countries. And yet the popularity of the government had risen and the public standing of its leader, Margaret Thatcher, was at an all-time high. The run of Alliance gains was halted at Beaconsfield and at Merton, Mitcham and Morden in May and June 1982 and by January 1983 the Conservatives enjoyed a substantial 12.5% lead over Labour in the national opinion polls (see Table 15).

**Table 15   Quarterly Party Opinion Poll Ratings, 1979–83 (%)**

|  | 1979 | | | 1980 | | | | 1981 | | | | 1982 | | | | 1983 | |
|---|---|---|---|---|---|---|---|---|---|---|---|---|---|---|---|---|---|
|  | II | III | IV | I | II | III | IV | I | II | III | IV | I | II | III | IV | I | II |
| Con | 45 | 43 | 40 | 39 | 39 | 37 | 35 | 32 | 30 | 28 | 27 | 31 | 43 | 43 | 42 | 42 | 43 |
| Lab | 38 | 44 | 45 | 45 | 45 | 47 | 50 | 41 | 38 | 36 | 28 | 32 | 29 | 30 | 34 | 30 | 27 |
| Lib[1] | 14 | 10 | 12 | 13 | 13 | 14 | 14 | 24 | 29 | 34 | 38 | 34 | 27 | 24 | 22 | 25 | 25 |

[1] From March 1981, The Alliance

There were two explanations for this apparent paradox. The first could be found in the obvious disarray of the Labour Party, from the leadership downwards. This was highlighted in February 1983 by the well-publicised activities in Bermondsey when Bob Mellish, the party's moderate former chief whip, resigned his seat in opposition to the local CLP's selection of the ultra-leftist Peter Tatchell as its next prospective parliamentary candidate, despite Michael Foot's disapproval. In the subsequent by-election Mellish gave his backing to an Independent Labour candidate, resulting in a split Labour vote and the election of the young Liberal 'community politician', Simon Hughes, as MP for a previously solidly Labour 'inner city' constituency, the Liberals' share of the vote rising dramatically from 7% in 1979 to 57%. The second explanation for this remarkable resurgence in Conservative fortunes was what came to be called the 'Falklands Factor'. The public, led by the popular press, rallied around their embattled leader who emerged as a Churchillian figure in what was seen as a quixotic fight of high principle in defence of the right of 'self determination'. Margaret Thatcher had restored a sense of national pride and purpose and had given clear and decisive leadership.

The 'Falklands Factor' remained strong throughout 1982, with Mrs Thatcher standing head and shoulders above her rivals in the other parties, so that, although she had often declared her intention to continue into a fifth year, there were strong voices within her party urging an early election. A long-awaited report from the Boundary Commission had resulted in a redistribution of constituencies likely to give the Tories 30 more seats[1] and the rate of inflation seemed set to show a rise in the foreseeable future. It was not surprising, therefore, when, after satisfactory returns in the local elections, Mrs Thatcher asked the Queen to dissolve Parliament on 13 May 1983. A general election was fixed for 9 June.

[1] The Boundary Commission had been established to effect a more equitable distribution of seats in terms of population size so as to reflect the demographic changes of the previous two decades, which had seen a movement away from city centres towards the suburbs and countryside and a faster rate of population growth in the south and east than in the 'de-industrialising' north. The Commission began its work in 1976 and ended up increasing the total number of seats in Parliament from 635 to 650: raising the number in England from 516 to 523, in Scotland from 71 to 72, in Wales from 36 to 38 and in previously under-represented Northern Ireland from 12 to 17. In all, only 53 constituencies remained unchanged in delineation, while a number of 'inner city' Labour MPs found their seats removed. The Labour Party leadership challenged the proposed new boundaries in the courts, attempting to hold off the changes until after the election. However, the Boundary Commission's recommendations were accepted by Parliament in March 1983.

## The June 1983 General Election

The British constitution has a built-in advantage for the government of the day which seeks re-election and the 1983 general election provided a textbook illustration of this. From Day One of the campaign Labour was showing signs of disarray, with Michael Foot as the shambling amateur compared with Margaret Thatcher who headed a well-oiled machine.

In charge of this Conservative machine was the skilled meritocrat, Cecil Parkinson. Since becoming Party Chairman in September 1981 he had set up a new marketing department, headed by Chris Lawson (a former managing director of Mars in the US), to draw upon modern American opinion poll research and direct mailing techniques. This department sent out 'Impact 80' to the constituency parties: a kitbag of useful suggestions on fund-raising, how to use the local media and how to produce local newsletters. It also set up a selection board system to train and scrutinise potential parliamentary candidates. Finally, it carried out sophisticated surveys to find out what targeted groups were thinking and how best to project the party. By January 1984, Central Office, in combination once more with Saatchi and Saatchi, had decided upon its campaign strategy. The emphasis was to be on continuity and the qualities of decisive leadership under the dual themes 'Stay on Course' and 'The Resolute Approach'. Perhaps surprisingly, research was showing that the public was blaming unemployment as much, if not more, on individual shortcomings and international factors as on government policies, so it was decided to be positive and aggressive even on this issue.

The Labour campaign, in contrast, seemed improvised and uncoordinated. The party was using the Johnny Wright advertising agency, which had covered the 1982 local elections, but the decision had been so long delayed that the agency had barely enough time to make the necessary preparations. The Liberal-SDP Alliance, public support for which had dipped to between 20–25% since the heady days of 1981, had to operate on a much smaller budget than the other two parties.[1] It had the added problem of identifying the leadership to a confused electorate. Roy Jenkins had

[1] By the time the campaign had ended the Conservative central party machine had spent £3.8 million (£2.2 million of which had been on advertising by Saatchi and Saatchi), the Labour Party campaign headquarters £2.2 million (£1 million by Johnny Wright), the Liberals £0.25 million and the SDP £1 million. Local spending by the Conservatives was put at £2.1 million, Labour at £1.9 million and the Alliance at £1.6 million (£0.55 million being drawn in grants from the central headquarters).

been elected head of the SDP in July 1982, defeating David Owen by 56% to 44% in a party postal ballot, and had developed a good working relationship with David Steel. Steel thus suggested that the experienced Jenkins should assume the title 'prime minister designate' while he became campaign leader. This arrangement was later to be regretted by the Alliance partners.

The Conservative Party produced an unusually cautious and low key manifesto, 'The Challenge of Our Times', emphasising a theme of 'business as usual' if re-elected to office: firm public expenditure control, tax cuts, privatisation and trade union reform. In addition, it developed the slogan of 'Freedom and Responsibility', emphasising the need for citizens to take responsibility for their decisions and actions in both the economic and social spheres. The Labour Party's manifesto, 'The New Hope for Britain', was by contrast a lengthy, detailed and unusually radical document. It took full account of the decisions taken by the recent party conferences and called for withdrawal from the EEC, unilateral nuclear disarmament, the re-nationalisation of privatised firms and the abolition of the House of Lords. Michael Foot, unlike previous leaders, did not attempt to dilute the programme. On economic matters, it promised a vague new National Economic Assessment between government and unions, which would be concerned with the distribution of national resources and the planning of growth targets, as well as an emergency public spending programme designed to reduce unemployment to a level of one million within five years. Jobs were to be provided through the launch of a major house-building drive, through expansion of the health and education sectors, through the creation of a new two year 'Student Traineeship' scheme for 16 and 17-year-olds and through state industrial investment under the guise of a projected National Investment Bank. Appended to the manifesto were promises to attack the problems of low pay, extend women's rights through 'positive discrimination' and address the issue of racial prejudice. The document proved to be political dynamite. The Conservative Party successfully cast scorn on the feasibility of its economic pledges, attacked the extremism of its defence, EEC and institutional reform proposals and warned voters not to vote for the Alliance in case it let Labour in.

The key issue in the campaign was naturally the economy. However, although unemployment stood in excess of three million, Labour could not convince the public that its Emergency Programme would not lead to a new increase in inflation. It did, however, raise concern over government intentions by leaking damaging CPRS documents which contemplated substantial cuts in welfare benefits and the dismemberment of the National Health Service, and Treasury papers, envisaging unemployment rising to 6 million. It alleged that the Conservatives were concealing a 'secret manifesto' of far right, market-centred reform, but this was vigorously denied by the Tory campaign team.

The other great issue was that of defence. The question of nuclear disarmament was very much in the public's mind in 1983, with Cruise missiles due to be stationed at Greenham Common in the autumn of that year. CND was at the peak of its popularity, its membership having increased tenfold between 1980–2 to 300 000, and had organised a series of effective marches. However, despite the strong feelings of the committed, opinion polls showed only 16% of the public favouring unilateralism. Labour's adherence to unilateralism and its support for withdrawal from the EEC, which was depicted by the government as likely to result in the loss of thousands of manufacturing jobs, thus proved to be major vote losing commitments. In addition, they led to rifts among its campaign team, with Denis Healey and, most pointedly, James Callaghan failing to support the manifesto line.

The campaign itself was disastrously run by the Labour Party. It lacked clear themes and a coherent strategy and its quirky leader, Michael Foot, concentrated on stump speeches to the party faithful rather than attempting to project himself on television. Most serious of all, Foot's continuation as leader became a subject of frequent questioning, with disaffected colleagues showing few signs of open support and General-Secretary, Jim Mortimer, being forced on 26 May to re-affirm to a press conference that Foot was still in charge. Within four weeks the party's efforts managed to reduce their share of the likely vote from 36% to 28%. The SDP-Liberal Alliance campaign also had its problems. Its policy programme, as set out in the manifesto 'Working Together for Britain'[1], was seen as vague

---

[1] The Alliance manifesto pledged to reduce unemployment by one million within two years through the launch of a crash growth programme of targeted investment in housing and environment improvement and employment subsidies to firms taking on new workers. This was to be funded through increasing the level of government borrowing from the current £8 billion to one of £11 billion per annum. It proposed, in addition, a statutory incomes policy to be backed up by a 'counter inflation tax' to be imposed on firms breaching the set norm; the encouragement of industrial democracy; compulsory secret ballots for union elections; the introduction of proportional representation; and greater decentralisation, promising to establish a directly elected Scottish (as did Labour) Assembly as well as assemblies for Wales and the regions.

and confusing and its two parties as lacking credibility as a future government. In addition its patrician leader Roy Jenkins remained aloof and awkward. Thus, after three weeks, David Steel was forced to call a meeting at his Ettrick Bridge home in Scotland to persuade Jenkins to drop the title 'prime minister designate' and allow the comforting, photogenic Steel to take a greater share of the spotlight. This was successful in boosting the Alliance share of the polls up from 20% to 25%, as the party benefited from a late surge in support at the expense of the disintegrating Labour campaign.

It was, however, Margaret Thatcher who emerged as a landslide victor. Her campaign was skilfully managed in a presidential fashion, with special 'media events' being arranged for each day, ticket-only youth and celebrity rallies staged by Harvey Thomas (formerly publicity director for the American Evangelist Billy Graham) and Central Office retaining tight control over the agenda of debate. On polling day the Prime Minister succeeded in gaining a huge overall majority of 144 seats (see Table 16). During the postwar era, only Labour, in 1945, had exceeded this margin of

**Table 16   The June 1983 General Election (Turnout 72.7%)**

| Party | Total Votes | % Share of Vote | Candidates | Av. % Vote Per Candidate | Number of MPs | Av. Vote Per MP |
|---|---|---|---|---|---|---|
| Conservative | 13.011m | 42.4% | 633 | 43.5% | 397 | 32,772 |
| Labour | 8.457m | 27.6% | 633 | 28.3% | 209 | 40,461 |
| Alliance | 7.781m | 25.4% | 633 | 26.0% | 23 | 338,337 |
| (Liberals) | (4.210m) | (13.7%) | (322) | (27.7%) | (17) | (247,647) |
| (SDP) | (3.571m) | (11.7%) | (311) | (24.3%) | (6) | (595,166) |
| SNP | 0.332m | 1.1% | 72 | 11.8% | 2 | 166,000 |
| Plaid Cymru | 0.125m | 0.4% | 36 | 7.8% | 2 | 62,500 |
| Ecology | 0.054m | 0.2% | 108 | 1.0% | 0 | — |
| National Front | 0.027m | 0.1% | 60 | 1.0% | 0 | — |
| British National | 0.014m | 0.0% | 53 | 0.6% | 0 | — |
| Communist | 0.012m | 0.0% | 35 | 0.8% | 0 | — |
| Others (GB) | 0.091m | 0.3% | 221 | NA | 0 | — |
| Others (NI) | 0.765m | 2.5% | 95 | 17.9% | 17 | 45,000 |
| Total | 30.669m | 100.0% | 2,579 | — | 650 | 47,183 |

victory. She retained the support of 30% of trade unionists and 40% of skilled manual workers (see Table 17), many of whom were attracted by her tough leadership style, firm approach to law and order issues and the government's sale of 500 000 council houses in 1979–83, and polled particularly strongly in the Midlands and southern half of England and among young, 'first time' voters. It should be noted, however, that the Conservatives captured only 42.4% of the vote, less than in 1979. This was thus an equivocal, and in many ways a defensive, rather than clear positive, vote for 'Thatcherism'. It was rather the staggering slump in the Labour vote, the split in the centre-left anti-Tory vote and the boon of boundary changes which led to this resounding victory.

**Table 17   Party Share of Votes by Social Groups in June 1983***

| Social Group | Conservative | Labour | Lib-SDP Alliance |
|---|---|---|---|
| Men | 42% | 30% | 25% |
| Women | 46% | 26% | 27% |
| Professional/Managerial (AB) | 60% | 10% | 28% |
| Office/Clerical (C1) | 51% | 20% | 27% |
| Skilled Manual (C2) | 40% | 32% | 26% |
| Semi/Unskilled (DE) | 33% | 41% | 24% |
| Owner Occupiers | 52% | 19% | 28% |
| Council Tenants | 26% | 47% | 24% |
| Private Tenants | 41% | 33% | 23% |
| Trade Union Members | 31% | 39% | 29% |
| Unemployed Workers | 24% | 48% | 24% |
| 18–24 Year Olds | 42% | 33% | 22% |
| 25–34 Year Olds | 40% | 29% | 29% |
| 35–54 Year Olds | 44% | 27% | 27% |
| 55 + | 47% | 27% | 24% |
| Pensioners | 51% | 25% | 23% |

**Table 18   Party Share of Votes by Regions in June 1983**

| | Conservative | Labour | Lib-SDP Alliance | Nat. |
|---|---|---|---|---|
| SCOTLAND | 28.4% | 35.1% | 24.5% | 11.8% |
| WALES | 31.0% | 37.5% | 23.2% | 7.8% |
| ENGLAND | 46.0% | 27.0% | 26.4% | — |
| North/Northeast | 34.6% | 40.2% | 25.0% | — |
| Northwest | 40.0% | 36.0% | 23.4% | — |
| Yorks & Humberside | 38.7% | 35.3% | 25.5% | — |
| West Midlands | 45.0% | 31.2% | 23.4% | — |
| East Midlands | 47.2% | 28.0% | 24.1% | — |
| East Anglia | 51.0% | 20.5% | 28.2% | — |
| Southwest | 51.4% | 14.7% | 33.2% | — |
| Southeast | 54.5% | 15.9% | 29.0% | — |
| Greater London | 43.9% | 29.9% | 24.8% | |

Labour's vote collapsed to 27.6%, its lowest share since 1918, with its average constituency vote in seats contested at its lowest level since the party was founded in 1900, and it captured a mere 209 seats to the Conservatives' 397. In southern England the party fared disastrously, capturing only three seats (Ipswich, Thurrock and Bristol South) outside inner London in the area below the Severn-Wash line, and finished in second place in only 18 of this region's remaining 151 constituencies. Its performance in Scotland, the north west and 'inner city' areas was more favourable, as disparities in regional voting patterns continued to broaden.[1] The party, nevertheless, still lost substantial middle class and skilled working class support to the Alliance, as well as a record 119 deposits (in 1979 it had forfeited only 22 deposits). The Alliance, in contrast, made a substantial breakthrough, finishing in first or second place in more than half (335) of the nation's constituencies and losing only 11 deposits, but its vote was too evenly spread to collect a corresponding number of seats. The Liberals held all but one of their 13 seats contested (William Pitt losing in Croydon) and made five gains (including two in Scotland and one in Wales). However, only 5 of the SDP's ex-Labour Party defectors were re-elected, Shirley Williams, in Crosby, and William Rodgers, in Stockton, being among those defeated. The party's representation in the Commons fell from 28 to 6, one gain being made in Scotland. In areas where the Alliance had already built up bedrock support they encountered, as the Liberals had before, the 'plateau effect', i.e. a smaller than average rise in their share of the vote. It thus could boast only a 3.5% share of parliamentary seats, despite capturing 25.4% of the national vote (the best third-party Liberal performance since 1923): an event described by the 'Sunday Times' as representing 'a new order of unfairness'.

For the other minor parties, despite a record number of candidates, the election was a disappointment. The SNP and Plaid Cymru (PC) each secured the re-election of both their two sitting MPs as a result of strong personal votes, but support for the SNP as a whole slumped to only 11.8% of the Scottish total, while that for PC remained stuck at 7.8%. The National Front, which had been split by the emergence of the new British National Party, polled lamentably, some of its support being siphoned off to the newly strident post-Falklands Conservative Party. Only, controversially, did Sinn Fein, the newly-formed political wing of the Provisional IRA, make any impact, its leader Gerry Adams unseating the moderate Catholic socialist Gerry Fitt in West Belfast.

[1] The progressive regionalisation of the Labour and Conservative vote resulted in the number of two-party 'marginal seats' falling from an average of 160 between 1955 and 1970 to only 80 in 1983. During the 1983 election the overall swing to the Conservatives was 4.4% below the Humber-Mersey line compared with only 2.8% above.

## The Aftermath of June 1983

The opposition parties were, not surprisingly, bitterly disappointed with the results of May 1983. A drained and depressed David Steel toyed with the idea of relinquishing his party's leadership, but decided, on reflection, to take a short three-months sabbatical to recharge his batteries while chief whip Alan Beith temporarily took over his leadership duties. Change in the other two opposition parties was more dramatic. Both Roy Jenkins and Michael Foot tendered their resignations in the election's immediate aftermath. David Owen, the forceful former Foreign Secretary, who had enjoyed a 'good Falklands' and had exhibited strong personal rivalry to Jenkins, was immediately elected the new SDP leader in an unopposed contest on 21 June 1983. The Labour Party's transfer of leadership was protracted, but equally smooth.

Denis Healey, now aged 66, decided not to challenge for the post, while Tony Benn (58), the standard-bearer of the left, who had lost his boundary-changed Bristol East constituency in the general election, was ineligible. The fight for the party's leadership thus centred on the younger generation: the centre-right Croslandite Yorkshireman, Roy Hattersley (50), and the 'soft left', Neil Kinnock. Kinnock, the 41-year-old son of a Welsh miner, was an articulate television performer with no ministerial experience. He was an acceptable choice for the trade unions and constituency parties and thus emerged a clear victor at the Brighton conference on 1 October 1983, capturing 71% of the Party's electoral college vote to Hattersley's 19%.[1]

Roy Hattersley also, however, stood for the deputy leadership, which had been vacated by Healey, and was successful, defeating Tony Benn's protégé, Michael Meacher (43), by 67% to 27%.[2] These results left the Labour Party with a stable and well-balanced 'dream ticket', which would provide the basis for its slow rebuilding in preparation for 1987 or 1988.

---

[1] Kinnock took 29% of the trade unions' 40% vote, 27.5% of the constituency parties' 30% vote and 14.8% of the PLP's 30% vote. The centre-right Peter Shore (59) and the 'hard left' Eric Heffer also stood, capturing 3% and 6% of the college vote respectively.

[2] The centrist Denzil Davies and Gwyneth Dunwoody also contested the deputy leadership, capturing 3.5% and 1.3% of the college vote respectively.

# Part Five

# THE SECOND THATCHER ADMINISTRATION: 1983-7

## This Lady's Not For Turning

### Starting a New Chapter or Rewriting the Old?

When Parliament reassembled on 15 June 1983 it had a new look. There were 157 new members[1], 101 on the government side, and a new Speaker, Bernard Weatherill (62), was rapidly elected to replace George Thomas, who retired with an hereditary peerage, as Viscount Tonypandy. The government front bench also had a changed appearance.

Francis Pym (61), who had had the temerity to suggest during the election campaign that a landslide victory might not be desirable, was unceremoniously banished to the back benches by a Prime Minister who was slowly learning how to 'carve the joint'. His departure allowed Sir Geoffrey Howe to fulfill his ambition and take over as Foreign Secretary. Howe was replaced as Chancellor by the abrasive monetarist hardliner, Nigel Lawson. Michael Heseltine had already been moved to Defence, following the announcement of the retirement to private business of John Nott in January 1983, and the Environment portfolio, after being briefly held by Tom King (50), was now in the hands of the 'dry' and loyal Patrick Jenkin. This promised to be a most demanding post, with controversial legislation to 'rate cap' local councils and abolish the metropolitan county councils due to be piloted through Parliament. Another important change was the elevation of the party's deputy leader, William Whitelaw, to the House of Lords as an hereditary peer.

[1] 50 sitting MPs had retired at the June 1983 election. These had included Sir Harold Wilson, Sir John Nott, Sir Angus Maude and Jo Grimond (Grimond, Maude and Wilson were subsequently raised to the Lords in the 'dissolution honours list'). 8 Labour MPs had been de-selected.

Whitelaw lost his Home Office portfolio, but remained a central figure in the new government. He had the brief, as the new Leader of the Lords, to impose discipline over an increasingly rebellious upper chamber and continued to serve as an important ad hoc adviser to the Prime Minister and party power broker through his post as chairman of the 'star chamber' cabinet committee MISC 62, a body which hammered out compromise deals on spending cuts with departmental ministers each autumn. Whitelaw was replaced as Home Secretary by the young, loyal and vigorous Leon Brittan. The final two important changes were the reluctant promotion of the dissident Peter Walker to the Energy Department, replacing the ousted David Howell (47), and the much more enthusiastic elevation of Mrs Thatcher's protege, Cecil Parkinson, to head a new combined, Heath-style, Trade and Industry Department. Parkinson was replaced as Party Chairman by John Gummer (43), a parson's son and the Prime Minister's former speechwriter.

In all, ten ministers changed their portfolios and there were three new entrants to the cabinet of June 1983 (see Table 19): Jopling (the former chief whip), Rees (the former Minister of Trade) and Parkinson. This represented a radical shake-up, in which the ranks

**Table 19    The Thatcher Cabinet of June 1983**

| | |
|---|---|
| Prime Minister | —Margaret Thatcher (57) |
| Chancellor of the Exchequer | —Nigel Lawson (51) |
| Foreign Secretary | —Sir Geoffrey Howe (56) |
| Home Secretary | —Leon Brittan (43) |
| Trade & Industry Secretary | —Cecil Parkinson (51) |
| Employment Secretary | —Norman Tebbit (52) |
| Agriculture Secretary | —Michael Jopling (52) |
| Environment Secretary | —Patrick Jenkin (56) |
| Defence Secretary | —Michael Heseltine (50) |
| Welsh Secretary | —Nicholas Edwards (49) |
| Education Secretary | —Sir Keith Joseph (65) |
| Transport Secretary | —Tom King (50) |
| Energy Secretary | —Peter Walker (51) |
| Northern Ireland Secretary | —James Prior (55) |
| Scottish Secretary | —George Younger (51) |
| Social Services Secretary | —Norman Fowler (45) |
| Lord Chancellor | —Lord Hailsham (75) |
| Leader of Lords | —Viscount Whitelaw (64) |
| Commons Leader | —John Biffen (52) |
| Treasury Chief Secretary | —Peter Rees (56) |
| Chancellor of Duchy of Lancaster | —Lord Cockfield (66) |

of the older generation of land-owning 'wets' were further thinned, giving a strong 'Thatcherite' bias to the new team. In particular, the Treasury and major spending departments were dominated by the new crop of business or legally trained 'dry' parvenus.

Margaret Thatcher further strengthened her position in 1983 in a number of ways: through the appointment of two new, young, like-minded permanent secretaries to head the Treasury and Defence Department, Peter Middleton (49) and Sir Clive Whitmore (48); the appointment of Robin Leigh-Pemberton as the new Governor of the Bank of England; the abolition of the CPRS 'think tank'; and the addition to her Number 10 Policy Unit (now headed by the former 'Spectator' editor Ferdinand Mount), of former UN Representative, Sir Anthony Parsons, as foreign policy adviser and Roger Jackling as defence aide.

## Policies for the Second Term

Mrs Thatcher's programme for her second term was to be similar in tone to that of 1979–83, concentrating on holding down public spending and reducing the PSBR. This time, however, it was to be more zealously pursued. Cecil Parkinson, the new Trade and Industry Secretary, unveiled plans for a fourfold increase in the privatisation schedule to a level of £2 billion per annum, with the envisaged sale of British Telecom, British Airways, the Royal Ordnance Factory and British Gas. In addition, he was keen to progress with de-regulation and the creation of a new 'enterprise culture', and to tighten the purse strings of the nationalised industries, with the aim of selling off each enterprise as it returned to profitability. At the Environment Department, Patrick Jenkin was set to make spending economies through his controversial new legislation and to examine the possibility of major reform of the system of local rates. At the Home Office, Leon Brittan was ready to re-introduce a tough new Bill designed to increase police powers, the 'Police and Criminal Evidence Bill', which had had to be temporarily abandoned as a result of the early election, as well as new measures for curbing terrorism. At Employment, Norman Tebbit was preparing to introduce a further, third, Trade Union Reform Bill, intended to force the holding of secret ballots before strike action if unions were to retain legal immunity from civil action for damages, and decennial ballots for the maintenance of unions' political funds. Finally, at the Defence Department,

Michael Heseltine was determined to see Cruise missiles installed and the peace movement defeated.

This radical programme, which was unveiled in the Queen's Speech of 22 June 1983, was, however, greeted with concern by the public and by many Conservative MPs and peers. There were widespread fears about possible health spending cuts and the social consequences of the continuing high level of unemployment, while the controversial metropolitan county councils abolition Bill was skilfully opposed in a media campaign orchestrated by Labour's GLC leader, Ken Livingstone. The government, with the Prime Minister adopting a more forceful leadership stance and the decimated, demoralised and, because of its reduced numbers, Select Committee-bound opposition unable to play a significant role in Commons' debates, was made to appear arrogant, insensitive and bludgeoning in the use of its large majority. Its opinion poll ratings dramatically slumped and were further lowered by the popularity of the new Labour leader, Neil Kinnock, and by a series of unfortunate 'banana skins'.

The first and most damaging of such 'banana skins' was the enforced resignation of Cecil Parkinson, the 'wonder boy' of the Conservative Party, in October 1983. This followed press revelations of an affair with his now-pregnant secretary, Sara Keays, and an ineffective attempt by Mrs Thatcher to persuade him to stay on. Parkinson's departure was damaging to the image of the party of 'Victorian values' and deprived the Prime Minister of the services of her most trusted adviser. In addition, it necessitated another rapid reshuffle: with Norman Tebbit taking over at Trade and Industry, Tom King at Employment and Nicholas Ridley at Transport. John Gummer was also given a cabinet seat as an Employment minister.

Two more 'banana skins' appeared in January and March 1984 with, first, the decision to ban trade unions operating at the government's 'secret' communications headquarters (GCHQ) in Cheltenham, each employee being offered £1,000 in compensation; and then a decision to prosecute Sarah Tisdall, a junior clerk at the MOD, under Section 2 of the Official Secrets Act, for providing 'The Guardian' newspaper with a copy of an embarrassing minute relating to the arrival of Cruise missiles at the Greenham Common air base. Tisdall was subsequently sentenced to six months imprisonment. These actions were seen as further evidence of the government's high-handedness, and led to a further slump in its poll rating as well as a worsening in its relations with the trade unions, who were to temporarily boycott Neddy meetings.

### The Miners' Strike

These events were, however, rapidly overshadowed by one major industrial dispute which dominated the political scene for a whole year and divided the country: the coal miners' strike. It began amid a euphoria of optimism, on 12 March 1984, and ended, in disillusion and bitter acrimony, on 5 March 1985.

As the drama unfolded, two principal actors emerged: Arthur Scargill (46), the evangelical Yorkshireman and avowed Marxist, with the power to hold and move mass audiences, and Ian (later Sir Ian) MacGregor (72), the Scottish expatriate with an industrial relations sense honed on the harsh realities of American business and with an almost embarrassing inability to communicate with any kind of audience. Backstage, but central to the dispute, was Margaret Thatcher, with a new opportunity to display her resolution and attack the 'enemy within', this time on her own ground. The dispute has now been widely recorded but the central features, and their impact on British politics, deserve consideration.

After the Heath government's demise, following the miners' strike of 1973–4, and her own, less damaging, capitulation in February 1981, over proposals to close 23 pits, Mrs Thatcher was determined to win the next battle. A secret policy group, chaired in 1978 by Nicholas Ridley, had already devised a strategy to inflict a cautionary defeat on the miners at a chosen date. This involved building up maximum coal stocks at the power stations; making contingency plans for the import of coal; encouraging the recruitment of non-union lorry drivers by haulage companies; introducing dual coal/oil firing in all power stations, cutting off the supply of social security funds to strikers; and the creation of a large mobile police squad to uphold the law against violent picketing. Arthur Scargill succeeded the pragmatic Joe Gormley as NUM president in 1982 and Ian MacGregor, fresh from his victory over the steelworkers in 1980, took over from the retiring Norman Siddall as NCB chairman in September 1983. The scene was thus set for a bitter confrontation in 1984.

MacGregor, on a three-year secondment, was determined to make the coal industry rapidly profitable by investing in new 'super mines', closing down smaller, uneconomic pits and reining back production from the levels envisaged in the 1974 'Plan for Coal' and retiring older workers on generous redundancy terms. Scargill and other NUM hardliners opposed this strategy, which, when announced on 6 March 1984, sought to reduce output by 4 million tonnes in 1984–5 and close 20 pits, with the loss of 20000 jobs. The

NUM had already started a national overtime ban on 31 October 1983 and a national strike commenced, on a 'rolling' regional basis, on 12 March 1984. A week later 90 of the 174 NCB collieries were on strike, involving 100000 of the 183000 workforce. The Nottinghamshire miners, however, based in an area of productive, low-cost pits, voted 3:1 not to strike and continued working. On 8 April a call for a strike ballot came from moderates on the NUM national executive and three days later the supervisors' union (NACODS) voted in favour of strike action but, because the vote did not meet the required two-thirds majority, it was ineffective. The following day, 12 April, the NUM president ruled against a strike ballot, despite entreaties from Neil Kinnock.

The strike became characterised by massive picketing by the NUM, including the use of 'flying pickets' from Yorkshire and other areas to the Midlands, a tactic devised by the young Scargill in 1972. It was met this time, however, by a firm and nationally co-ordinated police response. The government continued to claim its 'neutrality' but seemed ready to support both the NCB management and costly policing arrangements. Talks between the NCB and NUM proved abortive and the level of violence escalated, reaching riot proportions at Orgreave on 2 May. The miners received patchy support from the dockers', railwaymen's and seamen's unions, but failed to gain the allegiance of hauliers, steel or power workers. In addition, their finances were stretched both by court sequestration of their assets, in October, and by changes in the social security rules, which prevented single miners from receiving benefit and, in November 1984, reduced the sums given to married miners' wives and children. Special miners' support groups and 'soup kitchens' were thus established, with the help of donations from the TUC, the public and overseas.

The strike dragged on through the autumn and winter months of 1984, with a brief and menacing NACODS walk-out in September-October being ended by the NCB's agreement to a new pit closure review procedure. It became clear, however, that the government would remain firm and that there would be no power cuts. Thus a slow trickle back to work began before Christmas, encouraged by the NCB's offer of special seasonal bonuses. This exacerbated the tensions in pit villages, but by February 1985 the trickle became a flood and on 5 March there was a final, organised return to work by the 50% still on strike. The 'pit dispute' was over.

The strike, which was the longest in the coal industry since 1926, left scars, which promised to take long to heal, in addition to the immediate tragedies of three deaths and 600 men dismissed. It destroyed the national unity of mineworkers, leading to the creation of two separate union organisations: the NUM and Roy Lynk's Nottinghamshire-Derbyshire based Union of Democratic Mineworkers (UDM). It damaged relations between the police and the public in the pit villages. It gave a temporary boost to the Conservative government and a reverse to the Labour opposition, although the long-term effects remained less clear. It brought great hardship to many mining families and made it virtually unthinkable that its national union would take similar industrial action in the foreseeable future. Finally, it was a very costly strike: difficult to justify in industrial or governmental terms. The government spent £3000 million or more to make an annual saving of £250 million. It had given blank cheques to the NCB and other severely affected nationalised concerns, for example the Central Electricity Generating Board (CEGB), the British Steel Corporation (BSC) and British Rail, to write off the huge losses suffered that few private corporations could have endured. As with 'Fortress Falklands', Parliament was to be told by the Chancellor that the miners' dispute had been a 'worthwhile investment for the nation'.

An important question is, could this dispute have been avoided or, at the very least, restricted? Given a different leadership on one or both sides, the answer must be, possibly yes. It is unlikely that Joe Gormley would have chosen to strike in the coal and oil glutted circumstances of 1984–5 or, if he had, would have become so outmanoeuvred as the strike developed. It is also unlikely that Norman Siddall would have allowed the dispute to escalate as it did. But even with Scargill and MacGregor as the opposing leaders, the strike might have been over much sooner, and in the miners' favour, if the NUM president had not been guilty of three cardinal failures: firstly, to hold a national ballot in April, a ballot which he may well have won; secondly, to condemn all violence; and, thirdly, to show flexibility on the question of 'uneconomic pits'. Scargill shied away from a national ballot, having already lost three votes in 1982–3, since he argued that a pit closure was a regional rather than a national issue. He refused to condemn picket violence out of intense loyalty to his members. Both actions were, however, fatal, forfeiting the support of other trade unions and of public opinion and displayed an innate arrogance in Scargill's approach to the strike which transcended industrial action and took on the form of a direct political challenge to the elected government. Mrs Thatcher, in turn could be criticised for failing to see the future of

Britain's coal industry in a long term, human, context, and for not displaying the magnanimity which was required of a national leader.

## Mid Term Blues: 1984–6

### Restlessness in the Ranks

The miners' strike was of short-term benefit to the Thatcher administration. It united the Tory Party in the face of a shared enemy; it polarised the nation, squeezing support for the Liberal-SDP Alliance; it cowed the trade union movement; and, finally, it opened up right-left divisions in the Labour Party and called into question the strength of Neil Kinnock's leadership.

However, all was not cheer for the Prime Minister who faced rumblings from her backbenches over a number of controversial new policy initiatives. The Trade Union Reform Bill of 1984, piloted through the Commons by Employment Secretary Norman Tebbit, was designed to compel secret membership ballots for the election of union officials, for the calling of strikes and for re-affiliation (at five yearly intervals) to the Labour Party. It enjoyed firm backing from the Conservative backbenches as well as the sympathetic support of Alliance MPs. The measure was vociferously opposed by trade union leaders outside, but rapidly and successfully found its way onto the statute book. In stark contrast, the government's other principal reform proposal of 1983–5, the administrative restructuring and control of the financial basis of the local government system, encountered intense opposition both inside and outside Parliament, forcing significant changes to the original Bills.

### The Revolt of the Squires, Shires and Metropolis

During its first term in office the Thatcher administration, as a consequence of its monetarist convictions, had made strenuous efforts to control the level of local government spending. It believed that, with local administrations responsible for a quarter of all public expenditure, if the lower tiers were allowed to continue to spend freely, its entire fiscal strategy would be undermined. The new government, under the lead of Environment Secretary Michael Heseltine (1979–83), thus set in train a three-pronged offensive to bring local councils' spending under control. Firstly, the amount of funds sent out from the centre in the form of 'block grants' to local authorities was reduced in real terms in a staged manner, so that by 1985 the proportion of general local spending funded by Whitehall had fallen to 49%. This compared with a 1979 figure of 61%. Secondly, new computerised Environment Department (DOE) estimates, based on a complex combination of demographic, physical and social indices, termed 'grant related expenditure assessments' (GREA), were established to form a new basis for what local administrations were expected to spend, with authorities now being penalised, in the form of lost central grants, if they decided to exceed these limits. Thirdly, local bodies were encouraged to make more efficient use of their funds through adopting new managerial and accounting methods, an Audit Commission being established as part of this process in 1983, and through opening up many local services, for example cleaning and refuse collection, to the competition by both public and private tender.

The expenditure control measures of 1979–83 served to increase the interference of central government in local affairs in a fashion which contrasted sharply with traditional Conservative beliefs. More seriously for the government, these measures failed, in practice, to have their desired effects. The new GREA limits created a dilemma for councils in whether to comply with the new targets and impose stringent spending economies or whether to defy the central estimates and fund new, and what was seen as essential, spending through sharply increasing the level of local rates. Many councils adopted the latter course, with the consequence that rates rocketed between 1979–83, increasing in England and Wales by more than 90% at a time when the retail price index (RPI) advanced by only 55%. Taking the lead in this 'rate explosion' movement were a number of Labour-controlled 'inner city' councils, for example the 'New Left' dominated GLC and Sheffield metropolitan county councils, who acted in the knowledge that only a tiny minority of the local electorate in these run-down, unemployment riven areas actually paid rates directly themselves. Other councils, particularly in the Conservative or Alliance dominated shire counties, attempted to keep within or close to the GREA limits through savagely cutting back capital spending programmes or resorting to 'creative accountancy' procedures, building up, for example, special reserve funds which were to be drawn upon in years of central austerity. They were to find, however, that their reward for complying with DOE estimates was to be a decrease in their target level for subsequent years as the GREA was re-adjusted to take into account past spending performances.

By 1983, therefore, it had become clear to the Thatcher administration that the local government policies of its first term had failed to have their desired effect. They had adversely affected many pro-Conservative middle class ratepayers and rural and suburban counties, while, at the same time, were being defiantly disregarded and opposed by Labour city councils. A fundamental re-appraisal of policy was thus undertaken during the administration's second term. The Prime Minister had for long privately favoured a major overhaul of the system of local finance in order to restore democratic accountability to a tier of government in which barely a third of the electorate and only 17% of those who actually voted were directly taxed, and had pledged in the party's 1979 manifesto to abolish and replace local rates. However, the government's 1981 'Green Paper' on rates reform had uncovered seemingly insuperable administrative and financial obstacles and drawbacks to such a change. The new Environment Secretary Patrick Jenkin instead framed two major new initiatives directed towards the control of local spending during the government's second term. Firstly, a major 'rate-capping' bill was proposed under which the DOE would be empowered to draw up a blacklist of overspending councils and fix property tax rates for the ensuing year. The leaders of councils on the list would be allowed to subsequently negotiate with the Secretary of State on his funding decision on condition that they allowed the DOE to carry out a detailed examination of their financial books. However, if councillors defied the central government's spending limit they would become personally liable for such overspending and any rate increases levied above the permitted level would be deemed illegal. Secondly, the government announced its intention to introduce a Bill to abolish the metropolitan county council tier of local administration which had been established by the Macmillan and Heath governments in 1963 (in the case of the Greater London Council—GLC), and 1972, redistributing their functions to borough councils below and to a combination of partially elected or appointed QUANGOS and QUELGOS. Such a change, it was believed, would lead to substantial pecuniary administrative savings as well as bringing to an end a tier of government that had recently vaulted on to the political stage a group of vocal, media-orientated opponents of central government policy, Ken Livingstone, the leader of the GLC, David Blunkett, the leader of the Sheffield council, and Derek Hatton, deputy leader of the Liverpool council. All had used their metropolitan power bases to introduce radical interventionist economic and social programmes as well as promote fringe and minority group issues.

Many Conservative MPs strongly supported the government's attempt to exert greater control over such leftist-dominated metropolitan county councils. They were thus, in general, favourably inclined to the 'rate-capping' Bill of 1983–4, since all but one of the 18 blacklisted councils in 1984–5, and the 12 earmarked councils, were, in 1985–6, Labour-controlled. The 'rate-capping' Bill also included, however, a provision for wider 'reserve' powers for the Secretary of State and this was feared by a number of Conservative authorities. 13 Conservative MPs, including the former Prime Minister Edward Heath, who were concerned with the constitutionality of such an intrusion into local affairs, rebelled against the Bill in the Commons on 17 January 1984, a further 20 Conservatives abstaining. The measure passed its Second Reading, however, by 346 votes to 247 and subsequently became law. Fiercer opposition was experienced to the GLC-Metropolitan Counties Abolition (Local Government) Bill during 1984. The Bill's proposal to transfer functions currently undertaken to district bodies and to create new, non-elected 'Joint Boards' to run area-wide services such as fire, police and transport and to undertake strategic planning was acceptable to most Conservatives. However, the government, in its 'Paving Bill', sought, in addition, to abolish local elections for the metropolitan county councils due to be held in May 1985 and to transfer the running of the seven authorities during their final eleven months of existence to 'transitional councils' composed of members drawn on a proportionate basis from local metropolitan district and borough councils. Such an action, which would have transferred the GLC from Labour to Conservative control without any local ballot, was fiercely opposed on constitutional grounds by the Labour and Alliance opposition and by many traditional Conservatives. In the words of Edward Heath, it laid 'the Conservative Party open to the charge of the greatest gerrymandering in the last 150 years of British history'. The government had decided on such an approach in an effort to avoid embarrassing elections in which the abolition question would have emerged as a key issue. It succeeded, despite the revolt of 19 backbenchers led by Edward Heath, in forcing the measure through the Commons, but met sterner opposition on 28 June 1984 when the increasingly assertive House of Lords defeated the proposal at the committee stage. A compromise thus had to be patched up with the Upper House under which the government agreed to allow the metropolitan counties' existing councillors to remain in office until the authorities were finally abolished on 1 April 1986.

The GLC-Metropolitan Councils Bill was subsequently passed by Parliament in 1985 and the authorities abolished in 1986, a London Residuary Board (LRB) being established to run non-earmarked services for Greater London. The legislation had, however, generated fierce and acrimonious debate within both Houses and had proved unpopular outside. In by-elections deliberately engineered by the resignation of the GLC leader, Ken Livingstone, and three colleagues in September 1984, in borough elections during 1985–6, and in local opinion polls, a clear majority opposed to abolition was shown to exist. The government's new 'rate-capping' Act engendered equally fierce opposition. The Conservative-dominated Association of County Councillors and Association of District Councils spoke out against the measures as attacks on local democracy. It was, however, the Militant-controlled Liverpool Metropolitan Council, the 'hard left' Lambeth Borough Council, led by Ted Knight, and the 'New Left' GLC, Manchester and Sheffield Metropolitan Councils, which took the lead. These metropolitan and 'inner city' authorities argued, with considerable justification, that they had been unfairly discriminated against during the years between 1979 and 1985 in the level of grant support provided by the centre during a period when, as a consequence of recession and adverse demographic movements, social spending demands had increased dramatically. However, the overt politicisation and stubborn intransigence of a number of these authorities, which gained the epithet 'Loony Left' from sections of the popular press, proved to be self-defeating and served to dissipate public sympathy. During 1985–6 an attempt was made by leading metropolitan and borough councils to present a 'united front' of deliberate non-compliance with the government's imposed rate ceilings, but the unity gradually crumbled, leaving Liverpool and Lambeth in sole defiance. Their 81 councillors were eventually subjected, in March 1986, to High Court imposed surcharges of £200000, coupled with bans on their holding elective office for refusing to set a legal rate or attempting to balance their budgets. Despite a bumpy ride during 1984–5, the government had thus succeeded in imposing its will on the spending levels of local authorities.

## Thatcher Under Threat

In September 1984, three months after the government's humbling defeat in the Lords on the Metropolitan Councils 'Paving Bill', the Prime Minister was compelled to undertake the second cabinet re-shuffle of her second term as a result of the decision of James Prior, who had become disillusioned with his job in Northern Ireland, to leave and accept the chairmanship of the electrical conglomerate GEC, at a salary of £61 000. Mrs Thatcher replaced Prior with the mellifluent, former Etonian and career diplomat, Douglas Hurd (53): a politician of liberal instincts who had served as political secretary to Edward Heath between 1970–4. The Prime Minister also brought into the cabinet two fervent supporters of her entrepreneurial approach, David Young (52), head of the expanding Manpower Services Commission since 1982, as an unpaid minister without portfolio to be concerned with de-regulation, small businesses and job creation, and the Irish peer and Arts Minister, Lord Gowrie (44), as Chancellor of the Duchy of Lancaster.[1] Young, who was not an MP, was given a life peerage. One month later, on 12 October 1984, the devastating explosion of an IRA bomb at the Grand Hotel in Brighton, at which the cabinet was staying during the Conservative Party annual conference, left Trade and Industry Secretary, Norman Tebbit, and Chief Whip, John Wakeham, temporarily incapacitated, forcing junior ministers to take over their portfolios. Five Conservatives attending the conference, including John Wakeham's wife, lost their lives, and Margaret Tebbit, the wife of Norman, was severely paralysed.

The 'Brighton Factor', combined with the 'Scargill Factor', had a salutory effect on the fortunes of the Conservative Party during the autumn of 1984. In May 1984 the Conservatives had stood neck and neck in the national opinion polls with Labour at 38% and had recorded a net loss of 131 seats in local council elections. They performed more creditably in the June 1984 elections to the European Parliament (see Appendix B Table 35), heading Labour by 4.3%, but experienced a 16% fall in their share of the vote in the concurrent Portsmouth South parliamentary by-election and, as a result, lost a seat which the party had held since 1918 to the SDP city and county councillor Michael Hancock. During October and November 1984, however, as a direct consequence of the 'Brighton Factor', the Conservatives' national poll rating rose to

[1] Lord Gowrie took over the post vacated by Lord Cockfield, who had left to become the new British Commissioner to the EEC.

42% and a lead of 8% was temporarily opened up over the Labour Party in opposition, with the Alliance languishing with a national rating of only 20–22%. The government, more than a year into its second term, thus stood in a far more commanding position than it had enjoyed during 1980–1. This lead proved, however, to be transitory and from the closing month of 1984 the incumbent party found itself trapped in a downward spiral of mounting public antipathy and internal dissent caused by forced policy reversals, 'banana skins' of its own making and, above all, its continuing failure to bring down the still rising level of unemployment.

In December 1984, only days before the Christmas recess, the government experienced a major backbench revolt following an attempt by Education Secretary Sir Keith Joseph to radically restructure the system of funding higher education. A great admirer of the American system of college finance, Joseph sought ultimately to replace the state funding of university students with a system of student loans. In the interim, however, he proposed to make savings in the education budget by sharply increasing the contributions to be made by more affluent parents to the cost of their children's higher education. Within days Conservative constituency MPs from the Home Counties were engulfed in a torrent of mail from concerned parents making plain their opposition to such a move. In response, 93 Conservative back benchers signed a motion of protest and, fearing defeat in the House, Sir Keith was forced to beat a hasty retreat, announcing that the government had decided to reduce considerably the proposed increases. This episode graphically displayed the constraints within which the government was forced to operate, despite its 142 seat majority, when it came to tackling head-on the perks and privileges of its own supporters.

A month later, on 11 January 1985, the government slipped on a particularly embarrassing 'banana skin' of its own contrivance when the jury at the Old Bailey acquitted the former MOD 'high flying' civil servant Clive Ponting of the charge of 'leaking' papers on the 'Belgrano affair' (see page 99), in breach of Section 2 of the Official Secrets Act. Against a firm recommendation by the judge, the jury ruled that Ponting had acted in the state's interest in his passing of information to the Labour MP, Tam Dalyell. This verdict, coupled with the evidence presented during the trial, suggested that the government had not been fully frank in its disclosures on the subject and had been heavy-handed in its decision to prosecute. Later in the same year the clumsy attempt by the Home

Secretary, Leon Brittan, to prevent the BBC from broadcasting a 'Real Lives' documentary on the IRA sympathiser Martin McGuiness re-affirmed these impressions.

Equally damaging to the government was the continuing rise in the level of unemployment, which had breached the 3.2 million mark, and the Treasury's attempts to achieve further spending cuts following five years of belt-tightening. This pressure now forced reductions in the level of 'rate support grant' to the low spending Tory shire counties and encouraged the inauguration of a broad social spending review by the Social Services Secretary Norman Fowler, putting into question the government's continuing support for the state earnings related pension scheme (SERPS). The Minister also spoke of proposals to introduce greater means-tested selectivity in the grant of a number of welfare benefits. Such parsimony and policy rigidity rankled with moderate Tories. A number, including Sir Ian Gilmour, Francis Pym and Edward Heath, were, in consequence, persuaded to join the new all-party 'Employment Institute' which was established in April 1985 to, 'replace the tide of defeatism about unemployment and re-establish the notion that government policy can and does affect unemployment for good or ill'. This body, led by the LSE economist Professor Richard Layard and funded by the Rowntree Memorial Trust, sought to project alternative policy strategies, issuing its own 'Charter for Jobs', and included in its ranks prominent Labour and Liberal-SDP Alliance politicians, trade union officials and Keynesian economists.

A month later, following a disappointing performance in the shire county council elections, with the Conservative vote falling 13% on its 1983 level, Francis Pym established an intra-party pressure-group, called 'Centre Forward', with the support of more than 30 back bench colleagues, including the former ministers Sir Ian Gilmour, Geoffrey Rippon and Mark Carlisle. He launched the body with a strong speech at Oxford in which he criticised Mrs Thatcher's style of 'government by slogan' and called for greater public investment and borrowing to create new jobs. Six members, concerned at such a direct attack on the Prime Minister, rapidly left the grouping. However, the creation of this body, coupled with the concurrent formation of the former employment minister Jim Lester's 120-member Conservative Action for Revival of Employment (CARE), calling for a £2–3 billion education, training and infra-structure orientated reflationary package, was an indication of the rumbling discontent within the party's increasingly rebellious back benchers and at constituency level. Many of the new 'landslide intake' of 1983 began to fear for the retention of their seats in the next general election, a feeling which was strengthened by their party's loss of the Brecon and Radnor rural constituency in Wales to the Liberal Richard Livsey, in July 1985, following a 20% slump in Conservative support. They were also concerned about public and parliamentary outcry following the government's insensitive decision to award pay rises of up to 46% to senior civil servants and judges at a time when it was calling for poorer groups to take salary cuts and was scrapping Wage Councils, which had been established to protect the lowest paid.

Mrs Thatcher took notice of this mounting criticism of the presentation, if not the content, of her government's policy approach and carried out a major cabinet reshuffle in September 1985. The ineffective Peter Rees (58) and John Gummer, and the unpopular Patrick Jenkin were sacked and replaced by the articulate John MacGregor (48: formerly Minister of State for Agriculture) as Chief Secretary to the Treasury, Norman Tebbit, as Party Chairman, and Kenneth Baker (50), as Environment Secretary. Tebbit was a renowned 'dry' and MacGregor, although having headed Edward Heath's private office between 1970–4, a centrist figure with an avid grasp of statistical detail. Kenneth Baker was, by contrast, an interventionist 'Heathite'. An Oxford University educated historian and later successful merchant banker, Baker had served as the former party leader's PPS and campaign manager between 1974–5 before establishing a new reputation as an unusually active and enthusiastic Minister for New Technology, between 1981 and 1984, and as a successful deputy to Patrick Jenkin between 1984 and 1985. Baker was joined at Environment, in September 1985, by the green-tinged, liberal William Waldegrave (38), who was to serve as minister with special responsibility for environmental protection and nuclear safety. In addition, the September 1985 re-shuffle saw Leon Brittan being moved to Trade and Industry, Douglas Hurd promoted to the Home Secretaryship, Tom King relegated to Northern Ireland and Lord Young taking over the Employment portfolio, with the aid, in the Commons, of the new Paymaster-General, Kenneth Clarke (45: formerly Minister of State for Health). Lord Gowrie, pleading penury, left the cabinet to pursue a career outside. These changes represented, first, a desire to improve policy presentation through the promotion of a clutch of skilled and emollient television performers. Second, an increased concern to promote enterprise, small business and employment measures, with Lord Young being promoted into a key co-ordinating role. Third, evidence of a wish to revamp the party's organisation, under the heavyweight leadership of Norman Tebbit, a former Hemel Hempstead constituency colleague of the revered Cecil Parkinson. Mrs Thatcher also took the opportunity to bring in a new head of the Number 10 Policy Unit, the monetarist professor, Brian Griffiths (43), to replace the young merchant banker John Redwood (34) who had chaired the Unit since January 1984. She also inducted the bestselling novelist and former MP, Jeffrey Archer (45), into Central Office as the party's new Deputy Chairman.

These changes were followed by a number of policy concessions. It was announced in December that a scaled down SERPS scheme would be retained and, responding to the mounting calls for greater infra-structural spending, ministers began to talk vigorously about large scale investment plans for railway electrification, water pipelines, new hospitals and a Franco-British Channel tunnel. However, the outbreak of a renewed series of urban riots in Handsworth, Brixton and Tottenham, where a policeman was killed, in September and October 1985; the improved performances of the Labour leader, Neil Kinnock; and the outbreak of what became known as the 'Westland Affair' were to cause serious damage to the government.

## The Gravest Challenge: the 'Westland Affair'

The 'Westland Affair' proved to be the gravest internal crisis experienced by the government during its six years in office. It led to the loss of two key cabinet ministers in the space of a fortnight, the threatened resignation of the government's most senior Law Officers and called into question the integrity of the Prime Minister and her continued leadership of the Conservative Party. The crisis itself centred around two key issues: the administration's industrial strategy and the governing style of the Prime Minister. The immediate problem was the future of a troubled, Yeovil-based, helicopter manufacturing company, Westland, which was slowly slipping towards receivership and needed an injection of funds and secure new markets. The government refused to take a direct stake in the company, preferring a private sector solution. The most likely new partner was the American company Sikorsky, a branch of the United Technologies conglomerate, with whom Westland had worked in the past. Negotiations between the two companies were thus set in train during the summer and autumn months of 1985.

However, the Defence (MOD) Secretary, Michael Heseltine, was a keen supporter of pan-European co-operation and began trying to put together a European consortium in which Westland would participate. He gained initial approval for these efforts, but when, in December 1985, he began to press more definitely for this 'European option' he found himself thwarted by Leon Brittan, the Trade and Industry (DTI) Secretary, and the Prime Minister, who both preferred what they termed an 'even-handed', non-interventionist approach, which by its very nature tilted the balance towards Sikorsky.

Matters came to a head at a three-hour meeting of the cabinet's Economic Strategy Committee on 9 December 1985 which was chaired by Mrs Thatcher and attended by Leon Brittan and Michael Heseltine as well as Sir John Cuckney, Westland's chairman, who strongly favoured the 'Sikorsky option', and Marcus Agius, director of Westland's financial advisers, Lazards. The Prime Minister, siding with Leon Brittan and Sir John Cuckney, concluded that no great defence issue was at stake in the case and that the decision on whether to link up with Sikorsky or the European consortium or whether to accept receivership should be left to the company's board and shareholders. She added, however, that if the American option was chosen she would ensure that the MOD changed its purchase plans so as to provide a market for the new Black Hawk helicopters that Sikorsky planned to assemble at Yeovil. Michael Heseltine firmly opposed this tilting towards what he termed Sikorsky's 'metal-bashing' option. He thus secured, as a result of the support of fellow committee members Kenneth Baker, Kenneth Clarke and John Wakeham, agreement to delay a decision for four days, allowing him further time to put together a more appealing European solution. It was agreed that the cabinet would make a final decision on Friday 13 December at 3pm 'after the Stock Exchange had closed'. Two days later, however, Heseltine was informed by the Cabinet Office that this special cabinet meeting had been cancelled. Enraged by this decision, Heseltine attempted to raise the Westland question when the cabinet met in routine session on 12 December. He was told, however, by the Prime Minister that the subject, not being on the day's agenda, was out-of-order. He was later also to discover that the comments he had made on the issue did not find their way into the published cabinet minutes.

The actions of 9–13 December set the Defence Secretary and the Prime Minister, supported by her Trade and Industry Secretary, on a clear collision course. Despite the Westland board coming out clearly in favour of the Sikorsky offer on 14 December, Heseltine began a high-profile public campaign in favour of the 'European option', gaining support from the backbench Tory Defence Committee and all-party Defence Select Committee. The Prime Minister and Leon Brittan responded by exerting powerful behind-the-scenes pressure to influence the decision in Sikorsky's favour. This included the DTI's deliberate leaking on 6 January 1986 of damaging sections of a private letter written, at the Prime Minister's prompting, by the Solicitor-General, Sir Patrick Mayhew, and its lobbying of Sir Raymond Lygo, chairman of British Aerospace and part of the proposed European consortium, on 8 January, warning him that the stand he was taking would prove to be deeply damaging to the national interest. The breaking point came for the Defence Secretary on 9 January 1986, when at a meeting of a full cabinet the Prime Minister sought his agreement to a prepared brief that in future all ministerial statements on Westland should first be cleared with the Cabinet Office. Heseltine refused to accept such 'gagging' and, gathering his papers, stormed out of the meeting at 11am with the parting words, 'If you are insisting, then I can no longer remain a member of your cabinet'. Over lunch he sat down and prepared a detailed chronology of the events that had led to his eventual resignation which was subsequently read out at a hastily convened press conference. He spoke about his inability to raise the issue in full cabinet, alleging there had been a 'breakdown of constitutional government' and concluded that the Prime Minister's handling of the issue was 'not a proper way to carry on government and ultimately not an approach for which I can share responsibility'.

During the ensuing month, as MPs returned from the Christmas recess, a series of emergency debates was called in Parliament by the opposition parties, encouraged by a stream of new revelations by Michael Heseltine. The government was forced, in addition, to set in train an internal inquiry concerning the leak of the Solicitor General's letter and to accede to the matter being investigated by the Defence and Trade and Industry Select Committees. The greatest criticism during these debates was directed at the activities of the DTI and faced with an erosion of backbench party confidence, Leon Brittan decided to tender his resignation, on 24 January, for his role in the Mayhew and Lygo actions. This left the Prime Minister seriously exposed as she faced the Commons for a key 'make or break' debate on 27 January. Her position was saved, however, by skilful behind the scenes work by chief whip John Wakeham, who arranged for Conservative backbenchers to remorselessly barrack the Labour leader Neil Kinnock during his speech and for the rebel Michael Heseltine to return to the fold and deliver a statement of support. Through such means the Prime Minister survived intact, delivering a forceful speech in defence of her actions and rejecting any charges of wrongdoing. Two weeks later, following hectic and controversial share dealing, a modified Sikorsky bid was approved by the Westland shareholders at a long postponed meeting on 12 February. This brought the critical stage of the 'Westland Affair' to an end. The Defence and Trade and Industry Select Committees continued their work, but their efforts to call key civil servant witnesses were blocked by the Prime Minister's Office. The Defence Select Committee subsequently issued a highly critical report on the Affair during the summer recess, but concentrated its attack on the actions of civil servants, returning an open verdict on the culpability of the Prime Minister. Despite the uncertainty of the official verdict, however, the 'Westland Affair' had proved deeply damaging to the government and Prime Minister, reducing Mrs Thatcher's poll rating to pre-Falklands levels during February and March 1986 and leading to speculation of possible moves for her replacement at the Conservative Party conference in September.

The 'Westland Affair', taking a broader perspective, raised immediate questions about the government's laissez-faire approach to industrial matters and its readiness to allow the transfer of ownership to foreign buyers. It, secondly, provided clear evidence of the personalised manner in which Mrs Thatcher controlled the cabinet, but also paradoxical signs of weakness in her unwillingness to sack Michael Heseltine during the closing months of 1985. It, thirdly, raised queries about the relationship of ministers to their civil servants, with, for example, the DTI's press officer, Colette Bowe, being obliged to act in a deliberately 'political' manner through the selective leaking of the Solicitor-General's correspondence. Fourthly, it provided evidence of the potential investigative value of the new select committees, while at the same time revealing their continued weakness in comparison with their US congressional counterparts. This point was subsequently underlined by the success of the American investigative committees in unearthing wrongdoing at the highest executive levels during the 1986–7 'Iran-Contragate Scandal'. Finally, and more seriously for the government, 'Westland' appeared to mark a decisive and fatal turning point in its political fortunes.

In the midst of the affair Mrs Thatcher was forced to make a further major reshuffle to her cabinet (see Table 20), moving the Scottish Secretary, George Younger (54), to Defence and bringing in the Foreign Office Minister, Malcolm Rifkind (39), in his place and promoting Paul Channon (50) from number two slot to top position as the new Trade and Industry Secretary: all three were liberal, 'one nation' Tories. These changes, coupled with the warnings sent out by 'Westland', increased the influence of the 'wets' within the cabinet and promised to lead to a return to a more collective and co-operative form of cabinet government, with the moderate, 'consolidator' figures of John Biffen and Peter Walker gaining strength.

Outside the cabinet now stood Mrs Thatcher's most dangerous opponent, the flamboyant, 52-year-old, former publishing tycoon, Michael Heseltine: an effective public speaker and television performer, and the darling of the annual party conference. Heseltine might, in some respects, have been thought to have engineered the 'Westland Affair' as an issue of principle on which to resign at a time of continuing economic uncertainty. He would hope to assume the leadership if Mrs Thatcher failed to secure a third term.

## The Consolidators Take Charge: 1986–7

The first two-and-a-half years of the Thatcher second term had seen the Prime Minister, intoxicated by the landslide victory of June 1983, adopting a highly personalised and interventionist leadership style, supported dutifully by a predominantly 'dry' and like-minded cabinet. It had seen the government force through radical new trade union reform and public order Bills, two controversial local government measures and successfully withstand the fiercest and most protracted industrial dispute since 1926. This period had also witnessed the Thatcher administration in frequent conflict with the courts, television media and its own parliamentary back benchers; serious problems of public and industrial disorder; and a sharp polarisation in opinion, with support for the government and Prime Minister slumping to a level of barely 30%, in January 1986. The period of 'unbridled Thatcherism' was brought to an abrupt end by the 'Westland Affair'. Chastened by the events of January-February 1986, at one stage, prior to the 27 January Commons debate, during which she privately conceded that party pressure might have forced her to step down as leader, the Prime Minister adopted a more moderate, consensual and lower profile leadership style during the remaining period of her second term. Greater prominence began now to be given to departmental ministers in a collective fashion, radical and contentious policy proposals being hastily shelved and all efforts being concentrated on attempts to engineer a convincing economic recovery and dent the mounting unemployment total in time for fresh elections in 1987 or 1988.

Evidence of the new collectivist spirit of cabinet decision-taking became immediately apparent in February and April 1987, when, following an opposition outcry and open rebellion by backbench West Midlands MPs to news that the government had been surreptitiously negotiating to sell off Austin-Rover to Ford and Land Rover and Leyland Trucks and Buses to General Motors, the proposals were brought to full cabinet and rapidly abandoned, following warnings by chief whip, John Wakeham, that the measures could not be carried through the House. It was less clear on 15 April 1986 when a small inner grouping of ministers, Thatcher, Howe, Younger and Whitelaw, gave controversial approval to America's use of its F-111 aircraft stationed in Britain to launch air raids on Tripoli. This incident proved, however, to be the exception rather than the rule during 1986–7.

At the heart of the new, collective cabinet team of 1986–7, were the reassuring, centrist, 'communicator figures' of Kenneth Baker, Douglas Hurd and Kenneth Clarke, who now found themselves being pushed to the forefront as the new caring faces of Conservatism, and their departments' spending constraints being steadily relaxed as the government's tryst with the electorate moved closer. In particular, Kenneth Baker, who became Education Secretary (see Table 20) in May 1986, replacing Sir Keith Joseph who had announced his decision to retire from Parliament at the next election, emerged as the dominant and ever-visible public figure during the final year of the Thatcher government's second term. Inheriting an educational service that had been debilitated by more than a year of strike action and 'work-to-rules' over pay conditions and the introduction of the new GCSE examination, Baker secured a significant increase in his department's budget for 1986–7, waged a series of fierce attacks on alleged political indoctrination by a number of Labour controlled London 'inner city' councils and announced new schemes for 20 state and business funded City Technology Colleges (the Technical and Vocational Education Initiative: TVEI) and measures for improved educational standards and parental control. Baker's actions failed to bring an end to the enduring teachers' pay dispute. They did succeed, however, in pushing both the issues of education and the activities of 'far left' Labour councils to the centre of the political stage. At the Social Services Department the

**Table 20    The Thatcher Cabinet of May 1986**

| | |
|---|---|
| Prime Minister | —Margaret Thatcher |
| Chancellor of the Exchequer | —Nigel Lawson* |
| Foreign Secretary | —Sir Geoffrey Howe† |
| Home Secretary | —Douglas Hurd‡ |
| Trade & Industry Secretary | —Paul Channon‡ |
| Defence Secretary | —George Younger‡ |
| Welsh Secretary | —Nicholas Edwards† |
| Agriculture Secretary | —Michael Jopling† |
| Chief Secretary to the Treasury | —John MacGregor† |
| Social Services Secretary | —Norman Fowler† |
| Education Secretary | —Kenneth Baker‡ |
| Employment Secretary | —Lord Young* |
| N. Ireland Secretary | —Tom King‡ |
| Scottish Secretary | —Malcolm Rifkind† |
| Energy Secretary | —Peter Walker‡ |
| Environment Secretary | —Nicholas Ridley* |
| Lord Chancellor | —Lord Hailsham† |
| Leader of Lords | —Viscount Whitelaw‡ |
| Commons Leader | —John Biffen† |
| Transport Secretary | —John Moore* |
| Paymaster-General | —Kenneth Clarke‡ |
| Chancellor Duchy of Lancaster | —Norman Tebbit* |

*Thatcherite 'Dries'    †Cautious 'Dries'    ‡'Consolidators'

less telegenic figure of Norman Fowler, began to shelve longstanding plans for the restructuring of the benefits system and to concentrate, with Social Security Minister Tony Newton and Health Minister Barney Hayhoe, on stressing the spending achievements of the administration: accelerating the government's hospital construction programme; assuaging the pay claims of the nursing profession; launching a major publicity drive against the killer disease AIDS; and establishing a national breast cancer screening service. At Environment, where Nicholas Ridley replaced Kenneth Baker in May 1986, the proposed, but controversial, scheme to privatise the Regional Water Authorities, which seemed likely to meet fierce and protracted opposition from environmentalist groups and Conservative peers, was hastily shelved in July 1986. The Department began, instead, to launch new public spending drives on infra-structure and housing and eased the 'rate support grant' purse strings on the shire counties, in an effort to avoid unseemly pre-election central-local government disputes. Similarly, at the Defence and Trade and Industry Departments controversial proposals to sell off the Royal Ordnance Factory and the already noted Austin Rover/Leyland were quickly removed from the agenda, while backbench and external pressure forced the acceptance of a management buy-out of the Swan Hunter Tyneside shipbuilding firm instead of a private sector takeover sale.

Despite the importance of such presentational changes and the gradual relaxation of tight-spending discipline, so as to soften and improve the government's public image, the deciding factor in whether the government would be able to recover from its trough of unpopularity during January-February 1986 and regain sufficient support to achieve re-election in 1987 or 1988 promised to be its record on the economy and its ability to reverse the upward trend of unemployment. The Thatcher administration had been fortunate since its re-election in June 1983 to find itself holding power during a period of steadily expanding world trade, free from the oil shocks which had afflicted the Heath and Wilson governments in 1973–4, and itself during 1979–80. Each year since 1983 had witnessed a measure of industrial growth (see Table 32), although the performances of 1984 and 1985 had been alternately depressed and inflated by the miners' strike of 1984–5, a gradual fall in the inflation rate to a figure well below 5% and a marked improvement in real incomes for those in work. The one damning statistic that remained, however, was high and rising unemployment, which stood at a level of 3.3 million in April 1986. Top priority was thus now given in seeking ways of reducing this total to below what was seen as the politically decisive three million mark before the calling of the next election.

The central role in this unemployment reduction programme was given to one of Mrs Thatcher's most valued and trusted colleagues, Lord Young, who assumed the unofficial title of 'Jobs and Enterprise Minister'. A bullish and fervent believer in the competitive, self-help, free-enterprise system, Lord Young had already played an active part in establishing the Enterprise Allowance Scheme (EAS) for small businesses, a clutch of low tax, inner city development corporations on the 1981 East London's Docklands and Merseyside model, as well as a burgeoning number of Youth Training Schemes for 16–18 year olds. His efforts were now geared towards fostering a closer involvement of private industry in state training and education and in encouraging the small-firm, self-employed, service and tourism sectors, which he viewed as the future areas of principal job creation. In addition, in a more immediate effort to make a dent in the unemployment total, he now sanctioned the creation of 'New Workers' and 'Job Training' schemes to subsidise the employment of 18–25 year olds, a 'Jobstart' programme for the long term unemployed and a large-scale expansion of the number of places on the EAS and Community Programme. These efforts began to meet with mounting success during 1986 and 1987, although many of the new jobs created were part-time and lowly paid. Such positive and innovative reforms were buttressed by a series of less laudable 're-adjustments' to the basis on which the published unemployment totals were calculated, as well as by improving demographic trends, as the last of the 1960s 'baby bulge' generation reached working age. This combination of factors was to lead to the eventual checking of the remorseless upward movement in the seasonally adjusted unemployment total in August 1986 and to a slow downward trend which began to bring the jobless figure back towards the three million mark by the summer of 1987.

The funding of these new infrastuctural, welfare and job creation initiatives was made possible by continued buoyancy in external economic conditions during 1986–7, as a result of the boost to world commerce that was given by the sudden reduction in world oil prices during the opening months of 1986. Initially, this oil price slump perturbed the Treasury, which feared the fiscal consequences of the sharp contraction in its North Sea oil tax revenues. In practice, however, the price fall served, as a result of the concurrent fall in the sterling exchange rate, to give a counterbalancing boost to manufacturing exports. The most striking, and more important, feature of Treasury policy during 1986–7 was to be, however, its new-found fiscal pragmatism and the rapid expansion that was to take place in the privatisation programme as a means of providing the resources to fund an unprecedented period of public spending and tax-cutting munificence. First, 1986–7 saw the Chancellor's final abandonment of 'traditional monetarism' as his previously slavish adherence to the monetary indicators M3 and M0 (notes and coins) was now dropped and attention became concentrated, instead, on the more general goal of keeping in check public spending as a proportion of GNP. Second, and more importantly, the privatisation programme, which had been pursued in a steady but restricted fashion between

1979–84 (see Table 33), and had concentrated upon sales to institutional investors rather than the general public, was suddenly accelerated between 1985–7 and emerged as the centrepiece of the government's legislative and reform programme. The key event was the staggeringly successful privatisation of half the equity of the huge British Telecom utility in November 1984 for £1.5 billion, during which special efforts were made to attract the smaller shareholder. This sale, preceded by enormous television and newspaper advertising extolling the virtues of wider share-ownership and 'popular capitalism', opened the door to subsequent flotations of the Trustee Savings Bank (September 1986 for £1.5 billion, although the government itself received no funds from this sale); British Gas (December 1986 for £5.6 billion); British Airways (January 1987 for £0.9 billion); Rolls-Royce (May 1987 for £1.4 billion) and British Airport Authority (July 1987 for £1.25 billion). These sales, which brought substantial immediate 'windfall' premiums to purchasers, were viewed as valuable in creating a new populist basis of support for the government. More importantly, in the short term, they brought into the Treasury receipts totalling almost £5 billion per annum during 1986 and 1987. The funds raised, as with those derived from council house sales, were counted by the Treasury as 'negative public borrowing'. This enabled the government to meet, on paper, the annual public spending targets established under the MTFS, while, in reality, being able to fund a level of spending that was considerably higher. By such means, and through a judicious contraction in the size of the Treasury's 'contingency reserve fund', the Chancellor was able to announce reductions in the basic level of income tax by 1p and 2p in pound in March 1986 and March 1987 respectively, bringing down the standard rate to 27p, while, at the same time, announcing a £5 billion increase in public spending programmes in the expenditure White Paper of November 1986.

By the autumn of 1986 Chancellor Lawson and Employment Secretary Young, through a mixture of good fortune and bold design, had succeeded in engineering an appealing combination of steadily declining unemployment rolls, burgeoning public spending, inflation at an 18-year low, of less than 3%, falling mortgage and interest rates and rapidly rising real incomes for those employed. This elixir of economic success was to provide the basis for a dramatic recovery in support for the Conservatives in national opinion polls. During the spring and summer of 1986, however, the standing of the government and its leader still remained at abnormally low levels (see Table 21). On 10 April 1986 the party's vote slumped by 11% on its 1983 level in the Fulham parliamentary by-election, with the seat being captured by Labour's Nick Raynsford. Less than a week later, on 15 April, the government faced sharp public criticism for acquiescing in the US raid on Libya and was humiliatingly defeated in the Commons by a backbench revolt of 72 MPs over its deregulatory proposals to legalise Sunday trading. The lowest point for the government and Prime Minister during the second term was to come, however, on 8 May 1986. In two parliamentary by-elections held in safe northern Conservative seats at Ryedale (Yorkshire) and West Derbyshire, each boasting 1983 majorities of almost 16000, the party's vote slumped by between 16–18%, with Ryedale being lost to the Liberal, Elizabeth Shields, and West Derbyshire only being held by a mere 100 votes. In the concurrent local elections, held in England, Scotland and Wales, the Conservatives, defending seats captured four years earlier in the middle of the Falklands War, lost more than a third of their 2 300 sitting councillors and were left in control of only one of England's 36 metropolitan districts. These represented the worst combination of results experienced by the party under Mrs Thatcher's prime ministership and were to be immediately followed by national opinion polls which showed the Tories, at 28%, trailing Labour by eleven points and the opposition leader, Neil Kinnock, enjoying a rare three-point (27%: 24%) lead over the Prime Minister as the most popular national figure.

Table 21   Party National Opinion Poll Support, 1983–7 (Average % By Quarters)

| Party | 1983 | | 1984 | | | | 1985 | | | | 1986 | | | | 1987 |
|---|---|---|---|---|---|---|---|---|---|---|---|---|---|---|---|
| | III | IV | I | II | III | IV | I | II | III | IV | I | II | III | IV | I |
| Conservative | 43 | 41 | 40 | 38 | 39 | 39 | 37 | 34 | 31 | 33 | 31 | 32 | 34 | 39 | 39 |
| Labour | 32 | 37 | 38 | 37 | 34 | 36 | 36 | 36 | 35 | 35 | 37 | 39 | 38 | 37 | 32 |
| Alliance | 23 | 19 | 20 | 23 | 24 | 23 | 25 | 28 | 32 | 30 | 29 | 26 | 25 | 21 | 28 |

The local government and by-election defeats of May 1986 stimulated renewed infighting between the 'wet' and 'dry' wings of the Conservative Party and cabinet. Criticism was particularly directed at the abrasive campaigning style of Party Chairman, Norman Tebbit, who endured veiled criticism from the Leader of the Commons, John Biffen, stressing the importance of the party entering the next election with a 'balanced' leadership ticket. Tebbit also underwent a temporary rift with Mrs Thatcher over marketing and advertising strategies. The Prime Minister attempted to counteract this 'crisis of confidence' in the government by calling on her colleagues for a 'redoubling of effort' but for continued adherence to the established course. In reality, however, the events of April-May 1986, and the resulting backbench and constituency party pressures, were to give further impetus to the gradual shift in policy course and softening in presentational style that had been evident since the autumn of 1985. As 'spending round' negotiations for the 1987 budgetary year began, a semi-public battle developed between the 'consolidator' figures of Hurd, Baker, Walker, Younger, Fowler, Clarke, Biffen and King and those on the 'radical right', Lawson, Tebbit, Young and Moore, over whether to assign any 'free resources' to greater public and welfare spending or whether to maintain tight spending controls in order to achieve, instead, the government's long vaunted goal of reducing the basic rate of income tax to 25p. Majority opinion within the party at parliamentary and constituency level favoured the former course. In the end, however, a compromise was agreed, as the government published its Public Expenditure White Paper in November 1986. A 'balanced budget' strategy was chosen, in which substantial new funds were released for selective increased spending in the health, education, housing and local government spheres, while the defence budget was pruned and the privatisation programme accelerated so as to provide the basis for an eye-catching 2p income tax reduction in the budget of March 1987.

During July and August 1986 the national standing of the government and Prime Minister remained low, the Conservatives trailing Labour in opinion polls on 31 July by 9%. The intransigent refusal of the Prime Minister to join the remainder of the Commonwealth's leaders in imposing selective economic and diplomatic sanctions against South Africa, where a 'State of Emergency' had been imposed, at the 3 August Commonwealth Summit, failed to improve this position and served to create an embarrassing potential constitutional rift with the Royal Family. A month later, however, the corner was turned for the government and the Prime Minister and the Conservative Party began a steady ascent up the opinion polls from a figure of 31% in July (vis-a-vis 38% Labour and 28% Alliance) to one, at the head of the pack, of 39% in November (vis-a-vis Labour 36%, Alliance 23%). This recovery in fortunes, which was to continue during the opening months of 1987, resulted from three sets of factors: the progressive improvement in economic indicators, including that for unemployment; divisions and disarray in the ranks of the opposition parties; and the Conservatives' adoption of a skilled and carefully orchestrated campaign of policy presentation.

The economic performance of the British economy during 1986-7, as Table 22 shows, was unpredictable, industrial output fluctuating markedly from quarter to quarter. Its key features were a sharp decline in the inflation rate during the first three quarters of 1986, a marked increase in real disposable incomes as a result of above-average wage increases, and, most significant of all, a steady fall in the proportion of the workforce unemployed from the autumn of 1986. It remained a moot point whether the 15–20000 monthly decline in the unemployment total between August 1986 and May 1987 represented a real fall or was the result of transfers to the government's expanded special employment programmes. In political terms, however, the reverse in trend gave a significant boost to the Conservative Party and Prime Minister.

Table 22    1986–7 UK Economic Indicators (Average % by Quarters)

| | 1986 | | | | | 1987 | |
| | I | II | III | IV | All Year | I | II |
|---|---|---|---|---|---|---|---|
| NP/GDP | +2.2 | +1.4 | +0.7 | +2.8 | +2.0 | +2.8 | +3.6 |
| Industrial Production | +0.6 | +5.4 | −5.5 | +6.9 | +1.4 | −2.9 | +5.5 |
| Retail Sales | +4.4 | +7.0 | +10.0 | +7.4 | +7.2 | −0.5 | +4.7 |
| Consumer Prices | +2.7 | +3.9 | +1.2 | +4.0 | +3.5 | +5.4 | +5.3 |
| Wages/Earnings | +7.4 | +11.6 | +3.7 | +6.9 | +7.5 | +8.9 | +7.8 |
| Unemployment Rate[1] | 13.2 | 13.3 | 13.3 | 13.0 | 13.2 | 12.8 | 12.6 |
| Exchange Rate ($ per £) | 1.47 | 1.49 | 1.43 | 1.47 | 1.47 | 1.61 | 1.66 |
| Interest Rates | 12.5 | 11.0 | 11.0 | 12.0 | 11.6 | 11.0 | 10.0 |

Figures from 3rd quarter of 1986 have been adjusted to same % basis as those from first two quarters.

The second boost to the Conservatives' standing was delivered during the September-October 1986 party conference season by the opening of serious divisions within the Liberal-SDP Alliance, whose popularity had begun to menace Conservative marginal seats in southern England. On 23 September 1986, at the Liberal Party's annual assembly at Eastbourne, following CND activist pressure, a resolution was narrowly passed which came out controversially in favour of fighting the forthcoming election with a non-nuclear defence strategy. This policy was in sharp contradiction to that earlier agreed by the SDP-Liberal leadership, which had favoured replacing the current, ageing Polaris nuclear missile system with a minimum nuclear deterrent based upon an

Anglo-French alternative. The decision enraged SDP leader David Owen, whose conference had passed a pro-nuclear motion a week earlier. The two parties were forced to resume negotiations once more on a compromise package. The resulting policy confusion and temporary rift contributed to a sharp decline in Alliance support from its July-August level of 28% to a low of barely 20% in December 1986, with a number of waverers returning to the Conservative fold. A week later at Blackpool the Labour Party staged an unusually professional and united annual conference. With leadership backing, however, the delegates voted in favour of the removal of all nuclear weapons, British and American, from British soil, thus pushing defence towards the top of the political agenda.

The Conservatives responded with alacrity to the new opening afforded by the events of September 1986 and utilised their own conference at Bournemouth to launch ferocious attacks on the Labour and Liberals' 'defeatist' defence strategies. The opportunity was also taken to skilfully unveil a series of eye-catching ministerial policy initiatives designed to give the government a new positive, forward-looking image. The conference was orchestrated by director of communications, Harvey Thomas, and was to be followed by a concerted 'news management' drive directed at securing extensive television coverage of the opening of new hospitals, roads and infra-structural programmes and the shielding of government ministers from unexpected hostile receptions. All this accompanied a flurry of new 'Green Papers' proposing future radical de-regulatory reforms in the spheres of rent control, education, local services and the airwaves. This slick and positive presentational campaign was buttressed by a twin-pronged attack on the activities of radical left wing Labour councils by Education Secretary Kenneth Baker and Home Secretary Douglas Hurd. This was to reap unexpected dividends in February 1987 when the Labour Party endorsed the selection of one such radical councillor, Deirdre Wood, to contest the Greenwich by-election. Following a protracted, vitriolic and unprecedentedly expensive campaign, when polling day arrived, 26 February, Labour lost a seat which it had previously won from the Conservatives by a majority of 1,200. The unexpected victor was SDP-Liberal Alliance's Rosie Barnes, the Labour vote falling by 4.5%, the Conservatives' by 23.6% and the Alliance's rising by 28%.

The result in Greenwich was, on the surface, a disaster for the Conservatives, its vote falling by the largest margin ever recorded in any parliamentary by-election. In reality, however, it proved to be the springboard for the party's dominant advance in national polls during the ensuing months, as, with Labour's support slumping and the Alliance's sharply rising, the opposition vote became almost evenly divided at 30% apiece. Meanwhile, the government was exposed to a series of damaging external scandals—the MI5 case in Australia, the 'Zircon' raid on the BBC's offices in Glasgow and the Guinness sharedealing revelations—but succeeded in establishing a lead of six points in national opinion polls during February and March 1987. An additional three points were added to this lead during April, as a result of the favourable reception given to Chancellor Lawson's 17 March tax-cutting budget and Margaret Thatcher's well-publicised and hugely successful March-April visit to the Soviet Union. With Alliance support beginning to slip from its post-Greenwich high and Labour's position improving during April 1987, pressure began to mount for the Prime Minister to call an early election during May or early June 1987, to take advantage of the continuing split in the opposition vote. Mrs Thatcher appeared uncertain whether or not to delay until the autumn, but, following a strong party showing in the local elections on 7 May 1987, when it gained 75 seats, finally gave the green light to Party Chairman Norman Tebbit, calling on the Queen on 11 May to request a dissolution of Parliament, polling day being set for Thursday 11 June. For a Prime Minister and governing party that barely a year earlier had stood at the nadir of their fortunes, the months between May 1986 and May 1987 and, in particular, the period since August 1986 had seen a remarkable transformation in relative fortunes. They were an indication of the heightened volatility of the modern 'de-aligned' electorate and the complexity engendered by the new three-party system.

## The Opposition Parties: 1983–7

### The Labour Party: Reconstruction Under the Centre-left 'Dream Ticket'

The scale of the Labour's June 1983 defeat had led to serious speculation about the Party's possible terminal decline into a marginalised rump status, similar to that endured by the French Communist Party, with the SDP-Liberal Alliance emerging as the new dominant force on the re-aligned left-of-centre of British politics. Such a development was, however, averted between

1983–7 as a result of a series of determined organisational and policy changes that were accomplished by the Labour Party's new post-1983 leadership team and the uncertainty and drift that was exhibited within the Alliance camp.

The election of the young and inexperienced Neil Kinnock as Labour leader in October 1983 had been viewed by outside observers as a desperate and dangerous gamble by a party seeking to project a more modern and vigorous image, after more than a decade of dominance by the stale and elderly figures of Wilson, Callaghan and Foot. In retrospect, however, Kinnock's selection proved an inspired choice, the new leader emerging as one of the few figures capable of maintaining unity and balance between the party's left and right wings as well as being willing to undertake a major restructuring of its organisational machinery and a subtle reformulation of its policy stance, in an effort to broaden its electoral appeal.

Neil Gordon Kinnock (1942– ) came from a solid Bevanite, South Wales working class background, his father having been a miner and his mother a district nurse who had lived in a council 'prefab' in Tredegar. Benefiting from the expansion of educational opportunity during the early 1960s, he had attended University College, Cardiff, where he gained a degree and teaching diploma in history/industrial relations and served as president of the students' union, before being elected MP for Bedwellty in 1970. In Parliament Kinnock established a reputation during the 1970s as a fervent opponent of EEC membership, devolution for Wales and many of the conservative policy initiatives of the Wilson-Callaghan administration between 1974–9. This, coupled with his, and his wife Glenys', membership of CND and the CLPD, gave him impeccable left-wing credentials which were to prove of inestimable value in the leadership contest of October 1983 and in subsequent intra-party wrangles. Kinnock, although on the left, had always, however, aligned himself with the Tribunite 'soft left' majority grouping, retaining a scarcely concealed scorn for the activities of the middle class Bennite 'hard left' 'polytariat'. He rose to prominence through the oratorical skills he displayed at party conferences and during frequent CLP lecture tours and as a result of the close links he developed with his ascendant Bevanite patron, Michael Foot. During 1974 he worked as PPS to Foot at the Department of Employment and later as education spokesman in the 1979–83 shadow cabinet. Given this new responsibility, Kinnock began to drop his firebrand image and moderate his policy stance in a progressive and pragmatic manner, pointedly refusing to support the left's candidate, Tony Benn, in the 1981 deputy leadership contest against Denis Healey.

His election as Labour leader in October 1983, by the overwhelming margin of 71%:29% in the new 'electoral college', left him in a powerful position to impose his will on the direction to be taken by the party during the next four years. Under his leadership it embarked on a new, solidly centre-left, policy course and sanctioned radical organisational reforms. His efforts in these directions were helped by the swing towards moderation among trade union leaders, which had given the centre and 'soft left' a clear majority on the NEC since October 1982. In addition, the scale of Labour's 1983 defeat, in an election fought on a radical left-wing manifesto, had placed the 'hard left' on the defensive and shaken the rest of the party into action, making it receptive to new reform panaceas.

June 1983 had shown Labour to be out of touch with the increasingly important 'new middle and working classes': the upwardly mobile skilled and white collar workers, who had different aspirations from older manual workers, wanting to own their own homes and disliking nationalisation and militant unionism. The party would need to take heed of such attitudes if it was to break out of its 30% urban, blue-collar ghetto. Labour thus began a gradual re-appraisal and reformulation of its policy programme. It came to accept the popular desire for council house sales and continued membership of the EEC, and to reject the traditionalist call for blanket re-nationalisation and a crude repeal of Conservative trade union legislation, developing, instead, a more subtle and sophisticated approach. This involved support for a positive 'bill of rights' ('Workers' Charter') for trade unions, retaining the use of ballots, and, learning from Labour councils' local enterprise boards, the establishment of a decentralised partnership between private industry and the state, and the formulation of a new concept of 'social' rather than 'public' ownership.

The new party programme that was gradually evolved between 1984–7 placed priority upon reviving manufacturing industry through the establishment of a National Investment Bank (NIB) on the Japanese model; this would draw upon pension funds and exported capital, through a combination of tax incentives and interest guarantees and lend long term to companies at subsidised rates. The programme also called for greater state infrastructural and housing investment; improved technical training; and the holding of annual tripartite National Economic Summits between unions, employers and the government. This recalled Wilson's abortive 'white hot technological revolution' of the 1960s, but also borrowed significantly from the successful West German 'concerted action' system. The party, in addition, became more positive and confident in its approaches to law and order, where it advocated community policing and a 'safe estates' crime prevention programme, and defence, in which it united around support for a strong conventional-based policy and continued membership of NATO.

The overhaul of the party's organisational structure was even more radical. Larry Whitty (1944– ), a Cambridge University educated, former career civil servant and research officer with the General Municipal Boilermakers and Allied Trades Union (GMBATU), replaced the ineffectual Jim Mortimer as general secretary in June 1985 and proceeded to reduce the ten existing departments at Walworth Road to three 'directorates': administration, headed by Joyce Gould, publicity, Peter Mandelson, and research, Geoff Bish, shifting the emphasis away from policy formulation to campaigning. Robin Cook, Neil Kinnock's campaign manager in 1983, was placed in charge of this and worked with the former 'Weekend World' producer, Peter Mandelson (1953– ) and the former director of Friends of the Earth, Stephen Billcliffe, who became marketing manager. They set about targeting marginal seats and likely voting categories for support, and improved the flow of information sent to local branches and the party's use of television. A yellow bus was purchased for a new 'perpetual campaign'; sitting MPs began liaising in marginal constituencies; and training courses were arranged for prospective parliamentary candidates. A series of 'theme campaigns' was formulated; a pop-orientated 'Red Wedge' youth drive launched to win over the four million new first-time voters; and direct mail fund-raising was initiated.

The new Kinnock leadership team succeeded, in addition, in re-establishing party unity around its evolving centre-left policy programme. This was achieved by, first, deliberately marginalising the 'hard left' leaders Tony Benn, who, though re-entering Parliament after the Chesterfield by-election of March 1984, failed to gain election to the shadow cabinet, Arthur Scargill and Derek Hatton. Kinnock bitterly denounced the last two figures for their use of violence and their willingness to play 'politics with people's jobs' in a controversial, but effective, speech at the party's October 1985 Bournemouth conference. At the same time, continuing the programme instituted by Michael Foot in 1982, he orchestrated a campaign directed at the expulsion of leading members of 'Militant Tendency'. The campaign culminated in the NEC's withdrawal of party membership from eight Liverpool 'Militants', including Derek Hatton and Tony Mulhearn, during May–June 1986. Second, and in contrast, leaders of what could be termed the 'radical, but realistic, left', such as the community socialist, David Blunkett (1947– ) of Sheffield and the former Bennite, Michael Meacher, were warmly embraced and given important positions in the Kinnock team. This meant that the new unity achieved came to be based around a policy programme that remained radical in its adherence, for example, to unilateralism, 'social ownership' and decentralised planning, but which was presented by an attractive, and predominantly centre-right, shadow cabinet comprising the experienced Kissinger-like figure of Denis Healey (1917–: foreign affairs) as well as the 'new generation' figures of Roy Hattersley (1932–: the economy), John Smith (1938–: industry), Gerald Kaufman (1930–: home affairs) and John Cunningham (1939–: local government and the environment). The removal of policy formulation authority from the sole hands of NEC sub-committees to new 'joint policy committees', comprising both NEC and shadow cabinet members, further buttressed this movement to centre-left consensus.

Labour enjoyed an initial 'honeymoon' boost to its popularity during the autumn of 1983 and spring of 1984, following the appointment of Neil Kinnock as leader, its national opinion poll rating immediately rising ten points above its June 1983 level to a figure of 37–38%. The eruption of the miners' strike served, however, to halt further progress and the party also had to endure during 1984–5 the worry of re-selection contests and of trade union balloting on the political fund. It also had to come to terms with problems created by the breakaway UDM mineworkers in key East Midlands' constituencies. These storms were, however, successfully weathered. Only a handful of sitting MPs were forced to retire early; trade union members voted almost unanimously to maintain their political fund, with two extra unions even deciding to affiliate; and the party tactfully chose not to immediately expel UDM members and exacerbate pit village tensions. By the summer of 1985 Labour had thus succeeded in re-establishing itself as a credible opposition and alternative party of government. It headed national opinion polls with a level of support ranging from 35–37%, performed creditably in by-elections and in the May 1985 local elections recaptured Birmingham and gained control, for the first time ever, of Edinburgh. In addition, its leader, Neil Kinnock, though inexperienced, had emerged, through the skilful use of the television medium, as an engagingly popular figure and had succeeded in consolidating his dominance of the party, by the slow transfer of policy-making authority away from the bureaucratic NEC towards an 'inner circle' which incorporated his press secretary, Patricia Hewitt, economics adviser, Henry Neuberger, PPS, Kevin Barron and office director, Charles Clarke, as well as his parliamentary colleagues Cook, Healey, Hattersley, Smith and Cunningham. Indeed, Kinnock's ability to control the outcome of NEC and shadow cabinet debates and to secure the appointment of likeminded supporters to key posts, for example Derek Foster to the position of chief whip in November 1985, exhibited a hold over the party machine unprecedented since the Attlee era.

During the autumn of 1985 and spring of 1986 Labour achieved a further significant advance in national opinion polls, building up a 3–7 point lead over the Conservatives as it benefited from the favourable public reaction to Kinnock's combative Bournemouth conference speech and from the damage inflicted on the Prime Minister by the 'Westland Affair'. Heartened by these improved ratings, the party's organisational team began to move its publicity operations into top gear and add the finishing touches to its policy programme, in readiness for its hoped-for assumption of power. It launched three major policy campaigns: 'Freedom and Fairness', 'Jobs and Industry' and 'Investing in People'—in a glossy new media-style manner during 1986, with the aim of stressing the party's desire to combine its traditional concern for social justice and welfare provision with increased individual freedom and choice in a more modern 'enabling state' fashion. In addition, an attractive new party emblem, the Red Rose, set against a neutral, technocratic steel grey background was adopted to replace its outmoded, Soviet-style Red Flag. The October 1986 party conference at Blackpool was selected as a launching pad for an intensified period of pre-election campaigning. The conference was carefully stage-managed with the broader outside television audience in mind and characterised by studied displays of moderation and unity. Its centrepoint was Neil Kinnock's strong condemnation of the pernicious social consequences of 'Thatcherism' and his emotional appeal for the rallying to the party's banner of the country's 'moral majority, which doesn't expect politicians to deliver heaven on earth, but does expect politicians to work to prevent hell on earth.' The speech was designed to be followed by a rolling series of policy publicising 'Red Rose Rallies' and a clutch of presidentialist overseas visits by Neil Kinnock and Denis Healey under the skilled orchestration of the party's new campaign co-ordinator, Bryan Gould (1939– ) which were to peak in the summer of 1987 in readiness for a likely autumn general election.

Unfortunately for party strategists, however, Labour's post-1983 revival began to stall from October 1986. In retrospect, the party's fortunes peaked during April-May 1986, with Nick Raynsford's heartening by-election victory in Fulham, on 10 April, and the sweeping metropolitan district council gains in the 8 May local elections. During the autumn of 1986 Labour underwent a serious downward slide in national support that was to continue, in an accelerated manner, into the spring of 1987. Four factors explained this sudden reversal of fortunes. First, the widespread and adverse publicity given in the national press to the controversial anti-racist and anti-sexist activities of a number of Labour local 'inner city' councils, and the difficulties experienced in expelling the Liverpool 'Militants' between February and June 1986. Second, the close and critical scrutiny that was to be given to the party's proposed economic and defence policies as the election drew nearer. In particular, Labour's determinedly non-nuclear defence strategy, despite its stress on its commitment to increased conventional spending, met with increasingly fierce and wounding attacks from Conservative ministers from October 1986 as well as unprecedentedly open criticism from the US Reagan administration. Third, the leadership abilities of the inexperienced Neil Kinnock began to be questioned following the humiliating failures of his visits to Washington in November 1986 and March 1987. This led to the launching of a concerted anti-Kinnock campaign by Conservative Central Office in February 1987. Fourth, and most seriously, grave damage was inflicted upon Labour's poll standing and electoral credibility as a result of the re-emergence of the issue of its internal left-right divisions following events in Knowsley and Greenwich in November 1986 and February 1987.

In Knowsley-North the party's 'soft left' MP, Robert Kilroy-Silk, resigned in October 1986 to pursue a new career in television. Kilroy-Silk, formerly a rising figure within the PLP, left complaining of mounting harassment by his 'Militant' dominated CLP, who proceeded to select the radical left-winger Les Huckfield as his replacement to fight the ensuing by-election. Neil Kinnock moved swiftly and achieved NEC backing for a rejection of Huckfield's nomination, on the pretext that when selected as a Euro-MP candidate he had promised not to stand for Westminister before the next election, and the imposition of a 'centre left' local councillor,

George Howarth. The local party unsuccessfully challenged the NEC's decision in court, giving further adverse publicity to the issue. The subsequent by-election, on 13 November 1986, saw the sharpest decline, −8.2%, in Labour's vote endured since June 1983, although this stronghold seat was retained with a majority reduced from 17 191 (over the Conservatives) to 6 724 (over the Alliance).

In Greenwich, a by-election was occasioned by the death of the Labour MP Guy Barnett who had represented the constituency since 1971. The seat had been Labour since the war, but, as a result of 'gentrification', the party's majority over the Conservatives had been reduced to only 1,211 in June 1983. Ground had been made up in the similar constitiutency of Fulham in April 1986, by the adoption of an engaging centre-left candidate. In Greenwich, however, the local CLP selected as its prospective MP, Deirdre Wood, who, as a local councillor, had been on record as a supporter of many of the 'far left' policies that were under ridicule in the popular press. Labour's NEC gave firm, if reluctant, backing to Wood's candidature and attempted to steer her on to a more centrist policy course during the ensuing campaign. She was to endure, however, such fierce and scurrilous vilification by tabloid journalists that a bandwagon began to be successfully built up behind the SDP-Liberal Alliance's candidate, Rosie Barnes. When polling day arrived, on 26 February 1987, the Alliance achieved, as a result of a last-minute tactical transfer of Conservative support, a stunning victory, with a majority of 6 611. This result was to have momentous repercussions for the outcome and timing of the ensuing general election.

The divisions and adverse publicity engendered by Knowsley North and Greenwich effectively frustrated Labour's chances of building up its national support rating to the critical majority breakthrough level of 38–40%. It fell more than six points to 30% and all serious talk of victory in 1987 or 1988 receded. Instead, the party had to redirect its efforts to prevent a disastrous and possibly fatal slide to third party status behind the resurgent Alliance.

## The Alliance: A Force on the Centre-right or Centre-left?

In the immediate wake of the June 1983 election day-to-day control of the Liberal Party was assumed by chief whip, later deputy leader, Alan Beith. The deflated David Steel returned to his Borders home for a summer sabbatical to recharge his batteries, after suffering from a debilitating virus infection, and to rethink party strategy for the years ahead. Steel's absence from Westminister and the low media profile he was to deliberately adopt during the ensuing two years enabled the new SDP leader, Dr David Owen, to emerge as the dominant Alliance parliamentary spokesman. In addition, Owen began to mould the Alliance's policy outlook and electoral strategy in a significant manner.

While remaining committed to the need for a close electoral alliance with the Liberals, Dr Owen made it plain at the outset that he saw the two parties as distinct entities, emanating from differing philosophical traditions. He thus ruled out any question of immediate or pre-election merger. Instead, he concentrated during 1983–4 on a slow, but steady, transmutation of his own party's policy stance in a manner geared towards maximising its potential support base in 1987 or 1988. Aware that the Alliance had squeezed the 'soft Labour' vote close to exhaustion in 1983 and now stood second behind the governing party in 273 constituencies, Owen set out to woo 'soft Conservative' voters and in particular to win to his party's ranks the 'new working class' skilled manual 'swing voter' group who had voted Tory for the first time in 1979 and 1983. In an effort to achieve this, he adopted, what he termed, a 'tough and tender approach', praising elements of the post-1979 Conservative government programme, for example, its trade union reform laws, while strongly criticising its uncaring social policies and its hard-nosed attitude towards the unemployed and welfare services. In 1984–5, as part of this strategy, Owen backed the government's anti-NUM stand in the miners' strike. In addition, the new SDP leader emerged as a fervent advocate of the West German postwar governing principle of a 'social market economy': competetive free enterprise, tempered by selective state intervention to promote greater equality and social justice, to be financed by a determinedly redistributive tax system. His advocacy of this neo-liberal, market-centred policy strategy served to move the SDP significantly away from its Jenkinsite-Keynesianism roots of 1981–3. It gained the support of a number of senior colleagues, for example Ian Wrigglesworth, the economics spokesman, and John Cartwright (1933– ) the chief whip and defence spokesman, and began to be 'fleshed out' during 1985–6 by Dick Taverne's unveiling of a radical tax and social security reform package and by the party leadership's calls for enhanced market competition and acceptance of the Thatcher administration's privatisation programme.

147

David Owen made his influence felt on Alliance policy, strategy and style in three significant respects between 1983–6. First, by insisting on adherence to a firmly pro-nuclear defence strategy. This was to cause a serious rift between the SDP and Liberals in 1986. Second, by accepting that the Alliance, under the prevailing electoral system, had little realistic prospect of gaining power as a majority party in its own right in 1987 or 1988, and placing as its goal the capture of sufficient seats, circa 40–60, to enable it to hold the balance of power in a 'hung parliament' and setting out, in a detailed manner, the terms for its entry into a future coalition government. By such means, he hoped to force Labour and the Conservatives to make public their own strategies in such a situation and to 'talk up' the prospects of no single party being able to achieve an overall majority. Third, and most strikingly, Owen made a significant personal impact through his energetic and forceful leadership style. Aware of the limited media and parliamentary exposure that was given to the 'third force' outside election time, he worked energetically inside and outside the Commons to gain publicity for his party and to make his opinions known on all the pressing issues of the day. He was helped in this process by his past service in the key post of Foreign Secretary, which gave weight and significance to his pronouncements, and by his skilled use of the television medium. By such means, Owen was to emerge rapidly in the public's mind as the dominant force within the Alliance. At the same time, however, he was seen, because of his views on defence and the 'social market economy', and the admiration he displayed for a number of the leadership qualities of Prime Minister Thatcher, as moving progressively towards the Conservative Party, in sharp contradistinction to the pro-Labour leanings of David Steel and the Liberals. This depiction of David Owen was, however, unfair. He still retained a powerful Gaitskellite concern for social justice and egalitarianism that had been both inbred by his parents and deepened by his experience as an East London GP during the early 1960s.[1] He was

[1] Owen was born in Devon in 1938. His father was a GP who warmly supported the introduction of the National Health Service in 1948. His mother was a dentist and independent local councillor. Educated at boarding school and Cambridge University, Owen trained as a doctor, specialising in the study of neurology and psychiatry at St Thomas' Hospital, London. He was elected to Parliament for the Plymouth Devonport constituency in 1966 and was immediately appointed PPS to Defence Secretary Denis Healey. Between 1974–6 he served as Minister of State for Health and Social Security and between 1977–9 as Foreign Secretary. His American-born wife Debbie is a successful literary agent, numbering among her clients the former Conservative Party Deputy Chairman, Jeffrey Archer.

seeking, rather, to combine elements of Labour and 'New Conservatism' in a novel manner, as a means of achieving both economic efficiency and improved social provision.

Dr Owen, while proving remarkably successful in re-fashioning the public image and policy stance of the SDP, displayed less of an interest in more mundane organisational matters. This neglect was to have serious consequences for his party, which experienced a sharp contraction in membership between 1983 and 1984, falling from a high of 64 000 to a low of 50 000, and a consequential forced cutback in staff numbers at its Cowley Street central headquarters. Not until 1985–6 did membership rolls begin to increase once more: reaching 58 000 by mid-1986. The party did, however, recruit to its ranks the influential Engineers and Managers' Association (EMA) leader, John Lyons, a member of the TUC general council. It also gained the effective support of EEPTU leader Eric Hammond, and sent out feelers to the UDM rebel mineworkers. In addition, by holding its annual conferences at such 'mould breaking' inland venues as Salford and Buxton, the party made clear its desire to broaden its electoral base in the crucial Midlands and north west regions.

In terms of national popularity the SDP and Liberal Alliance suffered a marked drop in support during late 1983 and much of 1984. This was exemplified by its poor performance in the June 1984 Euro-elections, capturing only 19.5% of the vote and no seats, compared with Labour's 36.5% (32 seats) and the Conservatives 40.8% (45 seats). In by-elections, however, where it was able to pour in substantial central resources and personnel, the Alliance fared more strongly.

It gained significant publicity and forced tactical squeezes on major party support, particularly the Conservatives, between 1983–7. It won Portsmouth South in June 1984, Brecon and Radnor in July 1985, Ryedale in May 1986 and Greenwich in February 1987 and also came within less than a 1 000 votes of capturing the seats of Penrith (July 1983), West Derbyshire (May 1985) and Newcastle-under-Lyme (July 1986). Taken overall, in the 16 mainland by-elections between July 1983 and March 1987, support for the Alliance advanced 25% on its 1983 level, while the Labour vote fell by 16% and the Conservatives' by 49%. It captured 39% of all votes cast compared with the Conservatives' 30% and Labour's 29%.

During 1985 the Alliance made a broader advance in national popularity (see Table 21), benefiting in particular from a sudden mid-term slump in support for the government party. It was thus able to make sweeping gains in the May 1985 local elections, doubling its share of seats from 10% to 20%, and leaving it in effective control of five western counties, Cornwall, Devon, Somerset, Gloucestershire and Wiltshire, and sharing power in another 60 county and district councils. This experience of real political power at the local level served to make the membership of the two Alliance parties more hard headed and realistic. In the case of the Liberals, the decentralist, 'community politician' ACL wing, exemplified by David Alton, Simon Hughes and Michael Meadowcroft and led by Tony Greaves, became more pragmatic in outlook and moved closer towards the party leader David Steel. The SDP activists, many of whom were new to politics, became more vocal and began to flex their muscles, exerting increasing influence in the party's annual conferences.

**Table 23    Party Support in By-Elections 1983-7**
**(compared to 1983 result)**

| Constituency | Date | Con % | Lab % | Alliance % | | Majority |
|---|---|---|---|---|---|---|
| Penrith & the Border | Jul 83 | − 12.8 | − 5.9 | + 16.7 | Con Hold | 552 |
| Chesterfield | Mar 84 | − 17.2 | − 1.6 | + 15.2 | Lab Hold | 6,264 |
| Cynon Valley | May 84 | − 6.8 | + 2.8 | − 0.7 | Lab Hold | 12,835 |
| Stafford | May 84 | − 10.8 | + 3.7 | + 7.1 | Con Hold | 3,980 |
| Surrey South West | May 84 | − 10.4 | − 1.5 | + 11.3 | Con Hold | 2,599 |
| Portsmouth South | Jun 84 | − 15.7 | + 3.9 | + 12.2 | SDP GAIN | 1,341 |
| Enfield, Southgate | Dec 84 | − 8.5 | − 5.9 | + 12.2 | Con Hold | 4,711 |
| Brecon & Radnor | Jul 85 | − 20.5 | + 9.4 | + 11.4 | Lib GAIN | 559 |
| Tyne Bridge | Dec 85 | − 14.1 | + 1.3 | + 11.4 | Lab Hold | 6,575 |
| Fulham | Apr 86 | − 11.3 | + 10.4 | + 0.5 | Lab GAIN | 3,503 |
| Derbyshire West | May 86 | − 16.4 | + 2.7 | + 12.4 | Con Hold | 100 |
| Ryedale | May 86 | − 17.9 | − 1.9 | + 19.8 | Lib GAIN | 4,940 |
| Newcastle-under-Lyme | Jul 86 | − 17.4 | − 1.2 | + 17.2 | Lab Hold | 799 |
| Knowsley North | Nov 86 | − 13.8 | − 8.2 | + 19.8 | Lab Hold | 6,724 |
| Greenwich | Feb 87 | − 23.6 | − 4.5 | + 27.9 | SDP GAIN | 6,611 |
| Truro | Mar 87 | − 6.5 | + 2.5 | + 3.1 | Lib Hold | 14,617 |

Support for the Alliance reached its highest point in September 1985 when, in the immediate wake of the SDP and Liberals' highly successful Torquay and Dundee conferences, national polls showed it leading the pack with 35% support, compared with Labour's 33% and the Conservatives' 31%. This lead proved, however, to be short-lived. As the next election moved nearer difficult decisions had to be taken over candidate and campaign selection and policy formulation. These, particularly the latter, served to create serious rifts between the two parties, leading to confusion in the public's mind which was eagerly seized on by Labour and the Conservatives.

The apportionment of candidates to the mainland's 633 parliamentary constituencies went ahead in an unusually smooth and cordial fashion. By January 1986, 90% of constituencies had been allocated, with 'joint selection' by local party branches being utilised in 70 cases and with fewer local activist conflicts than in 1982–3. The formation of a joint campaign strategy team, chaired by Lord Harris of the SDP and John Pardoe of the Liberals, and an agreement on joint parliamentary spokesmen, from January 1987, also proceeded amicably. It was rather over policies for inclusion in the joint manifesto that serious differences emerged, as the divergences in outlook between Owenite 'social democracy' and broader Liberalism came to be highlighted. Joint SDP-Liberal 'policy commissions' were established at an early stage of the 1983–7 Parliament and succeeded in reaching agreement on the majority of issues. On the question of defence, however, a major rupture developed during 1986–7. In June 1986 the Alliance's Defence Commission, after months of bargaining, published a jointly agreed report, 'Defence and Disarmament', which sought to split the difference between the unilateralist-inclined Liberals and pro-nuclear SDP by deciding to maintain the British Polaris independent deterrent until it became obsolete in the mid 1990s, to cancel the Trident programme and to defer a decision on Polaris' replacement until the outcome of continuing East-West disarmament negotiations became clearer. Such a 'fudged' solution was, however, immediately criticised by the SDP leader, who saw the need for the parties to come out in favour of a clear alternative option to Polaris to retain credibility in the forthcoming election. Owen thus persuaded David Steel to support a hastily cobbled together Franco-British nuclear missile system scheme, but the proposal was narrowly rejected by the September 1986 Liberal Assembly at Eastbourne, which backed a non-nuclear defence motion. The Assembly's decision was not binding on its party's leader but created adverse publicity for the Alliance and opened serious divisions within the Liberal Party. A new Liberal-SDP joint compromise was subsequently hammered out by Steel and Owen in December 1986, committing the parties to the maintenance of a minimum nuclear deterrent, if necessary, until it could be negotiated away. The damage had, however, been done. The Alliance's poll ratings (see Table 21) slumped to a low of 20% in November 1986, as many 1985 'Conservative defectors' returned 'home'. Only in January 1987, with the Alliance's 'relaunch' at London's Barbican Centre to the strains of Purcell, and its publication of a detailed joint policy programme, 'Partnership for Progress', did it begin to recover public support. This recovery gained momentum with the events in Greenwich during February 1987, and significant successes in local elections, but its base of support still appeared fragile as the 1987 election campaign moved officially underway.

## The 1987 General Election

### The Campaign: The Media Consultants Take Charge

The May–June 1987 election campaign promised to be the most bitterly fought and divisive of the postwar era. The two major parties, Conservative and Labour, offered starkly diverging visions of the economic and social future: individualism and consumer primacy versus collective provision. Their differences on defence and foreign affairs were equally stark and they were led by leaders who displayed a strong and scarcely concealed mutual contempt. In reality, however, while the personal and policy exchanges proved to be intense, the campaign was to be remembered, in retrospect, for its style. The Labour Party, learning the lessons of the Conservative victories of 1979 and 1983, assiduously embraced commercial advertising and presentational techniques to an unprecedented degree and May–June 1987 was to emerge as the most expensively packaged and tightly organised television orientated campaign in British electoral history. While total spending remained well below the levels of contemporary US Congressional and Presidential campaigns[1] and

---

[1] During the 1987 election campaign the Conservative Party central headquarters spent upwards of £7 million (£3.5 million of which was on press advertising), Labour £5 million (£1.5 million on press advertising) and the Alliance in the region of £2 million (£0.25 million on press advertising). Local spending by candidates—which was limited to £5 800 in each rural and £5 300 in each urban constituency—is likely to have reached £9 million. This compared with spending of £300 million during the November 1986 US Congressional elections. In Britain, however, the grant of free party election broadcasts (PEPs) on television served to save considerable advertising funds.

while policy debate still retained its central place, the media consultants emerged as central figures, serving to soften and cloud many of the crucial issues of the campaign.

The early running in the May–June campaign was made by the Alliance. Buoyed by their recent success in the local elections and by an opinion poll rating of 25%, the Alliance's leaders looked forward, as in preceding contests, to adding a further 5–10% to this support level as the campaign progressed and elbowing aside Labour to establish themselves as the clear alternative party to the Conservatives. They set a target for themselves of capturing between 50 and 70 seats and achieving, as a consequence, a share of power in a possible 'balanced parliament'. The Alliance, with an electoral fighting fund of barely £2 million, lacked the financial resources of the two main parties. They hired, however, as advertising director, the renowned copywriter David Abbott (48) whose list of clients included Volvo, Sainsburys and British Telecom, and established a central campaign headquarters at Cowley Street under the direction of John Pardoe. In addition, their 1987 campaign enjoyed the advantages of an agreement with the broadcasting authorities to grant it, on the basis of 1983 electoral performance, equal television time with Labour and the Conservatives, as well as the support of the new national tabloid newspaper, 'Today' (circulation 0.3 million), and sympathetic coverage by the new 'quality' daily, 'The Independent' (circulation 0.1 million). The Alliance leaders, David Owen and David Steel, set off on 14–16 May on an early, hectic whistlestop tour by airplane and 'battle bus' to 14 key regions of the country in an attempt to build up an early bandwagon of support which would sweep them into second place in the opinion polls. The two men projected themselves as joint leaders of the Alliance during the campaign, making sure to rendezvous each evening for joint television appearances in an effort to avoid the public divisions that had damagingly emerged between Jenkins and Steel during the 1983 campaign. Well before the campaign had begun, however, Owen and Steel made clear that, if the Alliance did subsequently achieve a parliamentary majority in its own right, it would be the leader of the party boasting the largest number of MPs who would lead the parliamentary grouping as Prime Minister.

Between 12–18 May, with Parliament still sitting and the campaign still not officially begun, the Alliance stole a march on its opponents and attracted useful media publicity through the judicious unveiling of selected highlights of its subsequent manifesto. Costings of its economic and social spending plans, independently audited by the accountants Coopers and Lybrand, were revealed on 12 May. On 13 May a package of ambitious proposed constitutional reforms, entitled the 'Great Reform Charter', embracing support for the single transferable vote (STV) system of proportional representation (PR), national and regional devolution, a Bill of Rights, reform of Parliament and replacement of the Official Secrets Act by a new Freedom of Information Act, was published. Five days later, a day in advance of Labour and the Conservatives, the Alliance issued its manifesto, 'Britain United —The Time Has Come', a lengthy and detailed document, the culmination of almost three years of research by the parties' joint policy commissions. As well as the need for radical constitutional reform, it placed particular emphasis on three key areas: the reduction of unemployment by one million within three years through the launch of a £4 billion per annum reflationary programme of targeted public spending, backed by an incomes policy and the power to impose a counter-inflation tax on uncooperative employers; the fostering of increased participation and partnership by workers in industry, through profit-sharing and new management schemes; and a major overhaul of the taxation and welfare benefits system to improve provision for the poor and elderly. These policy aims were wide ranging and ambitious. The Alliance failed, however, to decide on priorities in promotion, whether to concentrate on the issue of constitutional reform or to campaign on its economic and social programme, or on which major party, Labour or Conservative, to target its invective. Thus, after its initial opening days of frenzied activity, the Alliance campaign rapidly lost momentum and became increasingly confused in its strategy. It was damaged by the fact that its two leaders clearly differed in emphases and approach. Owen reserved his sharpest attacks for Labour's defence strategy and set as the Alliance's target the achievement of a 'hung parliament', while Steel concentrated his criticisms on Conservative economic and social policies and declared his aim to be an overall parliamentary majority. In addition, its campaigning style, based on daytime lightning visits to market towns and evening, open-door 'Meet the Alliance' public question and answer sessions, appeared low-key and outdated compared with the razzmatazz of the two major parties. In such circumstances support for the Alliance slumped seriously during the second and third weeks of the campaign to a level of barely 21%. Somewhat unexpectedly, the election of June

1987 emerged as a classic right-left two party struggle between the Conservatives and Labour. This was mainly the result of the skilful campaigning efforts of Labour and its leader Neil Kinnock.

The Labour Party, following its loss of 227 local council seats on 7 May, began the 1987 election from a lower base than in May-June 1983. In stark contrast to 1983, however, the party, benefiting from organisational changes between 1983-6, succeeded in mounting a disciplined and imaginative campaign. Firm central control was exercised by the party's Walworth Road headquarters, with the efficient, New Zealand-born, former Oxford don and career diplomat, Bryan Gould, at its helm, as 'Campaign Co-ordinator'. He was specially assisted by party General Secretary, Larry Whitty, communications director, Peter Mandelson, and a team of twenty young and ideologically committed advertising executives, led by Philip Gould, termed the 'Shadow Communications Agency'. In addition, a major pre-election fund-raising drive by direct mail and contributions of £4 million by Trade Unionists For Labour[1] (TUFL) ensured that the campaign would be well financed. The Labour team, learning the lessons of their disastrous 1983 campaign, determined at the outset to run a tight ship, with iron discipline and almost military precision.

First, Walworth Road was linked by computer to all key marginal constituencies with daily briefings being sent out to local agents to ensure close strategy co-ordination. Second, party strategists, utilising the findings of pre-election opinion polls which showed Labour leading the Conservatives on the 'caring issues' of health, education and unemployment, sought to make these the key issues of the campaign and set out to dictate the daily agenda through the deliberate scheduling of topics for discussion at daily press conferences, supported by 'photo-opportunity' leadership visits. Third, and most importantly, great attention was paid to the image projected by party spokesmen during their television appearances. Special 'Red Rose' backcloths and musical accompaniments by Brahms were arranged for speeches at key venues; television slots were restricted to an approved list of popular and television-skilled moderates; and large, ticket-only rallies of party supporters were organised to project the 'dream ticket' duo of Kinnock and Hattersley in the most favourable light.

---

[1] An organisation comprising the 35 trade unions affiliated to the Labour Party. The TGWU, £0.75 million, GMB, £0.64 million and NUM, £0.4 million were the principal donors.

The substance of the Labour campaign was contained in the party manifesto, 'Britain Will Win', which was unveiled on 19 May. This manifesto, based on the work of the NEC-Shadow Cabinet joint policy commissions and drafted in its final version by the Kinnock office, was, in contrast to its 1983 counterpart, an unusually succinct and sharply focused document, the shortest of all three parties' manifestos. It brought together in a coherent manner the various economic, law and order, and defence initiatives that the party had been promoting during 1985–6. Avoiding fringe issues, emphasis was given to a 'priority' jobs and anti-poverty programme to be put into effect during its first two years of power. This entailed the immediate summoning of an National Economic Summit with the TUC and CBI, to discuss investment plans and inflation control; the implementation of a £6 billion per annum reflationary package of housebuilding, training and infra-structural improvement directed towards reducing unemployment by one million within two years; enhanced pensions and welfare benefits; and the introduction of a statutory minimum wage. The programme was to be funded through reversing the March 1987 2p reduction in income tax and the post-1979 tax cuts given to the richest 5% in the country, and by increasing government borrowing (the PSBR) by £3 billion. The Labour manifesto proposed, in addition, significantly increased expenditure on the health service and educational system; a new 'safe estates' crime prevention policy; the establishment of a democratically-elected Scottish Assembly in Edinburgh; the creation of a new Ministry for Women and Ministry of Environmental Protection; a new 'bill of rights' for trade unions; annual local government elections; a Freedom of Information Act, with the repeal of Section 2 of the Official Secrets Act; and, most controversially, concentration on a non-nuclear defence policy.

It was the style rather than the substance of the Labour message, however, which caught public attention during the opening weeks of the 1987 election campaign. The Labour leader Neil Kinnock, who was despatched to the provinces to address all-ticket evening rallies while the articulate and persuasive Bryan Gould chaired the party's morning press conferences in London, made an immediate impression through the televised excerpts of his oratorical flourishes before the party faithful. Particularly impressive was the speech he delivered to the Welsh Labour conference at Llandudno on 15 May in which, in sharp criticism of what he viewed as the divisive, self-centredness of Thatcherism, he spoke pointedly of the lack of real freedoms endured by those left out of the recent economic revival and questioned why the 'new' policies of de-regulation and private provision had been abandoned fifty years ago. These themes of the 'two nations', the haves and the have-nots, the Dickensian values of 'Thatcherism' and of the need for collective, co-operative provision were to be constantly reiterated in the ensuing weeks by Kinnock in what became a revivalist-style moral crusade. This appeal to traditional Labour values struck a deep and rapturous chord among party activists, buoying spirits as the campaign progressed. It also touched, more importantly, a wider audience on 21 May with the showing of a pathbreaking party political broadcast, scripted by Colin Welland and directed by Hugh Hudson, both of 'Chariots of Fire' repute, projecting the personality, family background and leadership qualities of Neil Kinnock in an unprecedentedly presidential fashion. The broadcast, which included clips from Kinnock's Llandudno address and ended with the the simple slogan 'Kinnock' under a picture of the Palace of Westminster, had a dramatic impact on the viewing public, leading to an immediate 3-point advance in the the Labour Party's popular rating and a 16-point rise in the prime ministerial rating of Kinnock himself.

Labour's advance between 14–25 May occurred almost entirely at the expense of the Alliance, whose vote (see Table 24) was squeezed by 4%. It was achieved as a result of the party's ability during this period to force social issues to the forefront of the campaign agenda. Walworth Road strategists were aware, however, from their private poll soundings that Labour's defence policy, based on unilateral nuclear disarmament, was a clear vote loser. This was a time-bomb waiting to explode at some stage during the campaign, with potentially fatal consequences for the party's pretensions to victory. It was eventually, and unintentionally, detonated by Labour themselves on 24 May when, during a Sunday morning television interview with David Frost, Neil Kinnock, in reply to the question of how without nuclear weapons Labour would counter a threat of nuclear blackmail and invasion by the Soviet Union, gave the impression of a resort to guerrilla resistance, stating forcefully 'the choice is exterminating everything you stand for . . . or using the resources that you have got to make any occupation untenable'. These words were eagerly seized upon by Conservative Central Office which hastily commissioned a press and poster advertisement showing a British soldier with hands raised in surrender and a well-orchestrated series of speeches by Margaret Thatcher, Party Chairman Norman Tebbit and Defence Secretary George Younger to deride what they termed Labour's 'Dad's Army' defence policy.

Table 24  'Poll of Poll' Ratings of the Parties
During the 1987 Campaign[1]

| Sample Dates | (Number) | Conservatives | Labour | Alliance |
|---|---|---|---|---|
| May 1–12 | (4) | 42.5% | 30.0% | 25.3% |
| May 12–20 | (6) | 41.7% | 32.7% | 23.7% |
| May 20–27 | (7) | 42.5% | 34.0% | 21.2% |
| May 27–June 2 | (7) | 42.6% | 34.0% | 21.2% |
| June 3–10 | (7) | 42.9% | 33.6% | 22.0% |

[1] Based on national polls comprising samples in excess of 1,000

Labour decided not to try immediately to counter these challenges in its weakest policy area and sought instead to shift the campaign debate back to its own 'social agenda'. The strategy largely failed, however. Severe damage had been inflicted upon the party by the defence issue and Labour's advance of the first two weeks of the campaign was halted. The party proved to be unable to break above the 34–35% level of support and to win over wavering floating voters, thus leaving the field open for a clear Conservative victory.

The Conservative Party began the May–June 1987 enjoying a commanding lead of more than 12% in national opinion polls (see Table 24) over a divided opposition. However, the fickle volatility of the contemporary electorate and the relatively recent recovery in the party's fortunes from the mid-term nadir of 1985–6 ensured that there would be no complacency at Central Office in Smith Square. The preceding year had been one of great activity and change at party headquarters. In May 1986, in the immediate wake of the local elections debacle, morale had been at a low ebb and, with constituency branches and business benefactors withholding financial support, a cash crisis had emerged, Central Office running up a bank overdraft in excess of £1.5 million. A major fund-raising drive was thus launched, directed both at companies and at targeted social groups through direct mailing, and a radical overhaul of both strategy and personnel undertaken.

First, detailed quantitative research was carried out into the electorate's attitudes towards government policy and social issues by the advertising agency Young and Rubicam. This identified a core group of middle and skilled working class voters, dubbed the 'belongers', who, being characterised as patriots, homemakers and family-orientated with a sense of public spirit, were concerned with the government's uncaring attitude to the health and education services and threatened to defect to Labour. Such findings worried party strategicians and formed a key factor behind the government's shift towards a new, more caring, 'consolidator' policy course during 1986-7. Second, a clutch of new and returning advisers were brought into Central Office. These included Peter Morrison, the former Industry minister, who was appointed Deputy Chairman to assist Norman Tebbit and later to take the place of Jeffrey Archer who resigned as a result of an alleged sex scandal in October 1986, and Christopher Lawson, who returned as Director of Special Services in May 1986. Working with Director of Communications Harvey Thomas and Saatchi and Saatchi and special deputy co-ordinator Lord Young, this experienced team began during early 1987 to lay out plans for the campaign ahead. These included the advance booking of prime poster sites for June 1987 and the advance mail-shotting of a number of selected social groups; privatised company shareholders, young house owners and former tenants who had purchased their council houses.

The Conservative campaign began in May 1987 in a deliberately delayed and low key fashion, being designed to gather momentum and reach a crescendo during the final days before polling. The manifesto, which had been drawn up by a special 'A Team' of senior ministers (Thatcher, Tebbit, Howe, Lawson, Young, Whitelaw, Hurd and Wakeham), was released on 19 May and comprised two documents. The first outlined the achievements of the government's first two terms in office. The second, entitled 'The Next Moves Forward', outlined its plans for the third term and deliberately included a clutch of radical new initiatives in the spheres of education, housing and rates reform, as a means of demonstrating the continuing forward-looking vigour of the administration. The new reform proposals: the establishment of a new class of self-governing, breakaway schools directly funded by the Department of Education; the decontrol of private rents; the provision for council tenants to choose new non-local-authority landlords; and the replacement of rates by a local 'Community Charge' paid by all adults were geared towards fostering greater individual choice and responsibility, thus giving real effect to the Prime Minister's personal self-help vision. They were launched under the populist slogan 'power to the people'. The manifesto included, in addition, plans to establish a new national curriculum in secondary schools and private-sector orientated Urban Development Corporations to foster the regeneration of 'inner city' areas. It promised a further package of trade union reform, to give individual workers additional rights; an accelerated programme of privatisation, embracing the airports and water authorities and electricity industry; and more movement in the direction of reduced levels of income tax. Finally, it reiterated the Conservatives' commitment to a strong nuclear-based defence policy, founded upon the new Trident independent deterrent.

The inclusion of new reform measures in the education, housing and local government spheres was designed to avoid any potential charges of staleness and to shift the policy debate away from the government's past record towards the future. This it succeeded in doing, although the new policies, having not been fully worked over in a detailed manner, did lead to a number of embarrassingly contradictory statements by ministers as the campaign progressed. The principal themes of the Conservative campaign were, however, to be largely negative. Party strategists concentrated their fire upon attacking four aspects of the Labour programme. First, the surrenderist and destabilising dangers of its defence policy. Second, the possibility of increased inflation and taxation that might result from its reflationary economic strategy. Third, the potential losses that might be suffered by shareholders as a result of Labour plans to repurchase equity in British Telecom and British Gas at the original flotation price level. Fourth, the threat of renewed labour unrest that might arise from Labour's pledge to restore the right to secondary picketing. These hard-hitting anti-Labour campaign themes were underpinned by the broader suggestion, under the slogan the 'iceberg manifesto', that Labour's glossy packaging was being used to deliberately conceal a more radical, secret, policy programme and that if elected to office a new 'hard left' influx of MPs might seize power by ousting Neil Kinnock in the manner of Ken Livingstone's 1981 GLC coup. The Conservatives were more restrained in their attacks on the Alliance, seeking instead to characterise a vote for such a 'third force' as likely to be wasted and running the risk of letting Labour in by default.

The Conservative campaign followed closely along the lines of May–June 1983 in terms of presentation and style. Carefully arranged 'photo-opportunities' were arranged each day for the Prime Minister in selected locations of successful businesses and new hospitals. A vetted list of 'sound' and presentable ministers was drawn up for television debates; and, in the evening, carefully staged ticket-only rallies of the party faithful were organised, to coincide with television news programmes. The campaign, dominated by the twin figures of Margaret Thatcher and Party Chairman, Norman Tebbit, was forceful and strident. However, the television broadcasts and newspaper advertisements devised by Saatchi and Saatchi looked tired and dated compared with the innovative efforts of the young Labour campaign team. This, combined with a series of minor 'gaffes' by the Prime Minister on questions about health and education, resulted in a worrying narrowing of the gap between Labour and the Conservatives during the opening weeks of the campaign. The successful emergence centre-stage of the defence issue during the third week served to reassert the Conservatives' dominance. This confidence was seriously undermined, however, on 3 June by a Gallup poll which suggested that the party's lead over Labour had been more than halved to 4%. The next day, later termed 'nervous Thursday', witnessed momentary panic at Central Office. The Prime Minister savagely attacked Norman Tebbit's campaigning efforts and tore up Saatchi and Saatchi's new advertising proposals. She placed Lord Young in firm control of campaign coordination and, working covertly with her close friend, the former Saatchi advertising executive, Tim Bell, oversaw the design of a new set of advertising material emphasising the government's 1979–87 achievements with the slogan 'Don't let Labour wreck it' and began to project her own leadership qualities and sense of social concern.

These themes were given particular emphasis during the final week of the campaign. In a key party election broadcast on Tuesday 2 June the experience and statesmanlike qualities of the Prime Minister were forcefully exhibited in a montage of newsreel clips of oveseas visits set to a stirring, jingoistic musical score specially composed by Andrew Lloyd Webber. Six days later Mrs Thatcher flew to Venice to attend the world economic summit, gaining extensive media coverage. The final days of the campaign saw, in addition, an unprecedented blitz of newspaper advertisements by the Conservatives, stressing, with the slogan 'It's great to be great again', the economic upturn of recent years as well as a clutch of major television interviews by the Prime Minister who, to counter opposition criticisms of her high-handedness, adopted a determinedly restrained and caring demeanour. The Labour Party attempted to outflank this late Conservative offensive by placing continuing stress on the health service issue and by launching a concerted appeal to voters who had 'defected' to the Alliance in 1983 to 'return home', picturing Labour as the party which presented the only realistic electoral alternative to the Conservatives. This failed, however, to achieve its aim. Instead, the Alliance enjoyed a late upturn of support during the closing days of the campaign. This was the result of a deliberate change in campaigning strategy in which David Steel and David Owen abandoned the use of joint television appearances, which had projected the image, in the words of David Steel, of 'Tweedledum and Tweedledee', and adopted a more forceful, bullish style, criticising both Labour's defence strategy and the Conservatives' economic and social programme and presenting the Alliance as the party which offered a unique and attractive combination of 'sensible' and moderate policies.

## The Outcome: The 'Two Nations' Election

When polling finally took place on 11 June, turnout, at 75.4%, proved high. The vitriolic and personalised campaign had served to galvanise both Labour and Conservative supporters to vote in large numbers in their respective bedrock regions of support and resulted in the most sharply polarised electoral result of the postwar era. As the early results came through from Conservative marginals in the South and Midlands it was clear that the incumbent party's support was holding up in these critical regions and that the government was heading for a clear parliamentary victory. In contrast, the Conservative vote dipped sharply in the north, and particularly in Wales and Scotland, with Labour piling up increased majorities in its already safe stronghold constituencies. By the early hours of the morning of Friday 12 June the Conservatives had again secured a parliamentary majority. This time it was 102 (see Table 25), only 42 fewer seats than its 1983 total.

This substantial Conservative majority was achieved on a 42.3% share of the total UK vote, a figure which represented little change both on the party's June 1983 performance or its average standing in opinion polls throughout the four weeks of a campaign which, by all accounts, had been run in an unusually slipshod and uncertain fashion. The party saw its support fall significantly in Scotland, Wales, northern and south western England (see Tables 6, 18 and 26), but advance in the Midlands, eastern and south eastern England and particularly in Greater London. In terms of support by social groups (see Tables 5, 17 and 27), the Conservative vote held up among all categories, including the crucial skilled worker (C2) grouping, with the exception of women, particularly those under the age of 25 (support among whom slumped from 42% to 31%), and pensioners.

**Table 25    The June 1987 General Election (Turnout 75.4%)**

| Party | Total Votes | % Share of Vote | Candidates | Av. Vote Per Candidate | Number of MPs | Av. Vote Per MP |
|---|---|---|---|---|---|---|
| Conservatives | 13.787m | 42.3% | 633 | 21,780 | 376 | 36,668 |
| Labour | 10.034m | 30.8% | 633 | 15,851 | 229 | 43,815 |
| Alliance | 7.340m | 22.6% | 633 | 11,595 | 22 | 333,632 |
| (Liberals) | (4.169m) | (12.8%) | (326) | (12,788) | (17) | (245,235) |
| (SDP) | (3.191m) | (9.8%) | (307) | (10,394) | (5) | (638,200) |
| SNP | 0.420m | 1.3%[1] | 72[2] | 5,833 | 3 | 139,989 |
| Plaid Cymru | 0.124m | 0.4%[1] | 38 | 3,252 | 3 | 41,196 |
| Green | 0.088m | 0.3% | 133 | 661 | 0 | — |
| Communist | 0.006m | 0.0% | 19 | 316 | 0 | — |
| Others (GB) | 0.039m | 0.1% | 90[3] | 435 | 0 | — |
| Others (NI) | 0.726m | 2.2% | 77[4] | 9,428 | 17 | 42,706 |
| Total | 32.564m | | 2,327 | 14,006 | 650 | 50,098 |

[1] The SNP captured 14% of the Scottish vote (finishing in second place in 13 constituencies) and Plaid Cymru 7.3% of the Welsh vote.

[2] Includes one Orkney and Shetland Movement (OSM) candidate.

[3] The raising of the level of the electoral deposit from its 1983 level of £150 to £500 by the 1985 Representation of the People Act discouraged a number of minor and 'fringe party' candidatures in June 1987, the National Front, for example, deciding not to put up any candidates on this occasion. 290 candidates lost their deposits, despite the reduction in the threshold of votes cast from 12.5% to 5%. These included one Liberal, one SNP and five Plaid Cymru candidates.

[4] As usual, the Unionist parties entered into constituency stand-down agreements before the election so as to maximise their chances of success. In the Province as a whole the Official Unionist Party (OUP), led by James Molyneaux, captured 38% of the vote and nine seats (losing Enoch Powell's Down South seat to the SDLP); the Democratic Unionist Party (DUP), led by the Rev. Ian Paisley, 12% of the vote and three seats; the Social Democratic Labour Party (SDLP), led by John Hume, 22% of the vote and three seats; Sinn Fein, led by Gerry Adams, 11% of the vote and one seat; the Alliance Party, led by John Cushnahan, 10% of the vote and no seats; the Ulster People's Unionist Party (UPUP), led by James Kilfedder, 2.5% of the vote and one seat; and the Workers Party put up 14 candidates and captured 2.3% of the vote and no seats.

**Table 26    Changes in Party Support by Region Between 1983 and 1987**

| | Conservatives | Labour | Alliance |
|---|---|---|---|
| SCOTLAND | − 4.4% | + 7.3% | − 5.3% |
| WALES | − 1.5% | + 7.5% | − 5.3% |
| ENGLAND | | | |
| North/Northeast | − 2.3% | + 6.2% | − 4.0% |
| Northwest | − 2.0% | + 5.2% | − 3.0% |
| Yorks & Humberside | − 1.2% | + 5.3% | − 3.9% |
| West Midlands | + 0.6% | + 2.1% | − 2.6% |
| East Midlands | + 1.4% | + 2.1% | − 2.6% |
| Southwest | − 0.8% | + 1.2% | − 0.1% |
| East Anglia | + 1.2% | + 1.2% | − 2.5% |
| Southeast | + 1.1% | + 0.9% | − 1.8% |
| Greater London | + 2.6% | + 1.6% | − 3.5% |

Table 27    Party Support by Social Group in June 1987*
(Change from 1983 in brackets)

| Social Group | Conservative | Labour | Alliance |
|---|---|---|---|
| Men | 43% (+1%) | 32% (+2%) | 23% (-2%) |
| Women | 43% (-3%) | 32% (+6%) | 23% (-4%) |
| Professional/Managerial (AB) | 57% (-3%) | 14% (+4%) | 26% (-2%) |
| Office/Clerical (C1) | 51% (NC) | 21% (+1%) | 26% (-1%) |
| Skilled Manual (C2) | 40% (NC) | 36% (+4%) | 22% (-4%) |
| Semi/Unskilled (DE) | 30% (-3%) | 48% (+7%) | 20% (-4%) |
| Owner Occupiers | 50% (-2%) | 23% (+4%) | 25% (-3%) |
| Council Tenants | 22% (-4%) | 56% (+9%) | 19% (-5%) |
| Private Tenants | 39% (-2%) | 37% (+4%) | 21% (-3%) |
| Trade Union Members | 30% (-1%) | 42% (+3%) | 26% (-3%) |
| Unemployed Workers | 25% (NC) | 52% (+5%) | 20% (-3%) |
| 18-24 Year Olds | 33% (-9%) | 40% (+7%) | 21% (-1%) |
| 25-34 Year Olds | 39% (-1%) | 33% (+4%) | 25% (-4%) |
| 35-54 Year Olds | 45% (+1%) | 29% (+2%) | 24% (-3%) |
| 55+ | 46% (-1%) | 31% (+4%) | 21% (-3%) |
| Pensioners | 47% (-4%) | 31% (+6%) | 21% (-2%) |

* Based on MORI poll of 23,396

Labour, after running the most professional and well-received campaign of all the parties, achieved a 3.3% advance in its national vote, to 30.8%, and captured twenty more seats than in June 1983. The party's fortunes were, however, even more regionally differentiated (see Table 26) than the Conservatives, recording significant advances in popular support of between 5–7% in Scotland, Wales and northern England, compared with improvements of barely 1–2% in southern and central England. Helped by its special youth campaign and female rights initiatives, the party polled far more strongly than in 1983 among first-time voters and among women (see Table 27). Its most significant advance by social category took place, however, among its traditional working class clientele of unskilled manual workers (DE) and council house tenants, as well as among the unemployed.

For the Liberal-SDP Alliance the results of June 1987 were little short of disastrous. Despite starting the campaign from an unusually high base, the grouping, finding itself caught in a classic two-party squeeze, lost ground both in its initial poll rating and its June 1983 level of support. It ended up capturing only 22.6% of the national vote, a figure 2.8% below its 1983 total, and recorded a net loss of five seats from its total at dissolution. The Alliance's support slumped most significantly among working class groups; skilled (C2) and unskilled (DE) labourers and council house tenants. This was reflected in the regional differentiation in its loss of support which varied from between 4–5% in Wales, Scotland and northern England and 2.6% in the Midlands and East Anglia to an average figure of 2% in the suburban southeast. Only in its traditional base region of the southwest did the Alliance vote remain solid. Before the campaign began it was acutely aware of the drawbacks of its geographically even spread of support, and had hoped to achieve disproportionate gains in selected marginal constituencies through promoting the concept of tactical voting (TV). During the spring of 1987 a centre-left organisation, TV '87, was thus established to promote the concept of 'intelligent voting' and to disseminate the findings of local opinion polls in key marginals. The results of 11 June proved, however, that this campaign had been a clear failure. 17% of electors (11% Conservative, 17% Labour and 28% Alliance) did admit to voting tactically, but, in the key Alliance 'hit list' marginals, such as Richmond, Chelmsford, Clwyd Southwest, Derbyshire West, Edinburgh West, Erith & Crayford, Hereford, Hazel Grove, Fife Northeast, Renfrew West, Stevenage, Penrith & the Border, all of which were held with Conservative majorities of less than 2 500, only one gain was achieved. Overall, the Alliance ended up capturing three new seats, Fife NE and Argyll & Bute in Scotland and Southport, all of them gained by the Liberals, while losing eight existing seats. These losses comprised five SDP and three Liberal MPs and included the prominent figures of Roy Jenkins (SDP: Glasgow Hillhead), Ian Wrigglesworth (SDP: Stockton South), Michael Meadowcroft (Lib.: Leeds West) and Clement Freud (Lib.: Cambridgeshire Northeast), as well as the recent by-election gains of Portsmouth South and Ryedale. The Alliance's performance was made worse, in many respects, by the fact that the minor regional Scottish Nationalist Party and Plaid Cymru polled strongly in June 1987, each recording a net gain of one seat.

The key feature of June 1987 was, however, the geographical and social polarisation of support for the two main parties, which represented both a continuation and an acceleration of a trend that had been evident in all general elections since 1974. A sea of blue engulfed southern and eastern England between the Wash and the Bristol Channel, with the Conservatives capturing 170 (see Appendix Table 2) of the 176 seats contested, excluding Greater London. Labour captured only three southern seats, Bristol South, Norwich South and Oxford East, and finished in second place in only 27 constituencies. This was the region which had benefited most from the private industry, service and financial-sector-based economic expansion that had been evident since 1982 and which enjoyed the lowest average levels of unemployment. The region also boasted the highest proportion of owner-occupiers in the nation and a high take-up rate for the government's recent privatised company share issues. June 1987 thus, as in 1983. witnessed a positive vote for 'Thatcherism' in the southern third of England, the government enjoying a support-rating there of between 52–56%. Similar pockets of strong approbation for the 'Thatcher revolution' were to be found in flourishing rural and suburban sub-regions of northern England, as well as in the critical 'hinge region' of the Midlands. The Midland region, with its mixed blue-collar and service-sector-based economy, contained 18 Conservative-Labour marginals. By 1987 it was emerging from the worst of the job-shedding restructuring of the 1979–84 recession and beginning to enjoy a period of healthy export-led growth and rapidly rising consumer incomes. The skilled workers of the West Midlands, many of whom had switched to the Conservatives in 1979 and 1983, formed the backbone of the 'New Conservatism', attracted by the government's tax cutting and home and share ownership policies. In the East Midlands, with an economy geared towards light industry and, in places, profitable deep coal mining, the rift caused by the 1984–5 pits' dispute and the emergence of the Nottinghamshire and Derbyshire-based breakaway UDM proved useful in dividing the potential Labour vote in a number of colliery constituencies, such as Sherwood.[1] A third, and equally crucial, area of growing Conservative support was Greater London. Here three factors operated in the Conservatives' favour, enabling them to increase their share of the vote by 2.6% and gain three seats (see Table 28). First, the 'gentrification' of a number of riverside central London constituencies, such as Fulham and Battersea. Second, the adverse publicity given to Labour by the government's and national press 'Loony Left' campaign. Third, the emergence, to Labour's detriment, of the 'race issue' as a result of black candidates being chosen to contest seven of the party's key marginal seats.[2]

[1] In the mining constituency of Mansfield a UDM-backed candidate, Brian Marshall, stood as a representative of the newly formed Moderate Labour Party (MLP). However, despite his winning 1,580 votes, Labour narrowly held the seat from the Conservatives by 56. In the Conservative mining marginal of Batley & Spen in Yorkshire, however, an MLP candidature proved decisive in depriving Labour of an important gain.

[2] Above average Labour to Conservative swings were recorded in inner London seats where Labour black candidates stood, as white working class voters deserted the party ticket. In addition, while Labour captured, as in 1983, almost 90% of the Afro-Caribbean vote, its share of the Asian vote fell from 80% to 67%, this community switching support to both the Conservatives and the Alliance.

However, while the Conservatives collected the votes of the successful 'haves' on the basis of a policy programme which stressed the primacy of the twin issues of the continuing battle against inflation and the need for a strong nuclear-based defence policy (see Table 29), Labour, fighting on a platform of job creation and improved public services and welfare provision, achieved new dominance in the depressed regions of the northern industrial belt, Wales and Scotland and among the nation's 'have nots'. It gained 7, 4, and 9 seats respectively in these regions (see Table 28) and achieved almost total dominance in the major cities of Glasgow, Liverpool, Manchester, Sheffield, Bradford, Leeds, Leicester and Newcastle, capturing 36 of the 38 seats available. It was in Scotland, however, where Labour's advance was most striking, the party capturing 50 of the country's 72 seats, compared to the Conservatives' 10. The intense unpopularity of the southerner Margaret Thatcher and her government's centralised style of rule and apparent use of Scotland between 1983–7 as an experimental laboratory for its new rates revaluation and Community Charge initiatives, was one reason for the sharp fall in Conservative support north of the border and Labour's resurgence. In addition, the region's high and, as a result of the depressed state of the offshore oil industry, still rising, level of unemployment was a compelling factor. Above all, however, it was the distinctive socio-cultural milieu of Scotland, with its Presbyterian traditions of mutual support, its distinctive Labour-orientated local press and media and a housing structure still dominated by council tenants rather than

**Table 28    Seat Losses and Gains in the June 1987 Election**

|  | Conservative | | Labour | | Alliance | | SNP | | PC | |
|---|---|---|---|---|---|---|---|---|---|---|
|  | Gains | Losses | Gains | Losses | Gains | Losses | Gains | Losses | Gains | Losses |
| ENGLAND | (12) | (13) | (13) | (6) | (1) | (7) | (—) | (—) | (–) | (—) |
| North | 1 | 1 | 1 | 0 | 0 | 1 | — | — | — | — |
| Northwest | 0 | 2 | 1 | 0 | 1 | 0 | — | — | — | — |
| Yorks & Humberside | 2 | 4 | 5 | 0 | 0 | 3 | — | — | — | — |
| East Midlands | 0 | 3 | 3 | 0 | 0 | 0 | — | — | — | — |
| West Midlands | 1 | 1 | 1 | 1 | 0 | 0 | — | — | — | — |
| Southwest | 0 | 0 | 0 | 0 | 0 | 0 | — | — | — | — |
| East Anglia | 2 | 1 | 1 | 1 | 0 | 1 | — | — | — | — |
| Southeast | 3 | 1 | 1 | 1 | 0 | 2 | — | — | — | — |
| Greater London | 3 | 0 | 0 | 3 | 0 | 0 | — | — | — | — |
| WALES | 0 | 5 | 4 | 0 | 0 | 0 | — | — | 1 | — |
| SCOTLAND | 0 | 11 | 9 | 0 | 2 | 1 | 3 | 2 | - | — |
| TOTAL | 12 | 29 | 26 | 6 | 3 | 8 | 3 | 2 | 1 | 1 |

owner occupiers, which provided the basis for the Labour landslide of June 1987, as the region responded warmly to its traditionalist message of joint action and collective provision.

**Table 29    The Key Issues for Voters in June 1987\***

| All Voters | Conservative Voters | Labour Voters | Alliance Voters |
|---|---|---|---|
| Unemployment (42%) | Inflation (36%) | Unemployment (66%) | Unemployment(53%) |
| Health Service (23%) | Defence (29%) | Health Service (37%) | Health Service (30%) |
| Inflation (20%) | Nuclear Weapons (26%) | Education (22%) | Education (27%) |
| Nuclear Weapons (20%) | Taxation (18%) | Pensions/Welfare | Nuclear Weapons(17%) |
| Education (19%) | Law & Order (18%) | Benefits (18%) | Pensions/Welfare |
| Defence (17%) | Unemployment (16%) | Nuclear Weapons (14%) | Benefits (13%) |
| Law & Order (14%) | Education (11%) | Law & Order (9%) | Defence (13%) |
| Pensions/Welfare | Trade Unions (10%) | Housing (6%) | Law & Order (12%) |
| Benefits (11%) | | Inflation (6%) | Inflation (10%) |

\* Source: ITN/Harris Exit Poll

Thus, despite the substantial parliamentary majority achieved by the Conservatives, the party's victory contained a number of qualifications and warnings. First, it was achieved, as in 1983, on a clear minority share of the national vote, being unduly inflated by the absence of a single united opposition bloc.[1] Second, and more importantly, its regional and social basis was unusually lopsided, substantial regions and social groupings having conclusively rejected the Conservatives' message. The government would thus need to proceed with tact and care in the years ahead if it was to heal and overcome such dangerously widening divisions.

[1] Under a simple STV ('alternative vote') system of proportional representation (PR), as for example, recommended in the Alliance's manifesto, the Conservatives would have secured a majority, but at a reduced figure of 8 seats (Conservatives 329, Labour 220, Alliance 75, SNP/PC 9, Northern Ireland parties 17). If a system of full PR, on the West German 'party list' model based at the regional level, had been employed June 1987 would have produced a 'hung parliament' with the Conservatives as the largest single party with 269 seats, followed by Labour (206), the Alliance (145), the SNP (10), the OUP (7), the SDLP (4), Plaid Cymru (3), the DUP (2), Sinn Fein (2) and the Northern Ireland Alliance Party (2). This is based on a regional cut-off threshold of 5% support (in West Germany the threshold is based at the national level and would have excluded the nationalist parties).

# Part Six

# THE THATCHER THIRD TERM: 1987–

## Power to the People

The new Parliament which convened on 17 June contained a large and varied number of new faces. 83 MPs, among them the senior figures of James Prior, Francis Pym, Patrick Jenkin, Sir Keith Joseph, Edward du Cann (all Conservatives), Sir James Callaghan, Dame Judith Hart and Ian Mikardo (all Labour) had retired. Six Labour members had been de-selected and 40 incumbent MPs, including Roy Jenkins (SDP) and Enoch Powell (DUP), had been defeated. The new 'Class of '87', partly as a result of the constituency campaigning efforts of the feminist '300 Group', included a record number of 41 women MPs (21 Conservative, 17 Labour, 2 Alliance and 1 SNP).[1] It contained the first black and Asian male MPs, Bernie Grant (Tottenham), Paul Boateng (Brent South) and Keith Vaz (Leicester East), all Labour, since 1929 and the first ever female black MP, Diane Abbott (Hackney North; Lab.).[2] It comprised, in addition, on the Labour benches, several figures who had already established a national reputation through their work for pressure groups and in local government. They were, for example, the former CND chairwoman, Joan Ruddock (Lewisham, Deptford) and the former local government supremos, David Blunkett (Sheffield, Brightside) and Ken Livingstone (Brent East). Overall, 14% of Conservatives and almost 30% of Labour MPs were 'freshers'.

---

[1] There had been a record 325 female parliamentary candidates; the Alliance, which under its selection rules must include at least two women on its candidate shortlists, 105; Labour, 92; and the Conservatives, 46. This compared with a total of 255 in June 1983, 209 in May 1979, 161 in October 1974 and 143 in February 1974. During the period 1974–1983 the number of women MPs had varied between 19 and 27.

[2] 27 black and Asian candidates, Labour 14 Conservatives 5, Alliance 7 had contested the election. This compared with a total of 18 in June 1983.

The number of Conservative retirements (43) in June 1987 was not abnormal. What was notable, however, was the prominence and political experience of many of those departing, 11 of those leaving taking with them 78 years of accumulated ministerial experience, and the predisposition of many of them to traditional 'one nation' conservatism. They were replaced by an influx of well-educated and energetic MPs, mostly in their late 30s and early 40s, with backgrounds in business and finance, and mostly orientated towards the 'dry' Thatcherite wing of the party. The shift in the balance within the parliamentary party, although centrist 'consolidators' were still predominant, was soon underlined by the post-election cabinet reshuffle by the Prime Minister, on 13 June. The critical and outspoken 'conciliator' figure of John Biffen was dismissed and sent to the back benches, while the remaining prominent 'wet', Peter Walker, was demoted to the Welsh Office portfolio. Into the new cabinet (see Table 30) returned the rehabilitated Cecil Parkinson, as Energy Secretary, while the 'enterprise partnership' of Lord Young and Kenneth Clarke was moved from Employment to the large and important Trade and Industry Department. The other significant promotion was that of John Moore, a self-made, scholarship son of an East London bench hand,and a committed free-market privatiser who had worked for five years in the United States as a financial consultant, from Transport to the high-spending Social Services Department.

The new cabinet contained Thatcherite 'dries', not only in the key Treasury posts, as between 1979–87, but also now in a number of the major spending departments, most prominently Environment, DTI and Social Services. This, coupled with the party's June 1987 manifesto pledges, suggested that the Thatcher third term would witness a period of new, free-market radicalism to fulfil the Prime Minister's 1979 pledge of effecting a major and irreversible shift in the structural formation of the British economy and polity, away from collectivism towards a new, private-sector dominated individualism. During the fortnight between 11 June and the state opening of Parliament, on 25 June, the Prime Minister moved rapidly to establish policy priorities for the 1987–8 legislative session. At the top of the agenda, in what was an unusually full programme, were initiatives to encourage enterprise in depressed inner city areas, a fundamental reform of school and college education and the replacement of rates by a new 'Community Charge', to be levied on all adults. In addition, a further tranche of privatisation was heralded, including the British Airports Authority

(BAA), in July 1987; the government's remaining shareholding in BP, in October 1987; and the electricity industry and regional water authorities, between 1989–91. A reduction in the basic rate of income tax to 25p was promised, as well as a new trade union reform Bill and partial deregulation of the rented housing sector, local government services and airwaves.

**Table 30    The Thatcher Cabinet of June 1987[1]**

| | |
|---|---|
| Prime Minister | —Margaret Thatcher (61) |
| Foreign Secretary | —Sir Geoffrey Howe (60) |
| Home Secretary | —Douglas Hurd (57) |
| Lord Chancellor | —Lord Havers (64) |
| Lord President | —Viscount Whitelaw (68) |
| Chancellor of the Exchequer | —Nigel Lawson (55) |
| Defence Secretary | —George Younger (55) |
| Trade and Industry Secretary | —Lord Young (55) |
| Environment Secretary | —Nicholas Ridley (58) |
| Employment Secretary | —Norman Fowler (49) |
| Social Services Secretary | —John Moore (49) |
| Education and Science Secretary | —Kenneth Baker (52) |
| Welsh Secretary | —Peter Walker (55) |
| Northern Ireland Secretary | —Tom King (54) |
| Scottish Secretary | —Malcolm Rifkind (40) |
| Transport Secretary | —Paul Channon (51) |
| Energy Secretary | —Cecil Parkinson (55) |
| Commons Leader | —John Wakeham (54) |
| Agriculture Secretary | —John MacGregor (50) |
| Treasury Chief Secretary | —John Major (54) |
| Chancellor Duchy of Lancaster | —Kenneth Clarke (46) |

[1] Of those removed from the previous cabinet, Nicholas Edwards had retired from the Commons, Lord Hailsham had stepped down on the grounds of advancing age and Norman Tebbit had resigned, so as to be able to spend more time with his convalescing wife, but retained his post as Party Chairman. Two new members had not previously enjoyed cabinet rank: John Major, the former Social Security minister, and Sir Michael Havers, who had served in the previous Parliament as Attorney-General.

The new policy initiatives were based on the Conservatives' 1987 election slogan 'Power to the People' and designed to encourage greater individual initiative and responsibility within schooling and trade unions. Greater private sector involvement within the inner cities was also to be fostered, under the aegis of new Urban Development Corporations (UDC), of the type that had already been established in east London and Liverpool. However, many of the new measures were controversial. The promised new 'Great Education Bill', with its provision for individual schools to 'opt-out' from Local Education Authority (LEA) funding and control and be financed directly from London, and plans for a nationally established curriculum, promised seriously to diminish local government control over one of its key sectors of activity. The proposals to establish new UDCs in Manchester, the West Midlands, Teeside and Tyneside and for the Environment Department to directly provide new Urban Regeneration Grants (URGs) to private developers, promised, similarly, to remove another important sphere of activity from council control.[1] Most contentious of all, however, although, surprisingly, it failed to emerge as a significant issue in the general election campaign, was the government's plan to replace rates with a universally payable 'Community Charge'. The change was viewed as a means of fulfilling the Prime Minister's 1979 pledge to abolish rates and to achieve a broader distribution of the local taxes. This, it was hoped, would serve to ease the burden on local businesses and encourage greater accountability and popular participation in local government. Despite such laudable aims, however, the particular alternative to rates approved by the government, the 'Community Charge', or, as the opposition termed it, the 'poll tax', was particularly contentious. Involving the payment by all adults of a flat rate local charge regardless to their income, although for recipients of welfare benefits 80% of the charge was to be borne by the DHSS, the proposed new charge was particularly inequitable, promising to lead to a major shift in the local tax burden away from the affluent towards the poor, council tenants and large families. In addition, it would be expensive and difficult to administer, and likely to lead to considerable evasion, and even encourage deliberate non-registration on electoral registers. The new 'Community Charge' was to be supported by a new, nationally framed, uniform tax rate for businesses, which promised to lead to substantial rises in business charges in the low-tax shire counties of the east and southeast and corresponding falls in highly taxed northern and urban areas.

The Rates Reform Bill, being likely to create more 'losers' than 'winners' and to encourage a relocation of businesses away from the shire counties, seemed set to encounter a fierce challenge, not only from the opposition benches but also from the government's own supporters.[2] Thus, despite the large majority, passage of the

---

[1] Urban Development Corporations are centrally funded and unelected bodies dominated by boards of officials and businessmen, which enjoy extensive planning, land purchase and development powers outside the purview of local council control.

[2] If passed by Parliament in 1988, the changes would come into force in 1990–1 and be phased in over a four-five year period.

measure by the Commons without substantial amendment seemed very much in doubt. The other elements of the government's 1987–8 programme were less contentious for Conservative MPs, but appeared likely to meet with close scrutiny by the increasingly assertive House of Lords. This, when combined with the determined policy of 'guerrilla resistance' threatened by the opposition parties' 62 Scottish MPs to the government's conduct of Scottish affairs and the renewed calls for devolution, promised to make the 1987–8 parliamentary session an unusually turbulent one.

## An Assessment of the 'Thatcher Revolution'

### Governing Style: 'The Resolute Approach'

The most striking change effected by the Thatcher administration has been the clear break from the corporatist, 'middle way' consensus of the previous three decades and a shift towards a more rigid, ideological and confrontational approach to government. As the Prime Minister stated clearly in 1981: 'To me, consensus seems to be the process of abandoning all beliefs, principles, values and policies . . . (and) of avoiding the very issues that have got to be solved'. She entered office with a clear set of beliefs and priorities and an unquestioning vision of the society she wished to mould. Furthermore, she was determined not to be pushed off course. She required loyalty and industry from the cabinet and the bureaucracy, and gradually built up an inner core of like-minded advisers, ministers and officials to put these policies into practice.

The new advisers were centred in the eight-man Number 10 Policy Unit, with ad hoc advice being drawn from the CPS. The more eclectic CPRS was abolished and the role of the Conservative Research Department downgraded. This inner core of ministers was concentrated, initially, in the Treasury, a department which dominated and sought to control all others. By October 1981, however, 'Thatcherites' had also taken charge of the key spending departments. These 'dry' ministers, who included Lawson, Brittan, Tebbit, Parkinson, Fowler, Nott, Joseph, Ridley, Young, Moore and Major, were drawn predominantly from a professional or lower middle class background and represented a new form of 'meritocrat Conservative', whose influence within the party had been growing since the mid 1960s. 'Dry'-minded officials and executives were also gradually appointed at the top of the civil service, quangos, nationalised industries and to financial and judicial posts. These radical, new figures contrasted sharply with their consensual forbears and led to criticism of overt 'politicisation'.

In the formulation and determination of policy, Margaret Thatcher employed small standing and ad hoc committees. The number of full cabinet meetings thus fell to 40–45 a year, half the average of the 1960s, although major issues were still finally resolved through this body. In these committee meetings the Prime Minister dominated discussions by first setting out her views and putting the onus on the dissenting minister to persuade her to change her mind. She also started rapid policy initiatives through the establishment of small seminars in Number 10, involving interested outside bodies and individuals. These seminars have ranged from drug abuse to football hooliganism. She has also overseen the formation of special interdepartmental ministerial groupings to tackle pressing problems, such as inner city decay, in 1987. This inveterate resort to ad hoc bodies has reflected the Prime Minister's deep antipathy towards structured bureaucracies. The Thatcher years have also seen the creation and emergence to prominence of a powerful new mediating body, the 'Star Chamber'. Dominated by 'dries', this six-member cabinet committee has ensured tight control over departmental spending programmes.

In pressing for implementation of policies, the Prime Minister has maintained far closer links with her backbenchers than her predecessor as party leader, Edward Heath, and has made frequent and judicious use of her extensive patronage powers. In addition, she has been willing, on occasions, to go above the heads of her immediate parliamentary and ministerial colleagues and appeal for support to the wider public and to Conservative Party constituency activists, through skilled use of the media. Margaret Thatcher has maintained a raw, cross-class, 'populist' appeal through her known beliefs on issues such as patriotism, capital punishment, the EEC and immigration, and has also managed to distance herself, when forced to make strategic and pragmatic retreats.

Taken in total, the Thatcher style of government has been forceful, personalised and in, many respects, presidential. She has emerged as the most interventionist Prime Minister since the 'mobilising' wartime leaders, David Lloyd George (1916–22) and Winston Churchill (1940–5) and has significantly extended the frontiers of her office, assuming, for example, close control over foreign policy during her second and third terms. However, it should be noted that, from a longer perspective, many of the changes effected have been matters of degree. The move towards smaller ad hoc committees has been progressive during the last three decades as the executive's workload has burgeoned. So has the induction of outside advisers and the stress on the individual rather than on the cabinet as a collective body.

Margaret Thatcher entered office in May 1979 pledged to concentrate on three main policy areas: the halting and reversal of Britain's economic decline; the reform and weakening of the trade union movement; the improvement of the conditions of law and order. To what extent had she achieved these aims by 1987?

## The Economic Record

The Thatcher administration adopted a radical economic strategy which drew on both monetarist and free-market, supply-side economics It aimed, first, at reducing inflation through tight control of the money supply and through lowering the PSBR; second, at reducing the level of public spending and pruning the state sector through a programme of privatisation; and, third, at increasing incentives for industry and attempting to foster a new entrepreneurial and individualistic spirit by tax cuts and de-regulation.

The government's record on inflation has been its proudest: the rate, after suddenly jumping in 1979–80, falling to a stable level of between 3–5%. It is unclear, however, to what extent this has been the result of a tight monetary-fiscal strategy or caused by the sharp and generalised fall in world commodity prices after 1980.[1]

Its record on reducing government expenditure has been less satisfactory. First, spending has been drastically squeezed on housing, education, the bureaucracy, local government, transport and industrial support (see Table 31), but has increased on health, social security, defence, and law and order, from a mixture of necessity and choice. Thus, despite the introduction of new management efficiency systems (MINIS and FMI), the sub-contracting of many ancillary activities, and the pruning of public sector workforces and constriction of their pay, public spending rose from

[1] In comparative terms, the UK inflation rate in 1986, which stood at 2.4%, was still inferior to that recorded in the competitor nations of France (2.0%), USA (1.6%), Japan (0.8%), Belgium (0.8%), Switzerland (0.5%), West Germany (−0.5%) and Holland (−0.7%).

175

a figure equal to 43% of GNP in 1978 to 46.5% in 1982. It only began to fall after 1983 as economic growth resumed, finally returning to its inherited proportionate level in 1986 (see Table 32). Second, while on paper the government has significantly reduced the size of the PSBR as a proportion of GNP, much of this has been illusory and the result of counting council house and privatised company asset sales as 'negative public spending'. A more accurate measure of government borrowing, the Public Sector Financial Deficit (PSFD), which excludes asset sales, shows only a minor fall in proportionate terms between 1979–86.

Faced with this disappointing performance. some free-market Conservatives, such as the backbench '92 Club', called for a more radical attack on public spending, including a switch towards private medicine and education and a fundamental overhaul of the welfare benefits system. However, the Thatcher administration has shied away from a frontal assault on the popular welfare state. It has sought instead slowly to roll back the state sector and encourage private services through tax incentives.

Table 31    Public Spending During the Thatcher Years, 1979–86

|  | 1978–1979 | | 1986–1987 | | Spending |
| --- | --- | --- | --- | --- | --- |
|  | (£bn) | As % of | (£bn) | As % of | Change |
|  | Expenditure | Total | Expenditure | Total | 1979–86[1] |
| Defence | 14.1 | 11.4% | 18.1 | 13.2% | + 28% |
| Foreign Office | 2.0 | 1.6% | 1.9 | 1.4% | − 4% |
| EEC | 1.4 | 1.1% | 1.1 | 0.8% | − 24% |
| Agriculture | 1.5 | 1.2% | 1.9 | 1.4% | + 23% |
| Trade & Industry | 4.5 | 3.6% | 1.6 | 1.2% | − 65% |
| Energy | 1.0 | 0.8% | 0.2 | 0.1% | − 78% |
| Employment | 2.0 | 1.6% | 3.8 | 2.8% | + 90% |
| Transport | 4.9 | 4.0% | 4.8 | 3.5% | − 3% |
| Housing | 6.7 | 5.4% | 2.7 | 2.0% | − 60% |
| Environment | 4.3 | 3.5% | 4.0 | 2.9% | − 7% |
| Home Office | 3.8 | 3.1% | 5.7 | 4.2% | + 50% |
| Education & Science | 14.6 | 11.8% | 15.5 | 11.4% | + 6% |
| Arts | 0.6 | 0.5% | 0.8 | 0.6% | + 30% |
| Health | 14.0 | 11.3% | 17.5 | 12.8% | + 25% |
| Social Security | 31.0 | 25.0% | 43.2 | 31.6% | + 40% |
| Scotland, Wales & | | | | | |
| Northern Ireland | 13.9 | 11.2% | 15.1 | 11.1% | + 8% |
| Other Depts. | 3.5 | 2.8% | 3.5 | 2.6% | + 1% |
| Asset Sales | - | - | 4.7 | | |
| Planning Total | 124.0 | | 136.5 | | + 10% |
| General Government | | | | | |
| Expenditure[2] | 140.7 | | 159.9 | | + 14% |

[1] Adjusted to take into account inflation

[2] Includes debt interest

The two most striking initiatives in this field have been the privatisation and council house sale programmes. These have gathered momentum, so that by 1985 the government had raised more than £12 billion from council houses sales and £7 billion from the privatisation of state industries and was well on course to raising a further £12 billion between 1986–8 from the sale of British Gas, British Airways, the National Bus Company, Rolls-Royce and the

**Table 32    Economic Indicators, 1979–86**

| | 1979 | 1980 | 1981 | 1982 | 1983 | 1984 | 1985 | 1986 |
|---|---|---|---|---|---|---|---|---|
| GNP Growth | +2.2% | −3.4% | −1.6% | +1.7% | +2.8% | +1.7% | +3.3% | +2.0% |
| Ind. Growth | +2.5% | −7.0% | −3.5% | +2.1% | +3.3% | +0.9% | +5.4% | +1.4% |
| Unemployment | 5.1% | 6.4% | 10.0% | 11.7% | 12.4% | 12.7% | 13.1% | 13.2%* |
| Inflation | +13% | +19% | +11% | +6.6% | +5.8% | +5.4% | +5.5% | +3.5% |
| Wages | +18% | +21% | +13% | +9.4% | +8.4% | +6.1% | +7.0% | +7.5% |
| Public Spending† | 43.5% | 46% | 46% | 46.5% | 45.5% | 45.5% | 44% | 43.3% |
| PSBR† | 5.0% | 5.5% | 3.5% | 3.3% | 3.2% | 3.2% | 2.0% | 2.2% |
| MS Growth (M3) | 11.2% | 19.4% | 12.8% | 11.2% | 10.1% | 9.8% | 14.4% | 18.6% |
| Exchange Rate | $2.1 | $2.3 | $2.0 | $1.7 | $1.5 | $1.4 | $1.4 | $1.5 |
| Trade Balance $bn | −6.7 | +2.6 | +0.7 | +1.6 | −1.5 | −4.9 | −3.1 | −11.7 |
| Working Days Lost To Industrial Action | 31.2m | 12.0m | 4.3m | 5.3m | 4.2m | 27.6m | 6.8m | 2.7m |

* Adjusted to 1985 basis

† As a proportion of GNP

British Airports Authority. Further sales of key assets such as the Regional Water Authorities, the electric supply industry, the British Steel Corporation, Land Rover and the remaining shares in British Telecom appeared likely to bring in more than £5 billion per annum between 1989–91. The proceeds from these sales, while being criticised as dangerous 'short termism' by opponents of the government, have proved useful in reducing the PSBR and of allowing for a significant measure of reflation between 1986–7. The policies have also served to transfer more than 400 000 workers to the private sector, and significantly broaden the shareholding and home-ownership base.[1] It remains be seen how these newly privatised firms fare during the next downturn in the economy. What is certain, however, is that this major shift in the balance of the economy will take many years for any subsequent government

[1] Between 1979–87 the proportion of the UK housing stock held by owner occupiers rose from 55% to 65% of the total, while that held by council tenants fell from 32% to 25%. The proportion of the population holding shares increased from 4.5% to 12% between these dates.

to redress: by 1985, for example, the proportion of the population covered by private health insurance had doubled to 8% and the proportion of children attending private schools had increased to 6%, from a 1979 level of 5%, while by 1988 the proportion of GNP accounted for by state industries will have been almost halved from 10.5% to 6.5%.

These privatisation schemes have formed part of a broader government strategy aimed at fostering a dynamic and innovative private industrial sector and inculcating a new, market-orientated spirit. They have been supported by a series of de-regulationary actions: the reduction in employment, environmental and planning restrictions on small businesses, and the opening up of monopolies, such as house conveyancing, telephone supplies and bus and coach transportation, to a measure of competition. In addition, the income tax burden was significantly reduced at both its upper and lower levels in the budgets of 1979 and 1987, in an effort to increase incentives. However, such measures have once again been criticised as too limited by radical supply-siders. The latter have called for the total abolition of Wages Councils and the removal of rent controls, to foster a dynamic and mobile, American style, economy. They have also been critical of the fact that, although income tax has been reduced, total tax burdens, direct and indirect, have increased from, on average, 35p in every pound in 1979 to 38p in 1986, as a result of the failure to cut public spending more savagely.

What has been the effect of these radical supply-side reforms ? Have they helped to foster a new economic and entrepreneurial revival ?

The economic statistics of the years between 1979–87 would suggest an equivocal answer. The British economy was plunged into the most severe depression since the 1930s during the period between 1980–2. Manufacturing output slumped dramatically, thousands of firms were bankrupted and unemployment rose sharply. Since 1982 there has been a slow recovery, but manufacturing output in 1986 still stood 4% below that attained during Edward Heath's enforced three-day week in 1974 and the country boasted a novel and widening deficit on its manufacturing account. This decline contrasted with an output growth of between 16% and 61% in the West German, Italian, French, American and Japanese manufacturing sectors.

Between 1979 and 1985 the numbers employed in the manufacturing sector fell precipitately by 24%, from 7.1 million to 5.4

**Table 33   The Thatcher Government's Privatisation Programme, 1979–87**

| | Companies Privatised | Amount Raised (£m) |
|---|---|---|
| 1979–80 | 5% of BP | 276 |
| | 25% of ICL | 37 |
| | Others | 64 |
| | Total | 377 |
| 1980–1 | 50% of Ferranti | 55 |
| | 51% of British Aerospace | 43 |
| | North Sea Oil Licences | 195 |
| | Others | 112 |
| | Total | 405 |
| 1981–2 | 49% of Cable & Wireless | 182 |
| | 100% of Amersham International | 64 |
| | 24% of British Sugar | 44 |
| | Others | 204 |
| | Total | 494 |
| 1982–3 | 51% of Britoil | 334 |
| | 49% of Associated British Ports | 46 |
| | Others | 202 |
| | Total | 582 |
| 1983–4 | 7% of BP | 543 |
| | 49% of Britoil | 293 |
| | 25% of Cable & Wireless | 263 |
| | Others | 69 |
| | Total | 1168 |
| 1984–5 | 50.2% of British Telecom (first call) | 1500 |
| | 100% of Enterprise Oil | 380 |
| | 100% of Jaguar Cars | 297 |
| | 75% of Inmos | 95 |
| | Others | 172 |
| | Total | 2444 |
| 1985–6 | British Telecom (second call) | 1200 |
| | Others (incl. 48% of British Aerospace) | 1500 |
| | Total | 2700 |
| 1986–7 | British Telecom (third call) | 1200 |
| | 100% of British Gas (first call) | 2000 |
| | 100% of British Airways (first call) | 480 |
| | Others | 920 |
| | Total | 4600 |
| 1987–8 (Planned) | 100% of Rolls Royce | 1360 |
| | British Gas (second call) | 1800 |
| | British Airways (second call) | 420 |
| | 100% of British Airports Authority (first call) | 600 |
| | 31.6% of BP (first call) | 2000 |
| | Royal Ordnance Factories | 190 |
| | Total | 6270 |

million, affecting both the older 'smokestack' industries of coal, steel, shipbuilding and textiles, as well as the 'second wave' engineering, automobile, rubber and electrical industries of the West Midlands. There were, it is true, long- and medium-term factors behind this decline, low investment and productivity, poor marketing, the 'cold shower' of EEC entry and growing competition from Japan and the NICs, but government policies between 1979–80 exacerbated the situation. High interest and exchange rates and the failure to check wage increases reduced British firms' competitiveness by a disastrous 50%. The home market was deflated by fiscal austerity, and the government failed to step in to provide temporary support to ailing concerns. In subsequent years, 'rationalisation' and the installation of new, automated technology raised productivity by more than a third (1980–7), but further reduced workforce numbers.

The performance of the rest of the economy has been less disappointing. North Sea oil, production of which increased rapidly to a 1985 peak, has created 100000 new jobs and contributed 7% to GNP, 11% to to exports and 9% to government tax revenues. A similar number are employed in the new high-tech sector, although the country has a growing trade deficit on this account. It has, however, been the service and small firms sector which has been the most buoyant during the Thatcher era. 0.8 million additional jobs have been created in the service sector since 1979 and 0.7 million among the self-employed, while there has been a net increase of 140000 in the number of registered businesses operating.

There is thus evidence of a revival of entrepreneurship and the creation of a more business-orientated environment. However, such changes have been minimal when set against the large scale decline in manufacturing, which has traditionally been the major wealth creating and exporting sector of the economy. The Thatcherite supply-side strategy has been ill suited to the complex requirements of manufacturing industry in a modern world economy, where government promotion and support have become increasingly necessary.

## The Tamed Giant? Trade Unions under Thatcher

Perhaps the greatest success of the Thatcher administration has been its humbling of the once powerful trade union movement. Much of this has resulted from the government's determination to stand up to union coercion, exhibited by the infliction of serious and exemplary defeats on the steelworkers in 1980, the miners in 1984–5 and the printworkers, teachers and civil servants in 1986–7. The government was also helped, however, by contemporary economic forces which have decimated union numbers, cowed their members and enabled the new legislation to be enforced without successful challenge.

During the 1970s union leaders exerted tremendous economic and political power at a time of rising membership rolls, the proportion of the workforce incorporated in trade unions rising to a peak of 54%, 13.3 million, in 1979. Things changed after 1979. Severe recession and the shift in the economy towards the poorly unionised service, small firms and self-employed sectors reduced membership rolls to little more than 9.5 million (40% of the workforce).[1] The strike weapon became ineffective at a time of glutted markets, while the doors of government were closed and a stream of anti-union legislation introduced.

This legislation, the Employment Acts of 1980, 1982 and 1984, outlawed secondary industrial action, restricted picket numbers, removed unions' legal immunities and compelled the holding of ballots for strikes, internal elections, closed shop agreements and the political levy. It was met with initial union defiance at the April 1982 Special Wembley Conference, but this did not materialise into widespread industrial action among workforces subdued by mounting unemployment. Instead, strikes became fewer, ballots returned power to the rank and file members and a new kind of co-operative German style unionism emerged.

This 'new unionism', involving the regular use of ballots, the negotiation of single union no-strike agreements, and union funding of re-training, has been pioneered by the EETPU electricians and supported by the AEU engineers. It has challenged the older, but declining, 'smokestack' industrial unions and threatened to lead to a split in the TUC, with the emergence of a breakaway body, incorporating the AEU, EETPU, the rebel UDM and moderate nursing, banking and management unions. The Thatcher era has thus seriously weakened the union movement and created fissures. The TUC may still unite around a moderate and realistic

---

[1] Particularly sharp falls in membership numbers were recorded by blue-collar manual unions, such as the TGWU, AUEW and NUM, whose rolls fell by between 20–35% between 1979–85. By contrast, white collar and service sector unions, for example local government workers (NALGO) and bankworkers (BIFU), either held on or increased their membership numbers. This helped somewhat to shift the balance on the TUC's general council in a more moderate, 'new realism' direction.

programme, but the diminution in union power appears likely to continue as employment progressively shifts towards the service and small firms sector, and as privatisation and no-strike agreements are extended. Many of the government's reforms, including the use of ballots, appear likely to stick, although a compensatory statute of union rights may need to be constructed.

## Law and Order

The Thatcher administration's record on law and order has, by contrast, been a failure. Crime levels and drug trafficking have increased, the number of notifiable criminal offences rising by 40% in the UK between 1979–85, and a spate of unprecedented rioting has blighted the inner cities. This breakdown in public order has been, in part, the consequence of an unfortunate side effect of the 'Thatcher revolution', the widening of regional and social differentials and tensions.

Margaret Thatcher's tax-cutting and incentive-based economic policy has reversed a thirty-year trend towards narrowing income differentials, with the share of national income held by the top 20% of households rising from 44.4% to 48.8% and that of the bottom 40% falling from 10.2% to 6.4% between 1976 and 1984.[1] This trend has been exacerbated by high unemployment levels and a shift in the labour force away from the higher paid, male dominated, manufacturing sector to the lower paid, predominantly female staffed, service sector.

The decline of the 'smokestack' and second wave industries in the traditional industrial regions of the northeast, northwest, central Scotland, South Wales and West Midlands and the growth of the new high-tech and service sector industries in southern and eastern England have widened regional economic differentials, as reflected in unemployment, average income, home ownership and even health statistics (see Table 34). The new high-tech industries have been attracted to southern England by its environment, its proximity to the expanding European market and by the existence of a matrix of government, private sector and academic research institutes. They have followed market forces and the government, with the exception of central Scotland's Scottish Development Agency (SDA) which funded 'Silicon Glen', has done little to

[1] The numbers living on or just above the poverty line increased from 11.5 million to 16.3 million between 1979–83.

182

attempt to reverse this natural process. It has, instead, reduced the scope of regional aid grants and cut back central support to inner city areas, with baleful consequences for regions such as Teeside and Merseyside, where unemployment exceeds 20%. These broadening regional economic differentials were reflected in the sharpening of divisions between north and south in terms of party support in the June 1983 and June 1987 general elections and have led to renewed interest in devolution and the creation of new, regional economic and political bodies. It remains to be seen whether the government's declared concern to bring employment and new industries to depressed regions and urban agglomerations during its third term in office will do anything to reverse this widening trend.

**Table 34    Regional Trends During the Thatcher Years**

|  | May 1986 | 1979–86 | 1985 Av. Weekly | 1985 % | 1985 % | 1985 (per 1,000 births) |
|---|---|---|---|---|---|---|
|  | Unemploy ment Level | Job Losses or Gains | Household Income | Owner Occupiers | Council Tenants | Infant Mortality |
| SCOTLAND | 15.8% | – 149,000 | £198 | 41% | 50% | 9.6 |
| WALES | 17.3% | – 130,000 | £187 | 67% | 23% | 9.8 |
| N IRELAND | 21.7% | – 64,000 | £179 | 61% | 34% | 9.4 |
| ENGLAND | 13.5% | – 1,267,000 | £210 | 64% | 25% | 9.2 |
| North/Northeast | 19.1% | – 215,000 | £170 | 62% | 27% | 8.4 |
| Northwest | 16.3% | – 278,000 | £183 | 65% | 26% | 9.4 |
| Yorkshire & Humberside | 15.8% | – 266,000 | £173 | 55% | 34% | 10.3 |
| West Midlands | 15.5% | – 301,000 | £187 | 63% | 28% | 10.5 |
| East Midlands | 12.9% | – 118,000 | £203 | 66% | 24% | 8.3 |
| Southwest | 12.2% | – 39,000 | £209 | 69% | 18% | 8.5 |
| East Anglia | 11.2% | + 23,000 | £205 | 66% | 22% | 9.4 |
| Southeast | 10.1% | – 73,000 | £248 | 64% | 24% | 8.5 |

## The Success of Thatcherism?

In summary, the achievements of the 'Thatcher Revolution' remain partial and flawed. It has conquered inflation, tamed the unions and begun to foster a more entrepreneurial and self-reliant spirit. Its tight fiscal policy and lack of interventionism have, however, had serious consequences for the manufacturing sector and for specific regions and social groups. In addition, its overriding concern to check public spending has resulted in unprecedented intervention in the sphere of local government, through such levers as ratecapping and UDCs, and a marked centralisation of power, in stark variance with traditional Conservative principles. The government has been successful, however, in effecting a significant sea change in popular attitudes towards the role and abilities of governments. Through its constant repetition of homilies about balanced bookkeeping and the need for wage restraint and thrift, it has inculcated into the public mind a philosophy of limits and of diminished expectations, following the Keynesian growth-orientated 1950–76 era, and has begun to foster a new 'small government' and individualist consensus. Margaret Thatcher's securing of a third consecutive term in power, making her the longest serving Prime Minister since Lord Liverpool (1812–27), has given her a unique opportunity to establish decisively this consensus, shifting the socio-political ratchet firmly in a 'New Right', market dominated, direction.

## Party Prospects for the 1990s

### A New Era of Conservative Dominance?

The Conservatives' achievement of three consecutive electoral victories between 1979–87, based on a solid 40 + % share of the national vote, suggested to many political commentators that Britain was set for an extended period of one-party dominance, more pronounced than that achieved by the Conservatives during the interwar and 1951–64 eras, and similar to that experienced during the immediate postwar decades by the Christian and Liberal Democrats in Italy, West Germany and Japan. During the 1960s and 1970s Labour, helped by and responding to economic and demographic changes, such as the trend towards larger 'collectivist' factories, offices and housing estates, the expansion of the public sector, and the influx of a swathe of young electors seeking upward mobility and material betterment, seemed to have established itself as the 'natural party of government'. Its period of dominance proved, however, to be short-lived. Newly affluent middle and skilled working class voters, concerned at rising tax levels, began to desert the party to support, instead, the Conservatives or Liberal-SDP Alliance. At the same time, Labour's traditional bedrock of manufacturing-based manual support was inexorably contracting, as a result of industrial recession and factory rationalisation, the proportion of the UK labour force employed in manufacturing falling from 35% in 1970 to only 25% in 1985. Instead, the balance of the economy shifted towards the service (65% of the workforce in 1985 compared to 52% in 1970), small firms (25% in 1985) and self-employed (10% in 1985) sectors, as well as towards southern and suburban regions. Such demographic changes enabled the Conservatives to construct a new alliance of the successful and the upwardly mobile, comprising in excess of 40% of the electorate, and establish a vice-like hold over the southern third of the nation. With its 1979–87 privatisation and council house sale initiatives, involving the transfer of more than 750 000 council homes into private ownership, and the creation of more than four million new shareholders, it broadened the social base of its support. The prospects of further advantageous constituency boundary changes, to take account of north-south, city-suburbs migration, should help the party to add to its 1983 and 1987 level of national support during the 1990s.

The economic and demographic changes of the 1980s have been disastrous for Labour, but beneficial to the Liberal-SDP Alliance. Labour's slump in support in the 1983 and 1987 elections, to between 28–30% from its 1970s level of 39%, has reflected the contraction in the relative strength of its bedrock manual working class and council-home owning support. The Alliance, in contrast, added almost 10% to the Liberals' 1970s level of support during the 1983 and 1987 general elections, attracting to its ranks many of the white collar and middle class 'new wave' voters. The grouping's full breakthrough has, however, been frustrated by the first-past-the-post electoral system and the existence of the Labour Party, with its solid class support, as an effective left-of-centre 'blocker'. If the Conservatives' new hegemony is to be broken, it seems that one of the two opposition party groupings will need to achieve true ascendancy, driving down its rival's share of national support to a level significantly below 20%, and thus radically changing the vote distribution at constituency level.[1]

## A New Labour Party for the '90s?

In the immediate wake of the June 1987 election, both opposition groupings began to address these issues. Inside the Labour Party a thoroughgoing debate started on the way forward. The party's right

[1] On present voting distribution, and with the continuing decline in the number of marginal constituencies, a national swing of 8% in 1991 or 1992 would be required for Labour to achieve a parliamentary majority and a swing of 4% just to prevent the Conservatives achieving a majority. By comparison, the largest postwar swings have been 11.8% (to Labour), in 1945, and 5.2% (to the Conservatives), in 1979.

wing, based in many of the heartland seats of northern England and central Scotland, where encouraging advances had recently been made, called for a major reappraisal of policy and organisation in an effort to reassert moderate 'true Labour' values and to broaden the party's appeal to middle-income groups. In particular, they sought the abandonment of the policy of unilateral nuclear disarmament, which psephologists suggested had forfeited Labour at least 4% of national support in June 1987. They also pressed for the introduction of 'one member, one vote' in the selection of parliamentary candidates and conference delegates and for reform of the procedure for election to the NEC, so as to strengthen the influence of northern party members and weaken that of radical London and southern 'polytocrats'. The Kinnockite 'soft left', which remained the clear controlling grouping within the party, rejected the right's calls for abandonment of Labour's non-nuclear defence strategy, preferring to wait to see how international disarmament negotiations progressed during the next few years.[1] Aware, however, of the need for Labour to widen its geographical and social base, and escape from its present '30% working class ghetto', they supported the drive for extension of party democracy so as to give individual members a greater say, and reduce the influence of committed GMC activists. With these ends in mind, a new national party newspaper was launched during 1987 which was mailed directly and free to all members and Neil Kinnock came out firmly in support of the principle of 'one member, one vote' in parliamentary candidate selection and re-selection, making plain his intention to re-introduce a proposal for this measure at the autumn 1987 party conference. In 1984 such a motion had been narrowly defeated because of the opposition of the large TGWU and NUPE trade unions. On this occasion, however, Kinnock appeared to enjoy firmer trade union backing. The proposal would involve a weighted 'electoral college' system at the constituency level, so as to give unions a continuing voice, and acceptance of the reform seemed probable. The centre-right and 'soft left' hoped that this rule change would lead to a large new influx of members, enabling it to build up a momentum and establish a fresh new, moderate image, in readiness for the 1991–2 election campaign. However, the 'one man, one vote' reform, coupled with the proposed further rightward shift in the party's policy stance in the economic sphere, and continuing drives against members of the

[1] A number did, however, moot the idea of, if elected, putting the nuclear issue to a national referendum as a means of taking the heat out of this contentious subject.

'Militant Tendency',[1] seemed set to be sternly opposed by the party's 'hard left' Campaign Group. This faction remained well entrenched at GMC level and now boasted a 25% share (57) of Labour's parliamentary seats, an increase of 5% (16) on its 1986 total.[2]

## The Alliance Regroups

In the Alliance camp, the early initiative after the June 1987 election was seized by the Liberal leader David Steel. Barely two days days after voting had been completed, Steel issued a statement calling for a 'democratic fusion' of the Liberals and SDP into a new party to be termed, tentatively, the Liberal Democratic Alliance. He argued that the existence of two separate party structures between 1983–7, while not only being wasteful of resources, had created policy confusion in the public's mind during the May–June 1987 election campaign, to the detriment of the Alliance's poll performance. He proposed, therefore, that both parties' ruling councils should meet jointly during the summer of 1987 to devise a framework for a new merged party, which would incorporate the strengths of each existing organisation, blending the 'logical and coherent constitution of the SDP' with 'the more powerful, decentralised, grassroots organisation of the Liberal Party'. These proposals would then be sent for ratification at the SDP and Liberals' autumn annual conferences before being sent on to both parties' membership at large to be accepted or rejected through a one person, one vote ballot. The question of merger had occupied the Liberal leader's mind since June 1983, but had necessarily been formally held back as a result of the declared opposition of the SDP leader, David Owen. Owen's distaste for merger derived from his fears of the SDP, with its distinctive new 'social market economy' approach, being subsumed by a Liberal Party which he saw as dangerously 'soft' on defence, muddled in its economic thinking and dominated

---

[1] In 1986–7 a new 'soft left' dominated, 11-member disciplinary body, the National Constitutional Committee, was established to take over from the NEC the lead in prosecuting members of 'Militant', in a more efficient and expeditious manner.

[2] At the constituency level the 'hard left' established the new Labour Left Liaison grouping in 1986, linking readers of the radical 'Socialist Action', 'Socialist Organiser', 'Campaign Herald' and 'Labour Briefing' newspapers. It was attached to the Campaign Group of MPs by the Campaign Forum organisation. The 'soft left' Tribunites were represented, locally, by the Labour Co-ordinating Committee.

by an unpredictable, and almost anarchic, tail of rank and file activists. Thus, although at first maintaining a studied silence, he worked hard behind the scenes to orchestrate moves designed to discredit the merger option. His close parliamentary allies, John Cartwright (Woolwich) and Rosie Barnes (Greenwich) made clear their view that the large, 130 000 member, 17-MP strong, Liberal Party was seeking precipitately to 'bounce' the dispirited SDP into what would effectively be the 'takeover' of a party which could only boast five MPs. A rift thus rapidly developed between the two parties' parliamentary leaderships, with the SDP, for example, on 17 June, ending the system of joint parliamentary spokesmen that had been in operation since January 1987. On the same day the Parliamentary Liberal Party unanimously voted for 'full-blooded merger' of the two parties.

During the closing weeks of June 1987 an unedifying public squabble developed between the Liberals and SDP, and between anti-merger 'Owenite' and pro-merger 'Jenkinsite' wings of the SDP itself, which served seriously to damage the two parties' claims to support a new style of co-operative, consensual politics. The 'Owenites', who boasted considerable strength in the SDP's National Committee, proposed, instead of merger, a 'federal solution', in which separate party structures would be retained, but in which policies for the next election would be jointly agreed at an early date and a single leader selected by January 1990, to head the Alliance during the subsequent campaign. They moved quickly to organise an early ballot of party members during July–August 1987, inserting a form of question which, by talking of the 'abolition of the SDP', was deliberately loaded against merger. The 'Jenkinsites', who included William Rodgers and Party President, Shirley Williams, and who enjoyed substantial constituency-level backing, sharply rejected this form of wording and forced, the National Committee to delete the offending phrase. Nevertheless, the Committee made clear, by 18 votes to 13, its preference for David Owen's federation option, urging the party's 58,000 members to vote against merger.

The merger decision was put to the SDP membership-at-large during July–August, the ballot posing a choice between the retention of separate parties with closer cooperation between them (Option 1) or discussions leading to a full merger (Option 2). The result was a 57% vote for talks about merging and this was later endorsed at the annual conference in Portsmouth, at the end of August, by the larger majority of 60%. Immediately following the ballot result David Owen announced his resignation as leader, on the grounds that he no longer commanded the support of the majority of the party, and, at a time when most leading members were scattered on holiday throughout the world, attempts were made to find a speedy replacement. The party's constitution required the leader to be an MP so none of the original 'Gang of Four' was eligible and the only clear pro-merger parliamentarian was the young Scot, Charles Kennedy. He eventually persuaded Robert Maclennan, previously thought to be firmly in the non-merger camp, to be nominated. The Owenites resisted the temptation to oppose him and, in consequence, the 51-year-old MP for Caithness and Sutherland was automatically elected. The emergence of the quiet, self-effacing Scots barrister as interim leader and chief negotiator in the merger talks with the Liberals was undoubtedly a setback for Owen and his supporters. The party now appeared to have divided itself into three camps: the pro-mergerites; the anti-merger, Owenite, faction; and the 'wait and see what the talks produce' group, of which Maclennan was an obvious member.

The negotiations, which were set to commence immediately after the Liberal Party's annual conference in September 1987, promised to be difficult and keenly argued, with a final decision on their outcome set to be put before the policy-making Council for Social Democracy in January 1988. If accepted, merger promised to lead to the formation of an enlarged and more responsible, new model Liberal Party, founded on a more tightly worded and centralised constitution, designed to give the leadership firmer control over the outcome of conference debates. This new party, Steel hoped, would form the fulcrum on which a new centre-left majority could be constructed, with a future electoral pact with the Labour Party, in return for an agreement to introduce proportional representation, remaining a possibility in the 1990s. However, the deep antagonism generated by the 'Owenite' Social Democrats' opposition to amicable merger has seriously diminished the possible publicity and support boost to be derived from the formation of the new centre-left party. This, coupled with the threatened creation of new minor splinter parties by Owenite SDP members[1] and Liberal traditionalists, promises to weaken the 'third force' in British politics, providing an opportunity for a newly re-invigorated Labour Party to re-establish its dominance as the principal opposition.

---

[1] The creation of the 'Grassroots Uprising' organisation by several thousand Owenite SDP members and the Greenwich-based Campaign for Social Democracy mailing organisation during September 1987 promised to be the precursor of a breakaway SDP grouping led by Owen, Barnes and Cartwright and partly funded by the businessman trustee David Sainsbury.

## Everything to Play For

For both opposition parties, a key factor determining the outcome of the 1991 or 1992 general election will be the fate of the economy. With North Sea oil output having reached its peak and beginning a slow decline, the Thatcher administration will be forced increasingly to face the 'stop-go' balance of payments policy constraints that afflicted successive governments between 1951–79, but to which it itself has fortunately been immune. Continuing public asset sales between 1987–91 will, however, provide a useful financial buffer for the incumbent government's public spending plans. Another, possibly decisive, factor will centre on the leadership of the Conservative Party. Despite talk on Margaret Thatcher's part of her willingness to 'go on and on' as national leader during the early stages of the May–June 1987 election campaign, the heavy 'frontloading' of the 1987–8 legislative programme has left the option for the Prime Minister to step down in mid-term, in 1988 or 1989, with her reform programme completed, and to establish in power a new like-minded leader, who would diligently safeguard and uphold the 'Thatcher Revolution'. Cecil Parkinson or John Moore emerge as obvious heirs. If pressed into stepping down, however, as a result of adverse fortunes, the party's leadership banner would seem likely to fall to one of the less committed, and more pragmatic and interventionist, figures of Kenneth Baker, Douglas Hurd, Peter Walker or Michael Heseltine. Whatever the eventual succession, however, no obvious contender possesses the combination of intense drive, self-belief, commitment and dogged determination that is combined in the present leader, suggesting that the post-Thatcher era will witness significant changes, not only in tone and style, but also in content, with a shift back towards consolidation rather than reform.

## APPENDIX

# Additional Tables

### Table 35  British Parliamentary By-Elections 1970–87

| Parliament | By-Election Numbers | Party Share Before By-elections | | | | | | Party Share After By-elections | | | | | |
|---|---|---|---|---|---|---|---|---|---|---|---|---|---|
| | | Con | Lab | Lib | SNP | PC | Ind | Con | Lab | Lib+ | SNP | PC | Ind |
| 1970–74 | 30 | 13 | 16 | 0 | 0 | 0 | 1 | 8 | 15 | 5 | 1 | 0 | 1 |
| 1974–79 | 30 | 10 | 20 | 1 | 0 | 0 | 0 | 16 | 13 | 1 | 0 | 0 | 0 |
| 1979–83 | 17 | 7 | 10 | 1 | 0 | 0 | 0 | 4 | 9 | 4 | 0 | 0 | 0 |
| 1983–87 | 16 | 9 | 6 | 1 | 0 | 0 | 0 | 5 | 6 | 5 | 0 | 0 | 0 |

+ Incl. SDP from 1981

### Table 36  Party Seats by Region (excl. NI)

| | OCTOBER 1974 | | | | | MAY 1979 | | | | | JUNE 1983 SDP‡ | | | | | JUNE 1987 SDP‡ | | | | |
|---|---|---|---|---|---|---|---|---|---|---|---|---|---|---|---|---|---|---|---|---|
| | Con | Lab | Lib | PC | SNP | Con | Lab | Lib | PC | SNP | Con | Lab | Lib | PC | SNP | Con | Lab | Lib | PC | SNP |
| ENGLAND | 253 | 255 | 8 | — | — | 306 | 203 | 7 | — | — | 362 | 148 | 13 | — | — | 358 | 155 | 10 | — | — |
| North | 8 | 30 | 1 | — | — | 8 | 29 | 1 | — | — | 8 | 26 | 2 | — | — | 8 | 27 | 1 | — | — |
| Northwest | 26 | 51 | 1 | — | — | 31 | 45 | 2 | — | — | 36 | 35 | 2 | — | — | 34 | 36 | 3 | — | — |
| Yorks & Humberside | 15 | 38 | 1 | — | — | 19 | 34 | 1 | — | — | 24 | 28 | 2 | — | — | 21 | 33 | 0 | — | — |
| East Midlands | 15 | 21 | 0 | — | — | 20 | 16 | 0 | — | — | 34 | 8 | 0 | — | — | 31 | 11 | 0 | — | — |
| West Midlands | 21 | 35 | 0 | — | — | 31 | 25 | 0 | — | — | 36 | 22 | 0 | — | — | 36 | 22 | 3 | — | — |
| Greater London | 41 | 51 | 0 | — | — | 50 | 42 | 0 | — | — | 56 | 26 | 2 | — | — | 58 | 23 | 3 | — | — |
| Southeast | 83 | 17 | 3 | — | — | 96 | 4 | 1 | — | — | 106 | 1 | 1 | — | — | 107 | 1 | 3 | — | — |
| Southwest | 32 | 8 | 3 | — | — | 37 | 5 | 1 | — | — | 44 | 1 | 3 | — | — | 44 | 1 | 3 | — | — |
| East Anglia | 12 | 4 | 1 | — | — | 13 | 3 | 1 | — | — | 18 | 1 | 1 | — | — | 19 | 1 | 0 | — | — |
| SCOTLAND | 16 | 41 | 3 | — | 11 | 22 | 44 | 3 | — | 2 | 21 | 41 | 8 | — | 2 | 10 | 50 | 9 | — | 3 |
| WALES | 8 | 23 | 2 | 3 | — | 11 | 22 | 1 | 2 | — | 14 | 20 | 2 | 2 | — | 8 | 24 | 3 | 3 | — |

**Table 37  The European Parliament Elections of 1979 and 1984**

| | Turnout | CONSERVATIVES % Of Vote | Seats | LABOUR % Of Vote | Seats | LIBERALS % Of Vote | Seats | NATIONALISTS % Of Vote | Seats | OTHERS % Of Vote | Seats |
|---|---|---|---|---|---|---|---|---|---|---|---|
| **7 JUNE 1979** | | | | | | | | | | | |
| England | 31.3% | 53.4% | 54 | 32.6% | 12 | 13.2% | 0 | – | – | 0.8% | 0 |
| Wales | 34.4% | 36.6% | 1 | 41.5% | 3 | 9.6% | 0 | 11.7% | 0 | 0.6% | 0 |
| Scotland | 33.7% | 33.7% | 5 | 32.0% | 2 | 13.9% | 0 | 19.4% | 1 | – | – |
| (G.B.) | (32.1%) | (50.6%) | (60) | (33.1%) | (17) | (13.1%) | (0) | (2.5%) | (0) | (0.7%) | (0) |
| N. Ireland | 55.7% | – | – | – | – | 0.2% | 0 | – | – | 99.8% | 3 |
| U.K. Total | 32.7% | 48.4% | 60 | 31.6% | 17 | 12.6% | 0 | 2.5% | 1 | 4.9% | 3 |
| **14 JUNE 1984** | | | | | | ALLIANCE | | | | | |
| England | 31.6% | 43.1% | 42 | 35.0% | 24 | 20.4% | 0 | – | – | 1.5% | 0 |
| Wales | 39.7% | 25.4% | 1 | 44.5% | 3 | 17.4% | 0 | 12.2% | 0 | 0.5% | 0 |
| Scotland | 33.0% | 25.7% | 2 | 40.7% | 5 | 15.6% | 0 | 17.8% | 1 | 0.2% | 0 |
| (G.B.) | (31.8%) | (40.8%) | (45) | (36.5%) | (32) | (19.5%) | (0) | (2.5%) | (1) | (0.8%) | (0) |
| N. Ireland | 63.5% | – | – | – | – | – | – | – | – | 100.0% | 3 |
| U.K. Total | 32.6% | 39.9% | 45 | 36.0% | 32 | 19.1% | 0 | 2.4% | 1 | 5.6% | 3 |

# ABBREVIATIONS AND GLOSSARY OF POLITICAL TERMS

ACAS—Advisory, Conciliation and Arbitration Service. Body established in 1974 to help mediate in industrial disputes. Chairman, Sir Pat Lowry.

AEU—Amalgamated Engineering Union. The country's second largest trade union, with a membership (1985) of 0.97 million. Known as AUEW—Amalgamated Union of Engineering Workers—until 1986. General-Secretary, Gavin Laird. President (since 1986), Bill Jordan.

ALC—Association of Liberal Councillors. Umbrella organisation for Liberal local councillors, based at Hebden Bridge (Yorkshire) and led by Tony Greaves, which advocates 'community politics'.

ALLIANCE PARTY—Moderate non-sectarian party in Northern Ireland formed in 1970. Leader (1987), John Cushnahan. Membership, 12000.

BIFU—Banking, Insurance and Finance Union. Moderate financial sector union. Membership (1985), 0.15 million. General-Secretary, Leif Mills.

BNP—British National Party. Breakaway grouping from the National Front formed in 1982 by John Tyndall.

BOAC—British Overseas Airways Corporation (now part of British Airways)

BP—British Petroleum

CBI—Confederation of British Industry. Employers' association formed in 1965. Its membership comprises 300000 companies. Director-General (since 1987), John Banham.

CEPG—Cambridge Economic Policy Group. Radical Keynesian grouping of Cambridge economists who advocated an 'Alternative Economic Strategy' of import controls, state planning and industrial investment during the mid and late 1970s.

CLP—Constituency Labour Party

CLPD—Campaign for Labour Party Democracy. Left-wing umbrella group formed in 1973 to press for constitutional reform of the Labour Party.

CLV—Campaign for Labour Victory. Centre-right grouping within the Labour Party formed in February 1977 as a successor to the Manifesto Group.

CND—Campaign for Nuclear Disarmament. Peace and nuclear disarmament pressure group founded in 1958. Membership (1984), 100000.

CPRS—Central Policy Review Staff. Think-tank attached to the Cabinet Office which operated between 1970-83.

CPS—Centre for Policy Studies. 'New Right' Conservative think-tank established by Sir Keith Joseph and Margaret Thatcher in 1974.

CSD—Campaign for Social Democracy. Precursor to SDP established by the 'Gang of Four' in January 1981.

193

DEA—Department of Economic Affairs. Economic planning and co-ordination department established in 1964 and disbanded in 1969.

DHSS—Department of Health and Social Security

DOE—Department of Employment

DTI—Department of Trade and Industry

DUP—Democratic Unionist Party. Populist and militant Northern Ireland Protestant party formed by the Rev. Ian Paisley in 1971. Known originally as the Ulster Loyalist Party.

EEC—European Economic Community. Formed following March 1957 Treaty of Rome.

EETPU—Electrical, Electronic, Telecommunication and Plumbing Union. Moderate, skilled workers' union. Membership (1985) 0.38m. President (since 1984), Eric Hammond.

EMA—Engineers and Manager's Association. Moderate, Alliance-inclined labour union. Membership (1985), 0.04 million. General-Secretary, John Lyons.

GDP—Gross Domestic Product. Measure of total domestic output of a nation. Includes exports, but not imports.

GEC—General Electric Company

GLC—Greater London Council. Metropolitan council established in 1963 and abolished in 1986.

GMB—General, Municipal and Boilermakers union. Known as GMBATU (General, Municipal, Boilermakers and Allied Trade Union) until June 1987. The country's third largest labour union with a membership (1985) of 0.82 million. General-Secretary (since 1985), John Edmonds.

GMC—General Management Committee. Top constituency-level body within the Labour Party which selects parliamentary candidates.

GNP—Gross National Product. Total value of the final goods and services produced in the economy (includes income from abroad minus the income earned by foreign investors).

GREA—Grant Related Expenditure Assessment. DOE computerised assessment of spending needs of local authorities.

GREEN PAPER—Discussion document produced by government outlining a policy proposal.

GREEN PARTY—Environmentalist party formed as heir to the 1973-85 Ecology Party. Co-chairpersons: Heather Swailes, Lindy Williams and Jo Robins.

IEA—Institute of Economic Affairs. 'New Right', monetarist economic think-tank.

ILP—Independent Labour Party. Radical left-wing body formed in 1893 which was attached to the Labour Party after 1900, but later disaffiliated in 1932 in opposition to the MacDonald government's economic strategy. Many of its members later rejoined the Labour Party after the death of the ILP's leader, James Maxton, in 1946.

IMF—International Monetary Fund. Body formed by UN in 1945 to promote exchange rate stability and which makes funds available to countries in difficulty, subject to policy conditions.

IRA—Irish Republican Army. Extremist organisation formed in 1919 which is dedicated to the creation of a united Irish Republic.

IRC—Industrial Reorganisation Corporation. Government supported investment bank which operated between 1966-70.

LCC—Labour Co-ordinating Committee. 'Soft-left' policy-making body established within the Labour Party in 1978.

LEA—Local Education Authority

LRB—London Residuary Body. Quango established in April 1985 to take over the non-earmarked functions of the dissolved GLC.

LSE—London School of Economics and Political Science

M3 —Broad definition of the money supply which includes notes, coins and money deposited in current bank accounts, as well as deposits in banks and building societies, public sector deposits and foreign currency in the country.

M0—Narrow definition of the money supply comprising notes and coins in circulation.

MOD—Ministry of Defence

MP—Member of Parliament

MS—Money Supply

MSC—Manpower Services Commission. Quango established by Department of Employment in 1974 to promote skill-training and enterprise and to help the unemployed find work.

MTFS—Medium term financial strategy. Economic strategy adopted by the Thatcher administration after 1980 which involved the establishment of four-yearly targets for control of the money supply, taxes and public spending and borrowing.

NACODS—National Association of Colliery Overmen, Deputies and Shotfirers. Pit supervisors' union. Membership (1985), 0.016 million. President, Ken Sampey; General-Secretary, Peter McNestry.

NALGO—National and Local Government Officers Association. The country's fourth largest trade union with a membership (1985) of 0.76 million. General-Secretary, John Daly.

NATIONAL FRONT—Extreme-right nationalist party formed in 1966. Chairman, Martin Wingfield.

NATO—North Atlantic Treaty Organisation. 1949 grouping of West European nations with the United States and Canada to safeguard the security of Europe.

NBPI—National Board for Prices and Incomes. Independent board monitoring wage and price movements which operated between 1964-70.

NCB—National Coal Board. Chairman (since 1986), Sir Robert Haslam. Now called British Coal.

NEB—National Enterprise Board. State holding industrial body established in 1975. It was replaced in 1981 by the research-orientated British Technology Group.

NEC—National Executive Committee of the Labour Party

NEDC—National Economic Development Council. Tripartite discussion body comprising ministers, industrialists and union leaders which was established in 1962. In recent years the influence of and resources devoted to NEDC have significantly diminished. Director-General, J. Cassels.

NHS—National Health Service

NI—Northern Ireland

NIB—National Investment Bank. State investment bank proposed in 1987 by the Labour Party.

NIC—Newly Industrialising Country

NIRC—National Industrial Relations Court. Body established by the Heath government between 1971-4 to police its new Industrial Relations Act.

NUM—National Union of Mineworkers. Principal miners' trade union with a membership of 120000. President (since 1982), Arthur Scargill; General-Secretary (since 1984), Peter Heathfield.

NUPE—National Union of Public Employees. The country's fifth largest union embracing predominantly manual workers in the public sector. Membership (1985), 0.66 million. General-Secretary (since 1982), Rodney Bickerstaffe.

OECD—Organisation for Economic Co-operation and Development. Paris-based organisation comprising the leading Western nations.

OPEC—Organisation of Petroleum Exporting Countries. Grouping formed in 1960 to promote the interests of oil-exporting nations by regulating prices and production.

OUP—Official (Ulster) Unionist Party. Conservative, Protestant, Loyalist party, led by James Molyneaux, which traces its roots back to the Ulster Unionist Council founded in 1905.

PC—Plaid Cymru. Welsh Nationalist Party. Formed in 1925 and strongest in Welsh-speaking north-western Wales. Membership (1985), 35000. Leader (1987), Dafydd Elis Thomas.

PLP—Parliamentary Labour Party

PR—Proportional Representation

PSBR—Public Sector Borrowing Requirement. The difference between government income and spending (asset sales being treated as income, or 'negative public borrowing').

PSFD—Public Sector Financial Deficit. The difference between public receipts and expenditure (current and capital), excluding asset sales.

QUANGO—Quasi-Non-Governmental Organisation. Appointed bodies which carry out functions assigned by government.

QUELGO—Quasi-Elected Local Government Organisation. Bodies comprising both elected and appointed members to carry out tasks assigned by the government.

RATECAPPING—Policy of outlawing rate rises above a stipulated level imposed on high-spending local councils since 1985.

RFMC—Rank and File Mobilising Committee. Far-left umbrella organisation formed within the Labour Party in 1980.

RPI—Retail Price Index

SDA—Social Democratic Alliance. Centre-right organisation set up at the grassroots level within the Labour Party during the mid 1970s.

SDLP—Social Democratic and Labour Party. Moderate, Northern Ireland, Catholic, nationalist party formed in 1970. Leader (1987), John Hume.

SDP—Social Democratic Party.

SERPS—State Earnings-Related Pension Scheme

SINN FEIN—Radical, Catholic, nationalist party formed in 1905. Has emerged as the political wing of the IRA. Leader (1987), Gerry Adams.

SNP—Scottish Nationalist Party. Formed in 1928 and strongest in the rural north. Membership (1985), 40000. Chairman (1987), Gordon Wilson; President, Donald Stewart.

SPD—West German Social Democratic Party.

STAR CHAMBER—A six-member cabinet committee, MISC 62, chaired by Viscount Whitelaw, which has been employed by the Thatcher administration to hammer out public spending priorities during the summer months.

STV—Single Transferable Vote

TGWU—Transport and General Workers Union. The country's largest single trade union. Membership (1985), 1.43 million. General Secretary (since 1985), Ron Todd.

TUC—Trades Union Congress. Umbrella organisation for the trade union movement. In 1985 91 trade unions, with a combined membership of 9.85 million, were affiliated to the body. General-Secretary (since 1984), Norman Willis.

UDI—Unilateral Declaration of Independence.

UDM—Union of Democratic Mineworkers. Nottinghamshire/Derbyshire based 30000 member breakaway miners union formed in 1984. President, Roy Lynk.

UN—United Nations

UPUP—Ulster People's Unionist Party. Northern Ireland, Protestant, loyalist party led by James Kilfedder which campaigns for the full devolution of political power to Ulster.

VAT—Value Added Tax

WHITE PAPER—The published notification of a new legislative initiative agreed by cabinet which forms the basis of a bill to be subsequently placed before Parliament.

# RECENT BOOKS ON BRITISH POLITICS

## General

S Beer—*Britain Against Itself: The Political Contradictions of Collectivism* (London: Faber 1982)

H Berrington (ed)—*Change in British Politics* (London: Frank Cass & Co. 1984)

I Budge, D McKay et al—*The New British Political System* (London: Longman 1985)

JD Derbyshire—*The Business of Government* (Edinburgh: W & R Chambers Ltd 1987)

H Drucker, P Dunleavy, A Gamble & G Peele (eds)—*Developments in British Politics 2* (London: Macmillan 1986)

P Dunleavy & C Husbands—*British Democracy at the Crossroads* (London: Allen & Unwin 1985)

P Hennessy & A Selsdon (eds)—*Ruling Performance: British Governments from Attlee to Thatcher* (Oxford: Basil Blackwell 1987)

S Ingle—*The British Party System* (Oxford: Basil Blackwell 1987)

B Jones & D Kavanagh—*British Politics Today* (Manchester: Manchester University Press 2nd Edn. 1983)

D Kavanagh—*British Politics: Continuities and Change* (Oxford: Oxford University Press 1985)

S Pollard—*The Wasting of the British Economy* (London: Croom Helm 1981)

R Skidelsky (ed)—*The End of the Keynesian Era* (London: Macmillan 1979)

## Parliament, Prime Ministers and the Cabinet

M Cockerell, P Hennessy & D Walker —*Sources Close to the Prime Minister: Inside the Hidden World of the News Manipulators* (London: Macmillan 1984)

G Drewry (ed)—*The New Select Committees: A Study of the 1979 Reforms* (Oxford: Oxford University Press 1985)

D Englefield (ed)—*Commons Select Committees: Catalysts for Progress* (London: Longman 1985)

P Hennessy—*Cabinet* (Oxford: Basil Blackwell 1985)

J Jowell & D Oliver (eds)—*The Changing Constitution* (Oxford: Oxford University Press 1985)

A King (ed)—*The British Prime Minister* (London: Macmillan 2nd edn. 1985)

P Norton—*The Constitution in Flux* (Oxford: Martin Robertson 1982)

P Norton (ed)—*Parliament in the 1980's* (Oxford: Basil Blackwell 1985)

## Conservatism and Right-wing Politics

R Blake—*The Conservative Party from Disraeli to Thatcher* (London: Fontana 1985)

N Bosanquet—*After the New Right* (London: Heinemann 1983)

I Gilmour—*Britain Can Work* (Oxford: Martin Robertson 1983)

M Heseltine—*Where There's A Will* (London: Hutchinson 1987)

Z Layton-Henry (ed)—*Conservative Party Politics* (London: Macmillan 1980)

R Levitas—*The Ideology of the New Right* (London: Polity Press 1986)

P Norton & A Aughey—*Conservatives and Conservatism* (London: Temple Smith 1981)

J Prior—*A Balance of Power* (London: Hamish Hamilton 1986)

F Pym—*The Politics of Consent* (London: Constable 1985)

A Seldon—*The New Right Enlightenment* (London: Institute of Economic Affairs 1985)

S Taylor—*The National Front in British Politics* (London: Macmillan 1982)

## Liberalism and Alliance Politics

P Bartram—*David Steel: His Life and Politics* (London: W.H. Allen 1981)

I Bradley—*Breaking the Mould?: The Birth and Prospects of the Social Democratic Party* (Oxford: Martin Robertson 1981)

I Bradley—*The Strange Rebirth of Liberal Britain* (London: Chatto & Windus 1985)

V Bogdanor (ed)—*Liberal Party Politics* (Oxford: Clarendon Press 1983)

J Grimond—*A Personal Manifesto* (London: Martin Robertson 1983)

R Jenkins—*Partnership of Principle* (London: Secker & Warburg 1985)

D Owen—*Face the Future* (Oxford: Oxford University Press 1981)

D Owen—*A Future That Will Work* (London: Viking 1984)

D Steel (ed)—*Partners in One Nation: A New Vision of Britain 2000* (London: Bodley Head 1985)

H Stephenson—*Claret and Chips: The Rise of the SDP* (London: Michael Joseph 1982)

S Williams—*Politics is for People* (Harmondsworth: Penguin 1981)

## Labour and Left-wing Politics

J Callaghan—*The Far Left in British Politics* (Oxford: Basil Blackwell 1987)

M Crick—*Militant* (London: Faber 1984)

M Foot—*Another Heart and Other Pulses: The Alternative to the Thatcher Society* (London: Collins 1984)

B Gould—*Socialism and Freedom* (London: Macmillan 1985)

J Gyford—*The Politics of Local Socialism* (London: Allen & Unwin 1985)

R Harris—*The Making of Neil Kinnock* (London: Faber 1984)

R Hattersley—*Choose Freedom: The Future for Democratic Socialism* (London: Michael Joseph 1986)

D Kavanagh (ed)—*The Politics of the Labour Party* (London: Allen & Unwin 1982)

N Kinnock—*Making Our Way: Investing in Britain's Future* (Oxford: Basil Blackwell 1986)

D & M Kogan—*The Battle for the Labour Party* (London: Fontana 1982)

M Leapman—*Kinnock* (London: Unwin Hyman 1987)

A Mitchell—*Four Years in the Death of the Labour Party* (London: Methuen 1983)

J Tomlinson—*Left, Right: The March of Political Extremism in Britain* (London: John Calder 1981)

P Whiteley—*The Labour Party in Crisis* (London: Methuen 1983)

### The 1974–9 Labour Administration

N Bosanquet & P Townsend—*Labour and Equality: A Fabian Study of Labour in Power, 1974-79* (London: Heinemann 1979)

J Callaghan—*Time and Chance* (London: Collins 1987)

B Castle—*The Castle Diaries, 1974-76* (London: Weidenfeld & Nicolson 1980)

D Coates—*Labour in Power?: A Study of the Labour Government 1974-1979* (London: Longman 1980)

B Donoughue—*Prime Minister: The Conduct of Policy under Harold Wilson and James Callaghan 1974-79* (London: Jonathan Cape 1987)

J Haines—*The Politics of Power* (London: Jonathan Cape 1977)

M Holmes—*The Labour Government 1974-9: Political Aims and Economic Reality* (London: Macmillan 1985)

A Michie & S Hoggart—*The Pact: The Inside Story of the Lib-Lab Government, 1977-78* (London: Quartet Books 1978)

D Steel—*A House Divided* (London: Weidenfeld & Nicolson 1980)

P Whitehead—*The Writing on the Wall* (London: Michael Joseph 1985)

H Wilson—*Final Term: The Labour Government 1974-1976* (London: Weidenfeld & Nicolson 1979)

### The Thatcher Administration

M Adeney & J Lloyd—*The Miners' Strike* (London: Routledge 1986)

DS Bell (ed)—*The Conservative Government 1979-84: An Interim Report* (Beckenham: Croom Helm 1985)

J Cole—*The Thatcher Years* (London: BBC Books 1987)

P Cosgrave—*Thatcher: The First Term* (London: Bodley Head 1985)

G Goodman—*The Miners' Strike* (London: Pluto 1985)

S Hall & M Jacques (eds)—*The Politics of Thatcherism* (London: Lawrence & Wishart 1983)

M Holmes—*The First Thatcher Government 1979-1983: Contemporary Conservatism and Economic Change* (London: Wheatsheaf 1985)

P Jackson (ed)—*Implementing Government Policy Initiatives: The Thatcher Administration, 1979-83* (London: Royal Institute of Public Administration 1985)

D Kavanagh—*Thatcherism and British Politics: The End of Consensus?* (Oxford: Oxford University Press 1987)

W Keegan—*Mrs Thatcher's Economic Experiment* (Harmondsworth: Penguin 1984)

M Linklater & D Leigh—*Not With Honour: The Westland Affair* (London: Sphere 1986)

I MacGregor & R Tyler—*The Enemies Within* (London: Collins 1986)

K Minogue & M Biddiss (eds)—*Thatcherism: Personality and Politics* (London: Macmillan 1987)

P Riddell—*The Thatcher Government* (Oxford: Basil Blackwell 2nd Edn. 1985)

G Thompson—*The Conservatives' Economic Policy* (London: Croom Helm 1986)

A Walters—*Britain's Economic Renaissance: Margaret Thatcher's Economic Reforms, 1979-1984* (Oxford: Oxford University Press 1985)

N Wapshot & G Brock—*Thatcher* (London: Fontana 1983)

P Wilsher, D Macintyre & M Jones—*Strike: Thatcher, Scargill and the Miners* (London: Deutsch 1985)

H Young & A Sloman—*The Thatcher Phenomenon* (London: BBC Publications 1986)

### Election and Voter Studies

D Butler & D Kavanagh—*The British General Election of February 1974* (London: Macmillan 1974)

D Butler & D Kavanagh—*The British General Election of October 1974* (London: Macmillan 1975)

D Butler & D Kavanagh—*The British General Election of 1979* (London: Macmillan 1980)

D Butler & D Kavanagh—*The British General Election of 1983* (London: Macmillan 1984)

I Crewe & B Sarlvik—*Decade of Dealignment: The Conservative Victory of 1979 and Electoral Trends in the 1970s* (Cambridge: Cambridge University Press 1983)

I Crewe & M Harrop (eds)—*Political Communications: The General Election Campaign of 1983* (Cambridge: Cambridge University Press 1986)

M Franklin—*The Decline of Class Voting in Britain: Changes in the Basis of Electoral Choice 1964-83* (Oxford: Oxford University Press 1985)

A Heath, R Jowell & J Curtice—*How Britain Votes* (Oxford: Pergamon 1985)

H Penniman (ed)—*Britain at the Polls: 1979* (London: American Enterprise Institute 1981)

H Penniman & A Ranney (ed)—*Britain at the Polls: 1983* (Washington D.C.: American Enterprise Institute 1986)`

R Tyler—Campaign!: *The Selling of the Prime Minister* (London: Grafton Books 1987)

# CHRONOLOGY OF RECENT EVENTS: 1974-87

1974—Feb, Conservatives lose majority in 'Who Governs Britain ?' general election. Labour assume power as a minority government. March, miners' strike ended. Oct, Labour achieve parliamentary majority of three, following fresh elections.

1975—Feb, Margaret Thatcher elected Conservative Party leader. June, 67% 'Yes' vote in EEC referendum.

1976—March, Prime Minister Wilson announces resignation. April, James Callaghan elected new Labour Party leader and Prime Minister. May, Jeremy Thorpe resigns as Liberal Party leader over 'Scott scandal'. July, David Steel elected new Liberal leader. Sept-Dec, IMF crisis.

1977—Jan, Roy Jenkins leaves government to become EEC Commissioner. Feb, Tony Crosland dies, David Owen appointed Foreign Secretary. March, 'Lib-Lab Pact' formed to prevent government defeat. Aug, unemployment peaks at 1.6 million.

1978—Sept, 'Lib-Lab Pact' ends. Dec, 'Winter of Discontent'.

1979—March, Devolution referenda fail; Government defeated on 'confidence vote' in Commons. May, Conservatives win general election with a majority of 44. June, Major income tax cuts in budget, but VAT increased.

1980—Jan, Steel strike. Aug, Unemployment passes two million. Sept, Labour conference votes for re-selection of MPs. Oct, Callaghan retires as Labour leader: Michael Foot defeats Denis Healey in leadership contest.

1981—Jan, Labour Party Special Conference establishes electoral college: 'Gang of Four' leave. March, SDP launched. April, Brixton riots. May, Labour gain control of GLC. July, Toxteth riots. Sept, Major cabinet reshuffle: Healey narrowly defeats Benn for Labour Party deputy leadership. Oct-Nov, Alliance win by-elections.

1982—Jan, Unemployment passes three million. April-June, Falklands war. July, Roy Jenkins elected SDP leader.

1983—June, Conservatives win general election with majority of 144: Labour captures its lowest share of the national vote since 1918. Foot and Jenkins announce their resignations as party leaders: Owen is elected unopposed as SDP leader. Oct, Neil Kinnock elected Labour leader with 71% of the new 'electoral college' vote: Roy Hattersley is elected deputy leader. Cecil Parkinson resigns as Conservative Party Chairman over 'Keays' affair'. Nov, Cruise missiles arrive at Greenham Common.

1984—Jan, Trade unions banned at GCHQ. March, Sarah Tisdall found guilty under Section 2 of the Official Secrets Act: Coal strike commences. May, Violence at Orgreave. June, House of Lords revolt over GLC abolition Bill. Oct, IRA bomb Conservatives at Brighton. Nov, British Telecom privatised.

1985—Feb, Clive Ponting acquitted of breaching the Official Secrets Act. March, Coal strike ends with NCB victory. May, Local election reverses for Conservatives: Formation of Pym's 'Centre Forward'. Sept, Major cabinet reshuffle. Sept-Oct, Handsworth, Brixton, Tottenham riots. Nov, Anglo-Irish agreement signed with Dublin.

1986—Jan–Feb, Resignations of Michael Heseltine and Leon Brittan over 'Westland Affair'. Feb, Enforced shelving of plans to sell off Austin Rover to Ford. April, GLC abolished; British bases used for US bombing of Libya; Nuclear accident at Chernobyl in the Soviet Union. June, NEC expels Liverpool 'Militants' from Labour Party. Sept, Liberal Party conference votes for non-nuclear defence policy. Nov, Chancellor announces £5 billion increase in public spending.

1987—Feb, Alliance victory in Greenwich by-election. March, 2p tax cut in budget: Margaret Thatcher visits the Soviet Union. May, Local election setback for Labour. June, Conservatives win majority of 102 in general election: Cecil Parkinson returns to new cabinet. Alliance parties differ over merger issue.

# POLITICS IN THE UNITED STATES

## FROM CARTER TO REAGAN

Examines the changing political scene in the USA during the
Carter and Reagan eras and the different programmes
adopted. Charts the resurgence of congressional power and
the growth of political individualism; the operation of
presidential government; contests for national leadership; the
Republican/Conservative revival; the changing character of the
Supreme Court; the rise of ethnic politics; changes in America's
foreign policy. There is an analysis of the 1986/7 Iran-
Contragate scandal and a look at the 1988 presidential
candidates.

# POLITICS IN WEST GERMANY

## FROM SCHMIDT TO KOHL

Examines the different policy programmes followed during the late Schmidt and early Kohl eras; the growing fissures within the SPD and the emergence of the Green Party; the splits within the FDP and between the CDU and its Bavarian sister party, the CSU; the southward movement in the German economy; the Gastarbeiter question; foreign relations with France, East Germany and USA.

# FROM GISCARD TO MITTERRAND

Examines and explains the key changes in French politics over the most recent decade. Considers the varying fortunes of the major parties and ideological coalitions; changing policy directions; the dominant personalities. Looks in particular at the modernisation of the inherited Gaullist state and at the 1981-85 "Socialist Experiment" and the post-1986 "cohabitation" experience.

# POLITICS IN THE SOVIET UNION

## FROM BREZHNEV TO GORBACHEV

Political changes/defence
and foreign policies/economic
and social developments/
internal opposition.

# POLITICS IN CHINA

## FROM MAO
## TO DENG

Examines the key changes in the Chinese
political and economic system during the
years from 1972 to 1987.
Looks at the changing functions of political
institutions, at the modernisation
programmes of Zhou and Deng, at changes
in China's foreign policy.

CHAMBERS     POLITICAL SPOTLIGHTS

# CHAMBERS
# WORLD
# GAZETTEER

Editor Dr. David Munro

The international directory of facts,
figures, people and places. Over 800 pages
packed with information; 20,000 towns and
cities featured; profiles of every nation in
the world; 150 maps of key political and
administrative divisions; a 120 page atlas in
full colour.

# Chambers Commerce Series

The up-to-date series for school and college students, embracing the full range of business and vocational subjects.

## Business Studies
*Mark Juby*

A comprehensive introduction to all aspects of business activity. The book covers the GCSE National Criteria in Business Studies, plus key areas of GCSE Commerce and Understanding Industrial Society courses. *Business Studies* is also geared to BTEC, LCCI, O/Standard Grade, RSA and SCOTVEC Courses.

## Bookkeeping and Accounting
*Harold Randall and David Beckwith*

A comprehensive introduction, showing how financial records are made, maintained and used in business. The book is of especial value to students on AAT, BTEC, GCSE, LCCI, PEI, RSA and SCOTVEC syllabuses.

## Typing
*June Rowley*

An introduction to basic typing theory and practice, ideal for a wide variety of secretarial and vocational courses including BTEC, CPVE, GCSE, LCCI, PEI, RSA and SCOTVEC.

## Word Processing
*Barbara Shaw*

Covers everything from text editing to repagination and mail merge—all the practical word processing skills. Ideal for BTEC, LCCI, PEI, RSA and SCOTVEC courses.

# *Chambers* *Commerce Series*

**Business Calculations**
*David Browning*

A step-by-step guide to mathematics in business
practice, from simple arithmetic to elementary
statistics. Geared to courses of many varieties—CPVE,
BTEC, LCCI, RSA and SCOTVEC; GCSE and
O/Standard Grade Mathematics, professional training.

**Business Law**
*Janice Elliot Montague*

A practical introduction to the law, how it works and
influences business procedures. *Business Law* covers
relevant components of a host of syllabuses—ATT,
ALS, BTEC, ICA, ICAS, ICMA, ILE, IOB, IPS,
LCCI, SCCA, SCOTVEC.

**The Business of Government**
*J. Denis Derbyshire*

A straightforward introduction to British government,
how it works in practice and how it influences business
procedures. Covers key elements of Politics and Public
Administration syllabuses, including BTEC, GCSE,
RSA, O/Standard Grade, Modern Studies,
SCOTVEC; an ideal reference text for A Level and
Higher Grade courses.

**Keyboarding**
*Derek Stananought*

A book of exercises and advice on the skills needed in
the age of new technology and the electronic office.
Includes training material in basic keyboarding,
proofreading, speed development, practical application
of typing techniques. Ideal for secretarial and vocational
courses—BTEC, CPVE, LCCI, PEI, RSA,
SCOTVEC.

# *Chambers* Commerce Series

**Secretarial Duties**
*Penny Anson*

A complete guide to all the practical aspects of a
professional secretary's work. Covers the syllabuses of
the important courses, including BTEC, CPVE, LCCI,
PEI, RSA, SCOTVEC.

**Office Procedures**
*Ruth Martindale*

A straightforward explanation of the work involved in
running a modern office. Well illustrated, up-to-date,
takes full account of the latest technolgy and
procedures. Covers the syllabus requirements of BTEC,
LCCI, Pitman, RSA, SCOTVEC.

# Chambers Commercial Reference

Straightforward guides to all the essential terms used in the business world. Ideal for students on a wide range of introductory business and vocational courses.
Written in clear, simple English.

**Bookkeeping and Accounting Terms**
*Anthony Nielsen*

**Business Terms**
*John Simpson*

**Office Practice Terms**
*Elizabeth King*

**Office Technology Terms**
*Elizabeth King*

**Computer Terms**
*Sandra Carter*

**Business Law Terms**
*Stephen Foster*

**Printing and Publishing Terms**
*Martin H. Manser*